MENNONITE FURNITURE

MENNONITE FURNITURE

A Migrant Tradition (1766–1910)

REINHILD KAUENHOVEN JANZEN

JOHN M. JANZEN

Good Books

Intercourse, PA 17534

Design by Dawn J. Ranck

MENNONITE FURNITURE: A MIGRANT TRADITION (1766-1910)
Copyright © 1991 by Good Books, Intercourse, PA 17534
International Standard Book Number: 1-56148-047-9
Library of Congress Catalog Card Number: 91-74055

Library of Congress Cataloging-in-Publication Data
Janzen, Reinhild.
    Mennonite furniture : a migrant tradition, 1766-1910 / Reinhild Kauenhoven Janzen and John M. Janzen.
        p. cm.
    Includes bibliographical references (p.   ) and index.
    ISBN 1-56148-047-9 : $35.00
    1. Furniture, Mennonite—Europe—Themes, motives. I. Janzen,
John M. II. Title.
NK2525.J3 1991
749'.08'8287—dc20

                                                                91-74055
                                                                CIP

To Bernd
To Gesine
To Marike

Table of Contents

Table of Maps

Foreword and
Acknowledgments

June 16, 1991 in Zhdanovka, Orenburg Oblast, south Urals region, the Soviet Union. We visit the home of Heinrich Neufeld—worker in the agricultural collective "Progress," junior preacher in the local Mennonite Brethren congregation, young father of five children. The benches, stools and high chairs on which the family sits, the tables from which they eat, the sleeping bench, the glass cabinet, the wardrobe, the walker for the toddlers—all were built either by Heinrich's father Johann, his father-in-law or by Heinrich himself. A round pedestal table, built by Johann, also a preacher, was used to hold the Bible during religious meetings when the home served as a semi-secret house church in the 1960s. The large wooden chest for storing clothes was built by Heinrich in 1984, according to a pattern used by his father.

All the furnishings, including the central oven and the plan of the 100-year-old adobe brick housebarn, were a living historical record of the Mennonite building and furniture tradition which was brought to North America by Mennonite immigrants and which is the central focus of this book.

However, in Zhdanovka the tradition was also coming to an end. The Mennonites of this village, as well as the other 22 large villages of the region, were in the midst of emigration to Germany. Suitcases, half-packed, stood on the sleeping bench. The Neufeld's large chest was ready to become a travel trunk, just as the dowry chests in North America had served as travel trunks at the time of migration in the 1870s. Here, too, the tradition was being eclipsed by mass-produced factory furnishings, pushing the old-fashioned handbuilt wooden pieces into attics, junk piles and, at best, into the recently opened local museums.

How often has this scene been repeated in Mennonite history? Certainly in many of the places to which Mennonites migrated after the particular building tradition of our study synthesized in the Vistula Delta region of northern Poland

250 years ago: South Russia, Siberia and Kazakhstan; the North American prairies of Canada, the United States and Mexico; and the Central and South American jungles of Paraguay, Belize and Bolivia.

Our work concentrates on one slice of the story of this building tradition, namely, the central Plains of North America, principally the United States. We examine the historic origins of Plains immigrant communities settled in the 1870s and 1880s.

Research for this book began in 1988 with an inventory of furniture and related artifacts, known to have been handcrafted by Mennonites prior to or after immigration to North America, which were held in private and public collections in the prairie states (excluding extensive additional holdings in Canada and Mexico). At the time of this writing this inventory included approximately 500 items and continued to be a primary research effort of Kauffman Museum.

A research trip in the fall of 1989, funded in part by a University of Kansas sabbatical and the National Endowment for the Humanities, to examine museum collections and speak with scholars in Belgium, The Netherlands, North Germany and North Poland clarified the historic material culture sources of this tradition. A further research trip in June, 1991, funded in part by the Fritz Thyssen Foundation, to the Mennonite villages in the Orenburg region of the Soviet Union, clarified the extent of continuation of the tradition in the Soviet Union and revealed some unknown original features common to all branches of the tradition.

A ten-month planning project in 1990, sponsored by the National Endowment for the Humanities, brought Scott Swank of Shaker Village, Canterbury, New Hampshire; Jeremy Bangs of Plimouth Plantation; Anne Woodhouse of the Wisconsin State Historical Museum; and Nancy-Lou Patterson of Waterloo, Ontario, to Kauffman Museum to establish comparative perspectives for the interpretation of the inventoried body of Mennonite material culture. These scholars contributed much to our understanding of the materials presented in this book, and we thank them sincerely.

Currently the National Endowment for the Humanities is partially supporting the preparation of this book and the implementation of an exhibition *Mennonite Furniture: A Migrant Tradition 1766-1910* at Kauffman Museum.

This book would not have been possible without the generous, selfless help of very many persons who freely shared information and photographs of handcrafted furniture and furnishings from their collections. We are greatly indebted to all who have carefully preserved the tangible memory of their history and their roots.

Foremost among all of these we want to thank Ethel Ewert Abrahams who embraced and encouraged this pioneering project from its inception and who has given much of her time, energy and resources, volunteering as field photographer and collector of data for the past four years.

Similarly, the assistance of Lorin Epp, Donald and Margaret Huebert, Bill and Vera Hinz and Nada Voth has been invaluable. We also thank Walter Adrian, Agnes Dalke Bryan, Arthur Claassen, Sheridan Dell, Anna Grace Flickinger, Lucille Harms, Arthur Kroeger, Martha Lepp, Adina Meek, Martha Nielsen, Dale E. Schrag, Helen Swisher, John Schroeder and Joyce Watts. We also thank Valery and Irene Friesen, Tula, USSR; and Jacob and Agnes Friesen,

Zhdanovka, Orenburg region, USSR; Edmund and Camilla Kizik, Poland; and Arkadiusz and Zyta Rybak, Poland.

We are also grateful for George Vollmer's insightful assistance throughout all stages of this project, especially for his editorial comments and patience with a rough first draft.

We thank Rachel Pannabecker for her energetic and efficient management of the inventory materials. We thank her and the other Kauffman Museum staff members for continued support of this project which often diverted our attention from the everyday needs of Kauffman Museum.

We are further indebted and wish to thank the following museums, archives and colleagues for their assistance: The Mennonite Library and Archives, Bethel College, North Newton, Kansas; the Center for Mennonite Brethren Studies, Fresno, California; the Mennonite Heritage Museum, Goessel, Kansas; David Wiebe, the Adobe House Museum, Hillsboro, Kansas; Ralph Kauffman, the Heritage Hall Museum, Freeman, South Dakota; the McPherson Historical Museum, McPherson, Kansas; the Heritage House Museum, Mountain Lake, Minnesota; Peter Goertzen, the Mennonite Heritage Village, Steinbach, Manitoba; Steve Prystupa, the Museum of Man, Winnipeg, Manitoba; Heinz Hammer, Stadtarchiv Friedrichstadt, Friedrichstadt, Germany; Mark Laenen, Provincial Open-Air Museum, Bokrijk, Belgium; Theodor Kohlmann, Heidi Mueller, Konrad Vanja, Museum für Deutsche Volkskunde, Berlin; Helmut Ottenjann, Museumsdorf Cloppenburg, Cloppenburg, Germany; Ewa Gilewska, Ethnographic Museum Gdansk-Oliwa, Poland; Krystyna Mellin, National Museum, Gdansk, Poland; Maria Kwiatkowska, Krystyna Laskowska, Museum of Elblag, Poland; Kinga Turska-Skownonek, the Ethnographic Museum of Torun, Poland; Olga Penner and Katarina Sawatzky, Zhdanovka Museum, in the old Mennonite church, Zhdanovka, USSR; Katarina Gisbrecht, Chortitza Museum in the Culture Palace, Chortitza-Orenburg region, USSR; Alexander Chibilov, Padolsk Museum in the former farm house of Johann Wiehler, USSR; Marina Nikifarova, Kitschkass Museum in the Culture Palace, USSR.

Gratitude is extended to Edith Kauenhoven, Gunhild Kauenhoven, Berthild Kauenhoven Berger and Hendrikje Robrecht Kauenhoven, who have generously assisted this research effort with difficult library and museum inquiries in Germany, who have refreshed weary travelers and who have sustained our work, as did Hilda and Louis A. Janzen, by unquestioning faith in its validity.

A note on spelling place names: cities and places that have existed in the past 450 years under different political and linguistic regimes have been spelled in quite different ways; for example, Danzig and Gdansk or Marienburg and Malbork, in German and in Polish respectively. We have chosen to use the spelling that corresponds to the use that was current during the particular time period in question.

A note on spelling Low German *(Plautdietsch)* words: generally the Plains portion of this project deals with people who came from the Molotschna area of South Russia. We have tried to use words and expressions as we have encountered them, which may account for some inconsistency in spelling. Wherever we have needed to "impose" standardization or consistency of naming or spelling, we have used Herman Rempel's *Kjenn Jie Noch Plautdietsch? A Mennonite Low-German Dictionary.* When our sources used High German words instead of Low German words, we kept the High German.

A note on photographic sources: sources for the illustrations in Figs. 47, 50, 51, 52, and 56 could not be identified at the time of publication. For inquiries please contact the authors. All other photographic sources are listed in the endnotes for the figure captions.

Artifacts from both museum and private collections are identified in terms of their historic makers and/or owners, where known, as well as by the use of their identifying number in the Kauffman Museum Inventory of Mennonite Furniture and Furnishings.

Credits for drawings and original photography: maps by John M. Janzen; all drawings of artifacts and technical diagrams by Gesine S. Janzen; all color photography unless identified otherwise by Mark Wiens with the exception of Figs. 24, 103, 156, 157, 158 and 160 by Burton Buller.

August 6, 1991
Reinhild Kauenhoven Janzen and John M. Janzen
Heubuden, Kansas

Themes in the
Interpretation of an
Immigrant Furniture Tradition

This book is a case study of the emergence, the florescence and the transformation of the domestic furnishings and related material culture of the immigrant Mennonites of the prairies of North America, in particular those of the United States.

Mennonites of the North American Plains, like Mennonites worldwide, are an Anabaptist community with spiritual roots in the left wing of the sixteenth century Reformation. This movement emerged from a desire to radically separate the congregation of believers from the dictates of the state, through the act of adult baptism. (They were called re-baptizers or "anabaptists.")[1] The name "Mennonite" refers to followers of Menno Simons, a sixteenth century Netherlands priest, who became a leading figure among the Anabaptists for his emphasis on the congregation and on the doctrine of pacifist Christian witness. Anabaptist assumptions are at the historical basis of the modern separation of church and state, including the first amendment of the American Constitution.[2]

For their beliefs the Anabaptist–Mennonites were severely persecuted, forced to flee and even martyred. From their original homes in The Netherlands, Belgium, Germany, Switzerland, France and Italy, they scattered to places such as the Vistula Delta of Poland, Moravia and the New World where they found a tolerant political environment and where they could believe and live according to their consciences.

This work follows the northern European path of Mennonite migrations, first eastward to Poland in the sixteenth century, still further eastward to Russia in the eighteenth century and westward to the Plains of North America in the nineteenth century. The time framework of 1766-1910 suggested by the book title is based on the earliest and the latest authentic pieces of furniture in the Plains corpus. The first is a spinning chair made in the Vistula Delta which was taken to South Russia and subsequently to North America. The second is a desk

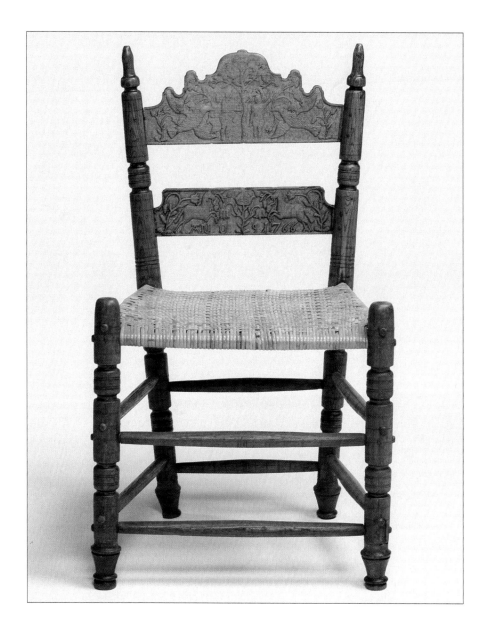

made by Peter Vogt of Inman, Kansas, for his daughter Nettie when, at the age of 16, she became a school teacher.

Furniture provides a unique material record of a way of life and a people. It may be presented as a medium with functions, forms and aesthetic sensibilities in its own right. For a fuller understanding furniture may also be interpreted in terms of the layers of context which shape it: the domestic architecture in which it stands; the materials out of which it is made; the family institutions which shape the pattern of commissionings and inheritance; the broader economic patterns of varied tastes determined by class or grouping. Furniture may also serve as a mirror of the culture in which it is found—a reflection of the sense of privacy, of domestic function and of family organization. Because of the intricacy of the migration story behind this Mennonite furniture tradition, and the fact that the co-authors are an art historian and a cultural anthropologist, respectively, this work addresses the full range of presentations suggested.

The material culture represented by immigrant Mennonite furniture may be seen as a tradition that comes into being at a given point, persists for a time and then changes. As it is now understood, this furniture tradition crystallized in the period 1750-1800 in the Vistula Delta of northern Poland where Mennonites had lived from the sixteenth century. From there it was taken by late eighteenth and early nineteenth century emigrant groups to central Poland and South Russia. Finally, it was taken from all three locations to the Plains in the late nineteenth century (see Maps 1 and 2), as well as to other locations in the Soviet Union and the Americas.

The North American prairie Mennonite immigrant domestic furniture, although now an extinct tradition which is no longer made by craftsmen, continues to provide a kind of mirror of the conditions that prevailed at the time of the tradition's emergence 250 years ago. In a manner comparable to Jean-Louis Flandrin's work on seventeenth century French society, we believe furniture and the domestic layout offer a way "to rediscover the characteristics of family life in former times on the basis of what is known of the material environment."[3]

The material record of pieces of furniture created over a period of 250 years and taken along at the time of migration, together with archival sources and oral traditions, may, like an archeological record of artifacts, reveal both the conditions at the time of the emergence of the tradition as well as the conditions of internal change and possible complete dissolution.[4]

To "read" furniture and the domestic layout in an effort to understand the formative setting and its later dissolution, we must look at the ways in which

Fig. B, Nettie Vogt's teacher's desk. back view.

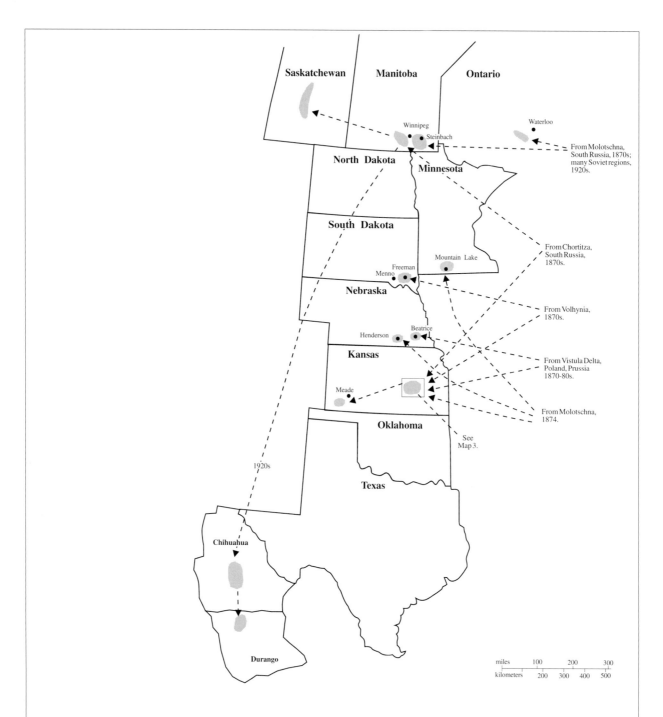

Map 1. Mennonite settlements and migrations from Russia and Poland–Prussia to the North American Plains, 1870s-1920s (see Map 3).

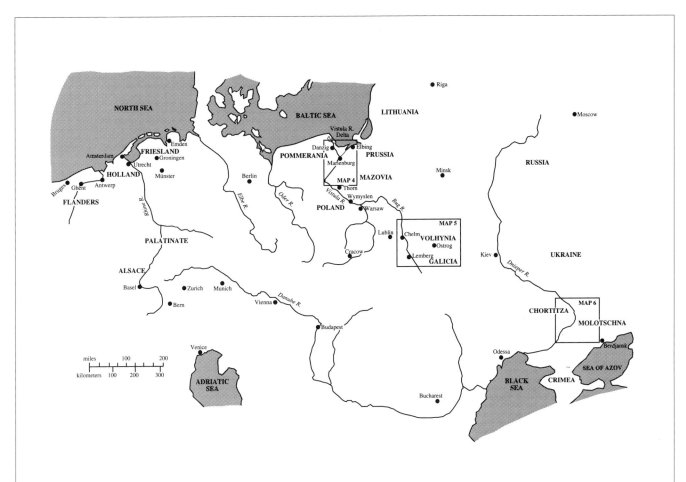

Map 2. Anabaptist–Mennonite settlements and migrations in central and eastern Europe, sixteenth to nineteenth centuries, as cited in text (see Maps 4, 5, 6 for details of Mennonite settlements).

the cognitive dimension of the tradition—beliefs, concepts, aesthetic patterns and principles—interacts with or inspires the material dimension of the tradition—the actual objects and the material conditions that go into the construction and use of the object. Initially, the two dimensions or realms are often closely associated. However, over time the cognitive may change and come to be out of phase with the material tradition. Subtle changes or abrupt, drastic changes may then appear in the record of material objects. For example, the intricate construction and fine aesthetic sense in Mennonite dowry chests of 1800 reflect both the central role of the dowry as an institution in the society of the time and the high value that was placed on bringing together all of the material needs for the new household prior to the time of marriage. Later, on the Plains of North America, the dowry as a chest-full of household items was replaced by readily available land which could be bought and sold and farmed to generate resources needed to furnish the household's goods. Thus the construction of new dowry chests came to an abrupt halt.

The artifacts for this inquiry of the immigrant Mennonite domestic tradition are found in prairie communities settled in the 1870s-80s by Mennonites (see Maps 1 and 3) who emigrated directly from South Russia, Prussia and Poland to central Kansas (Hillsboro, Goessel, Buhler, Inman, Moundridge, Pretty Prairie, Newton, Whitewater); western Kansas (Meade); Nebraska (Henderson, Beatrice); South Dakota (Freeman, Menno); Minnesota (Mountain Lake); Ontario (Waterloo); Manitoba (south of Winnipeg); and Saskatchewan. A secondary migration of "Old Colony" Mennonites from Manitoba in the 1920s took the tradition southward to the Chihuahua and Durango provinces in Mexico. Also included in this study are the Swiss Volhynians of Kansas and South Dakota, an immigrant group from Polish Volhynia who originated in the Alsace and the Palatinate. They came into close contact with the Vistula Delta Mennonites and seem to have adopted similar domestic furnishings. The Pennsylvania–German Amish and Mennonites, the Hutterites (a related Anabaptist group) and the "German Russians" (whose background is usually central Germany), who also settled on the central Plains, will not be considered here because their material culture traditions are different.

The North American Plains segment of this Mennonite furniture and furnishings tradition survives today mainly in museums and in private collections. Memories of those who built it are dim or totally obscure. A survey conducted by Kauffman Museum (see Appendices A and B) revealed that this furniture tradition's basic set of a dozen or so functional types and features (listed at the outset of chapter one) was represented consistently wherever it was introduced by Mennonites to the Plains.

The manufacturing of these pieces ceased rather abruptly a generation after the immigrants came to the Plains and was replaced by mass-produced American furniture.

Within the broader context of the immigrant Mennonite culture, furniture and furnishings also reflect differential rates and types of change. Land tenure and settlement practices associated with the immigrant tradition were abandoned almost immediately, whereas basic inheritance practices were continued for a far longer period. Other elements of the material culture, for example, church architecture, were also retained much longer. The Low German and Swiss German languages were the primary languages in most communities of this tradition for several generations and are still spoken today in some settings. Religious beliefs of Mennonites continue to influence contemporary North American and global realities. These particular rates of change hold a clue to the significance of the furniture pieces and to the manner in which they may reflect Mennonite cultural character and value priorities.

The outline of this book takes into account the interests and needs of a range of readers, most of whom will not have much prior knowledge of the subject.

The chapter on "Mennonite Furniture in the Rituals of Daily Life" introduces the core furniture types among immigrant Mennonites to the North American Plains, a set that we call the "canon." The notion of "rituals of domestic life," borrowed from Flandrin's study of seventeenth century French furniture, identifies the functional contexts within which these Mennonite furnishings existed and were used.

"Sources for a Vistula Delta Tradition" addresses the intricate, layered and, for most readers, strange world of the Vistula River Delta in North Poland,

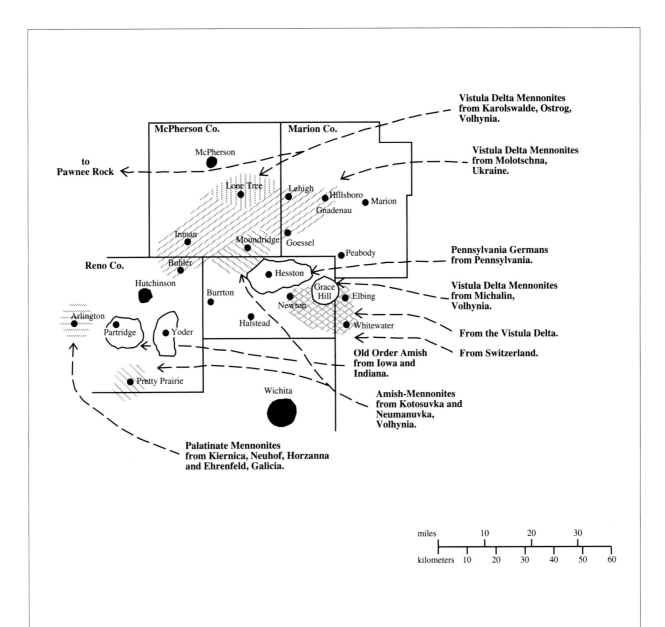

Map 3. (Detail of Map 1) Mennonite settlements and towns in central Kansas, showing origins of emigration.

The following labels appear on the map:

Vistula Delta Mennonites from Karolswalde, Ostrog, Volhynia.

Vistula Delta Mennonites from Molotschna, Ukraine.

Pennsylvania Germans from Pennsylvania.

Vistula Delta Mennonites from Michalin, Volhynia.

From the Vistula Delta.

From Switzerland.

Old Order Amish from Iowa and Indiana.

Amish-Mennonites from Kotosuvka and Neumanuvka, Volhynia.

Palatinate Mennonites from Kiernica, Neuhof, Horzanna and Ehrenfeld, Galicia.

McPherson Co.

Marion Co.

Reno Co.

to Pawnee Rock

McPherson

Lone Tree

Lehigh

Hillsboro

Marion

Gnadenau

Inman

Moundridge

Goessel

Peabody

Buhler

Hutchinson

Hesston

Grace Hill

Burrton

Newton

Elbing

Arlington

Halstead

Whitewater

Partridge

Yoder

Pretty Prairie

Wichita

miles 10 20 30

kilometers 10 20 30 40 50 60

where Anabaptist–Mennonite sixteenth century refugees from many regions of Europe settled and where their cultural traditions, including furniture, took shape.

"Making the Tradition Mennonite" describes the gradual emergence of a Mennonite way of life from the sixteenth to the eighteenth centuries. Although this was similar in many ways to that of most inhabitants of the Vistula Delta region, both urban and rural, the Mennonite imprint was particularly significant in the development of architectural forms such as the domestic longhouse and the religious prayerhouse and in the synthesis between immigrant and local forms.

"Furnishing a New Home" focuses on the central role of the dowry furniture, and on the sources of style and decoration among the Mennonites of the Vistula Delta in the late eighteenth and early nineteenth centuries.

"The Migration of the Tradition" traces the migration of Mennonites beginning in the 1780s to a number of sites southward and eastward of the Vistula Delta: up the Vistula toward Warsaw; to Volhynia, halfway between Warsaw and Kiev; and to the southern Ukraine. Several household inventories and historic accounts of these settings provide evidence for continuity and change in the furniture tradition.

"The Tradition Comes to America in Shipping Crates and in the Minds and Hands of Immigrant Craftsmen" features three immigrant craftsmen from the Molotschna Mennonite Colony—Franz Adrian, Heinrich Schroeder and Heinrich Rempel—and the circumstances of their continuing work on the Plains.

"Construction, Decoration and Style" offers a technical perspective of the Mennonite furniture canon and places it within the wider context of Western decorative arts.

"The Waning of the Tradition" analyzes the rapid decline of manufacture of the tradition around 1900 on the Plains, citing such elements as the availability and attractiveness of reasonably priced mass-produced furniture as reasons for the halt in production.

"Thoughts on Mennonite Aesthetic Identity" explores the character and focus of the aesthetic sensibility within this historic furniture tradition.

This book will fill a gap in written material about the furniture belonging to Mennonite immigrants of the central United States, and it will complement several book-length works on the Canadian extension of the tradition.[5] We hope that it will contribute to the understanding and appreciation of the historic way of living and building revealed in Mennonite furniture.

1
Mennonite Furniture in the Rituals of Daily Life

Our parents' house was 32 feet by 20 feet. The walls were of sod and the roof had a steep pitch. It was partitioned into two rooms with a mud brick oven with an open chimney in one room...the family lived on one end of the house and two horses and the cow stayed on the other end...Our parents had bought three chairs and a cook stove in Lincoln which were the only household goods that they owned...Then he [father] bought lumber to build bedsteads which could be pulled out on one side to make more room to sleep in, also a table, some benches, and sort of a sleeping bench. It was used as lounge in the daytime and three of us children could use it at night. This was about all the furniture we had by springtime...[1]

The Mennonite immigrants to the prairie states and provinces in the 1870s and 1880s either brought their furnishings with them, built their own after they arrived or purchased pieces from commercial dealers. Of the handmade pieces a distinct style is evident that has come to be called "Mennonite furniture" by antique dealers, connoisseurs and families who cherish heirlooms. Mostly, these are single pieces, seen in isolation.

Examination of several hundred examples of this Mennonite immigrant furniture in the Kauffman Museum survey reveals a central canon of a dozen types with distinct functions, forms and decorative styles. This chapter offers, first, a list of the canon in answer to the question, "What is Mennonite furniture?" or, more specifically, "What kind of furniture did Mennonites use?" since much of this furniture was similar to that used in other societies of eastern and northern European derivation.[2]

A mere list such as this needs to be understood in terms of the context within which the furniture was created and the purpose it served, as well as the forces of change that may have led to the replacement of a particular type by another.

These categories of activities and functions within which household furnishings may be understood have been referred to by Jean-Louis Flandrin as "the rituals of domestic life."[3] By ritual Flandrin means the repetitive and symbolic practices around central familial values and needs. In his work on eighteenth century French peasants he identifies the material context—the architecture and the furnishings—which articulated the growing need for privacy around three basic rituals: "sleeping," "eating" and "being together in the evening."

Immigrant American Mennonite households of the late nineteenth century, and their eastern European antecedents, reveal these and other domestic rituals and spaces, which will be developed in the second part of this chapter.

What we have identified as the canon of immigrant Mennonite furniture corresponds with earlier glimpses of this tradition, extending back at least 250 years to settlements in the Vistula Delta region of northern Poland, central Poland, Polish Russia, South Russia (the Ukraine) and all the Old and New World communities that stem from the tradition.[4]

The illustrations shown in this chapter suggest there are variations around a number of dimensions: plain or fancy; crudely made by a carpenter of necessity or finely built by trained cabinetmakers; and painted or inlaid. Despite such contrasts within the tradition, these pieces are decidedly different not only from what was available commercially in stores of late nineteenth century midwestern America, but also from what non-Mennonite craftsmen were building.

The Canon of Immigrant Mennonite Furniture

The typical forms that represent this furniture and furnishings tradition, their vernacular Low German terms and their functions include: (1) the chest (*Kjist*), for the dowry (of the women in particular) and for other storage needs; (2) the hanging corner cabinet *(Akjschaup),* for the personal effects, money and devotional books of the household head; (3) the pullout bed *(Bad, Loaga* or *Bocht),* space-saving double bed which stood in the "large room" or the "corner room" piled high with bedding—also called the *Himmelsbad* because of the cloud-like appearance of feather pillows; (4) the cradle *(Waej),* a basic archaic form reflecting sixteenth century derivation; (5) the common backless bench *(Benkj),* designated for varied seating purposes, such as "stove bench" *(Ofenbenkj)* or "milk bench" *(Melkbenkj),* according to use; (6) the sleeping bench *(Schlopbenkj),* which was used for children to sleep in and doubled as a daytime couch; (7) the couch or settee *(Ruebenkj,* literally "resting" bench), for daytime sitting; (8) the chair *(Stool),* a sewing or spinning chair, reflecting a Netherlandish influence; (9) the wardrobe *(Kjleedaschaup),* for clothes storage, an eighteenth century furniture type that expanded the function of the chest; (10) the built-in wall cabinet *(Miaschaup)* or glass cabinet *(Glasschaup)* for display and storage of china; (11) the table *(Desch),* an all-purpose functional type; (12) the utility cupboard for varied storage purposes, such as *Melkschaup* (literally, "milk shelf") near the barn entrance for milk and milk-product containers or *Aeteschaup,* in the kitchen for food and utensil storage; and (13) the wall-hung pendulum clock *(Klock),* reflecting English–Netherlandish clockmaking specifically manufactured by Mennonites and expressive of a high sense of time-consciousness. Other functional types that appear less systematically, such as the wash stand, commode or dresser and the desk, will be discussed in less detail.

Furniture in the Rituals of Domestic Life

How were these pieces arranged within the immigrant Mennonite household? What were their uses? What did they mean to the people who brought them along or built them after arrival? These questions are answered in terms of the following ten rituals and spaces of domestic life.

The Relationship of People to Animals in the Household

Most Mennonite immigrants to the prairies were farmers who needed to arrange shelter not only for themselves, but also for their horses, cattle, pigs and chickens. The most common northern European pattern of domestic architecture was one which reflected this dual and interrelated set of needs—the housebarn or *Langgebied* (longhouse), which combined the house and the barn under one long roof. Numerous examples and styles of the longhouse will be shown in this work.

J.J.Friesen, in the beginning quotation of this chapter, describes this household form in 1874-75, from his childhood memories in Henderson, Nebraska:

> The family lived on one end of the house and two horses and the cow stayed on the other end.[5]

The Hearth—a Family Space

The central hearth and the main hall functioned as the general cooking, eating and whole-family living space. The earliest record of this feature of Mennonite immigrant housing was made by Mr. H. Worrall of Topeka, Kansas, who visited the Mennonite communities in McPherson, Marion and Harvey counties soon after the immigrants arrived from the Ukraine in 1874. His sketches of the basic Mennonite adobe house capture the space as well as the spirit of the immigrant Mennonite home in central Kansas (Figs. 1, 2). What impressed him most was

Fig.1, Interior of Mennonite kitchen, 1878, central Kansas.[1]

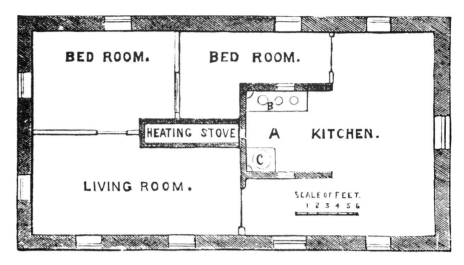

the use of straw, or grass, for fuel. His 1878 article was appropriately titled "How the Mennonites Warm Their Houses and Cook with Straw as Fuel."[6] He wrote:

> We first saw straw in use for fuel at the home of a Russian Mennonite bishop [elder] in the colony in McPherson Co., Kansas. Dinner for four of us was to be prepared. A vigorous young Mennonite girl vanished with a bushel basket, and returned with it full of loose straw, then placing her kettles, etc., on the top of the cook range, opened the fire door, and thrust in two large handfuls of straw, touched the match, closed the door and the kettle commenced singing almost immediately; in about two minutes the door was again opened and two more handfuls of straw were thrust in and the door closed. Our dinner consisted of ham, eggs, potatoes, Russian waffles, and excellent coffee, all cooked in less time than an ordinary stove could have been made "hot for buscuits." The fire was "dead out" before the dinner was half consumed and the house none the warmer for the fire, the surplus heat all escaping through the chimney [Fig. 3].

Worrall went on to describe the central chimney and heating stove:

> The cooking place and doors of the straw stove that heats the building, are all in the base of the chimney, which is eight feet square, with a stone floor; the walls are vertical for about 8 feet, when they are gradually brought in, reducing the interior of the chimney to about 12 inches at the comb of the roof...The upper portion of the chimney is the family smoke-house, in which are stored hams, shoulders, sides, and festoons of sausages hung on poles, permanently set in the walls, access being had to them by a ladder. On one side of the base is a large cauldron, for wash days, set in a furnace of adobe or sun-dried bricks; on the other side the cooking-range, also of adobe, having a sheet-iron top, with holes cut for the pots and kettles; both ranges, that for washing, and the one for cooking, have a flue of adobe four feet high. The heating stove is 9 feet long, 8 ft. 6 in. high, and nearly 3 ft. wide, and forms part of the partitions of the three rooms heated by it. The ovens in this stove are formed at top and bottom of narrow plates of rough cast iron, set loosely in the stove walls, to admit of expansion and contraction, the doors are of sheet iron, and the walls two bricks thick. In ordinary winter weather, fire is made in the stove every morning, when

(top) **Fig.3,** Mennonite woman cooking at hearth, 1878, central Kansas.[3]

(bottom) **Fig.4,** Section of Mennonite house, 1878, central Kansas.[4]

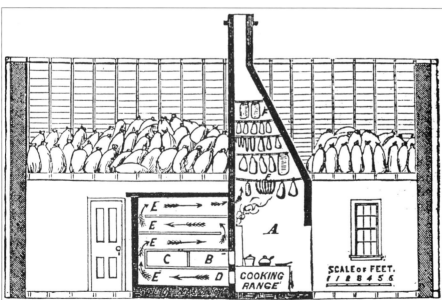

two good armfuls of straw are consumed in from 20 to 30 minutes, this heats the stove sufficiently for the whole day. In very cold weather, the fire is made two or three times each day, burning an equal amount of straw at each firing. So soon as the fire is out, the flue connecting the stove with the chimney is carefully closed by a damper, in order to retain the heat.

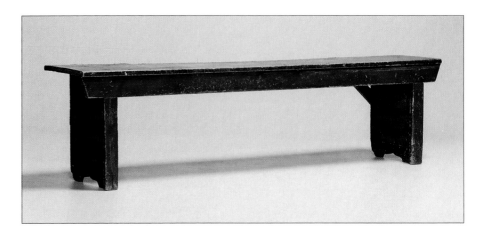

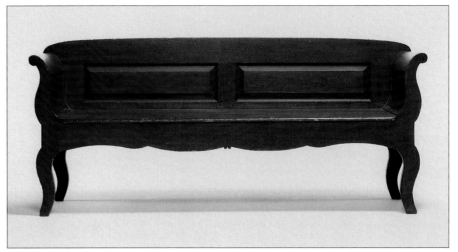

Bread is baked in the ovens, and also in the fire chamber of the heating stove, where it is placed immediately after firing, on a wrought iron stool, which will keep it above the ashes in the straw [Fig. 4].

The visitor Mr. Worrall was so thoroughly taken up with the food and the construction of the Mennonite house that he failed to comment on the obvious social fact that he was being treated as a guest. No doubt, his hosts were accustomed to receiving strangers and neighbors into their home.

Calling or visiting, in its common form, was called "neighboring." The space where this happened on weekdays was in the kitchen, around the table, seated on a plain bench or chairs (Fig. 5). We know from family records of the cabinetmakers Klaas Hiebert and Peter Unrau that they made chairs, as well as other furniture, both in South Russia and in North America.[7] On Sundays and holidays visitors were usually entertained in the special room, the *Grootestow,* where guests sat on the resting bench (Fig. 6) or sleeping bench.

In 1883 Marie Janzen, a new immigrant to the Whitewater-Elbing, Kansas community from West Prussia, wrote to relatives in Europe about a visit to a Russian Mennonite home in Gnadenau "ten miles north of Peabody:"

[Eduard Loeppke] has 40 acres of land and a modest house. He has rented out his land and is engaged in finish carpentry and furniture building. There are many of the Russian Mennonites in the area where he lives. Their style of building is much different from ours, partly because they do not have the funds to do otherwise. Loeppke's house also was covered with narrow boards on the outside as is custom here but on the inside his walls were of hollow brick [adobe] and painted white. They said this type of interior is much warmer in winter than the American way of doing it. Inside they have a stove made of bricks which heats two rooms and in the kitchen there was a brick cooking stove of the Russian type. Many houses in this settlement were also constructed of prairie sod, which is supposed to be very good also [Figs. 7, 8].[8]

If Marie Janzen had been able to recall the homes in the Vistula Delta of West Prussia from a century earlier, she would have recognized the common background with this "Russian Mennonite" home. However, during the nineteenth century the Prussian and Russian Mennonite settlements had developed some-

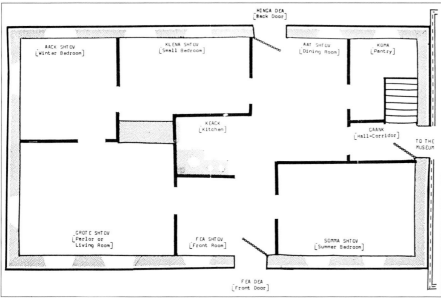

(top) **Fig.7,** Klaas Hiebert housebarn, built in 1877, Mountain Lake, Minnesota.[5] Left to right: cabinetmaker Klaas Hiebert, Anna Janzen Hiebert and their three younger children, Anna, Mary and Jacob.

(bottom) **Fig.8,** Floorplan of the restored Adobe House Museum in Hillsboro, Kansas, built ca. 1876.[6] Orginally the Peter Loewen house.

21

what different domestic building styles.

The emigres from the Vistula Delta to the Ukraine constructed their own buildings and often used indigenous materials, including adobe brick. It was natural for them to continue this vernacular architecture on the prairies, because they had used it in Russia in a similar pioneer environment.

The Mennonites who remained in the Vistula Delta, generally the more affluent families, adopted commercial building forms and furnishings in the course of the nineteenth century—part and parcel of the middle class revolution in what had become West Prussia. All of the 1870s-1880s emigrants from West Prussia to Whitewater, Elbing, Newton and the Bruderthal Community northeast of Hillsboro, Kansas, and those who came to Beatrice, Nebraska, were able to sell their farms before they emigrated and to hire American builders after they arrived. Their houses and barns (i.e., the Gustav Harder farm in Fig. 9) were made of solid contemporary wood frame or, occasionally, native stone construction.

Sleeping, Conjugal Privacy and Gender Separation

The pullout bed (Fig. 10), the sitting–sleeping bench (Figs. 11,12,16) and the cradle (Figs. 13-15) were three bed types found in Mennonite immigrant homes. In this realm of life, as in all others, the size of the house (i.e., the number of bedrooms) as well as the style of furniture reflected the differences between well-to-do and modest means. The pullout bed and the sitting bench or bed *(Schlopbenkj),* which could be pulled out to double its size, are often explicitly referred to as space savers. Cradles stood near the parents' bed.

Little mention of privacy may be found in the sources on immigrant living, so we need to make inferences from circumstantial evidence. The presence of several rooms to separate the sleeping quarters of family members suggests that these Mennonites of nineteenth century European origin had been thoroughly influenced by an increasing desire in the late eighteenth century for privacy, particularly in middle- and upper-class homes.[9] Even in poor Mennonite homes, the parents had their own sleeping quarters separate from those of the children. This contrasted to the open area of sixteenth century homes in northern Europe and to the seventeenth century French peasant sleeping arrangement in which everyone in the family, even the visitors and servants, reportedly slept together

(top) **Fig.10,** Pullout bed, 1875. Made by John Albrecht, Turner County, South Dakota. Pine, pegged construction, original red paint was removed.
H:34" L:72.4" D:28" (not extended).
#17.005, KM 2251.

(middle) **Fig.11,** Sleeping bench, ca. 1880-1890. Hinged seat stained dark brown, small flower decals decorate center of each recessed back panel. Pullout section makes the bench into a bed wide enough for two. Pine, pegs, nails, painted graining simulates two contrasting wood stains.
H:35" L:75" D:22½".
#6.003, Private collection.

(bottom) **Fig.12,** Sleeping bench, ca. 1876-1886. Made by Rudolph Riesen, Sr., or his oldest son, Rudolph. Made for one of the young sons to sleep in. Hinged seat, front section pulls out to make a wide bed. Pine, mahogany red stain, inside lid and inside box are painted white.
H:36" W:80½" D:21¾".
#6.006, KM 88.04.01.

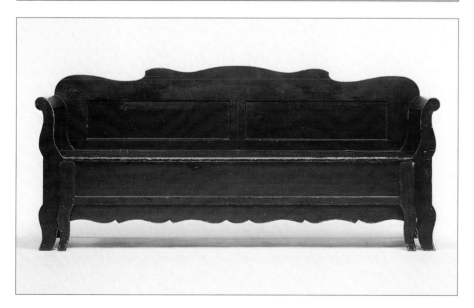

(top, right) **Fig.13,** Cradle, ca. 1880s. Made by Jacob Kauffman, Marion, South Dakota. Pine, reddish-brown paint, two porcelain pulls (served both as blanket fasteners and as a way to secure the infant).

H:20" L:36½" W:29" (width of rockers).

#18.003, KM 2263.

(bottom, right) **Fig.14,** Cradle, ca. 1880-1900. From the Moundridge, Kansas Mennonite community. Pine, painted graining, painted pink roses, dovetailed joints. Two carved hooks on each side were used to hold ribbon fasteners.

H:20½" L:36" W:18".

#18.029, McPherson Historical Museum.

(below) **Fig.15,** Doll cradle, ca. 1890s. Pine, painted graining, painted black accent line.

H:9" L:19" W:10 ½" (extension of rockers).

#18.021, KM 3206.

in one huge bed.[10]

In the immigrant Mennonite home the parents' bedroom was usually either the corner room *(Akjstow)* or the large room *Grootestow,* in which case the bed on which the extra bedding was stored had to be pulled out and made up nightly. If there were children, there was one bedroom for each set of siblings of the same gender, and they all slept together in one bed. Girls frequently received the corner room, and boys the unheated summer room or a room prepared in the unheated second story of the house.

Most immigrant homes had provisions for guests or other family members who visited. Often the *Grootestow* doubled as a guestroom. The room layouts shown in this chapter demonstrate how the basic three-room house, such as the

(top) **Fig.16,** Sleeping bench, ca. 1890. Probably by Mr. Becker of Goessel, Kansas. Pine, painted graining, wooden peg joints, few screws, turning "roller" armrests which are said to have been used for covers. "Covers were put over the rollers and thus easily pulled."[8] Recessed back panels are beveled on the back side of the bench.

    H:33" D:22" W:81".
    #6.017, Private collection.

(left) **Fig.17,** Kitchen cupboard, ca. 1876. From the Isaac and Agnetha Fast family summer kitchen. Pine, stained orange-red, four shelves. (The top one is notched to hold spoons, knives or forks.) Original door screens are missing.

    H:83" W:60" D:14".
    #14.009, KM 87.91.8.

(facing page) **Fig.18,** Wall cabinet, ca. 1880. Originally built into the kitchen wall of the Peter Voth home, Gnadenfeld village one mile east of Goessel, Kansas. The cabinet is said to have been painted by Emil Kym. Separately constructed gable, butt joints. The glass cabinet has two shelves and two drawers with porcelain pulls. The lower cabinet is fitted with shelves. Pine, painted graining, painted roses and forget-me-nots.

H:88" W:36" D:18".

#14.001, Private collection.

(left) **Fig.19,** Wardrobe, ca. 1890. Made by Reverend Dirk Tieszen or by his father; Marion, South Dakota. Pine, painted mustard yellow with black trim. Constructed of several component parts which are held in place by four wedges. Original pediment is missing. Clothes are hung on handcarved hooks which are fastened to short wooden swivel arms.

H:79½" W:51½" D:21".

#11.013, Heritage Hall Museum, Freeman, South Dakota.

one visited by Worrall (Fig. 2), could "grow" into the larger four- or five-room house, such as the Peter and Catherine Voth home shown at the end of this chapter.

Storage

There were, of course, different storage needs in the Mennonite immigrant household: food and provisions; clothing and household linens; and tools and utensils. Cupboards stood in every house, either in the large main room with the cooking stove and bake oven or in the smaller utility room (Fig. 17). These cupboards were usually home built, following a style that allowed them to be dismantled and moved easily. Doors were often board frames stretched with cloth or screen to keep flies out.

Every home also had a cabinet in which to store china and other tableware. The upper doors were of framed glass so that the chinaware was visible. The bottom cabinet was either fitted with drawers or with shelves and solid doors. Often built into the wall (the Low German *Miaschaup* literally means "wall cabinet"), these china cabinets followed a tradition that began at least as early as 1800 in Prussia and South Russia (Fig. 18).

Large storage boxes and trunks were also common in the immigrant Mennonite home. Grain chests for seed grain, storage boxes for tools, chests for clothing and the fancy dowry chests all provided additional storage spaces. The

(top) **Fig.20,** Gerhard Nickel, 1855-1935, cabinetmaker, Hillsboro, Kansas.[9]

(right) **Fig.21,** Wardrobe, 1889. Most likely made by Gerhard Nickel, who is known to have built wardrobes of exactly this style. The wardrobe was first owned by the Herb and Elizabeth Funk family in the Bruderthal community, northeast of Hillsboro, Kansas. The pine wood is painted with an amber ground color over which graining in a darker tone is applied. The recessed panels of the doors and the sides have "realistic" graining, whereas the graining on the rest of the surfaces assumes a vibrant pattern in its own right and has no other agenda than to be itself. The date "1889" is feathered into the painted graining in the center of the pediment, forming the focal point of the wardrobe.

H:90½" D:21½" W:54¼".
#11.004, Private collection.

chest or trunk may well be the oldest form of furniture in European history; certainly it had a central function in medieval and sixteenth century furnishings.

Many of the chests or storage boxes in early immigrant Mennonite homes had been built just prior to the migration:

> Through the winter and into the spring of 1874 preparations continued for the journey. Much time was spent making chests and cases for the emigration. Into their chests went all their personal belongings, clothes, smaller tools and heirlooms. In the bottom were often the seeds from their vegetables needed to start a garden in the new land next year. Many chests had an ample layer of toasted zwieback at the top as this would provide food for all the journey.[11]

Immigrant Mennonites also built or custom ordered wardrobes for their

28

clothes since houses of this period had no closets in the modern sense (Figs. 19-21). The wardrobes, like the other storage cupboards, were made of component parts so they could be moved into rooms where they were to stand and dismantled and moved again when necessary. Like the chests and the wall or china cabinets, the wardrobes received careful attention from builders and were prized for their elaborately painted graining and decorative motifs. The wardrobes stood in a number of rooms—the *Grootestow,* the parents' bedroom or elsewhere as needed and available.

There are not many stories about the construction of wardrobes, but the following anecdote told by Marie Harms Berg about her father is indicative of the love and attention that often went into their construction.

Wilhelm Harms had been a cabinetmaker in Russia but had to supplement his income in Kansas with farming. "He built a wardrobe with a beautiful key hole plate carved from a horn. He went into the pasture and found a cow's horn, sawed, cut and carved it to be a beautiful key plate. O how he must have loved grandma. He built her other things too, also for other people. I don't know if any of those things remain."[12]

Workspaces and Surfaces

The simple utilitarian table was a central piece in the immigrant Mennonite household (Figs. 22, 23). It served for food preparation, eating, washing dishes, sewing, writing and many other family activities. N.J. Kroeker describes the standard construction technique that resulted in these sturdy long-lasting tables:

One of the most essential pieces of furniture was the common kitchen table. It had to be sturdily built with a straight top that would not crack,

(top, right) **Fig.22,** Table with drawer, ca. 1883. Made by Jacob Friesen for his daughter Maria Friesen Schroeder at the time of her marriage in 1883. Cleated top, horizontal molding, shaped angle brackets and tapered legs are standard design features of "Mennonite" tables. Pine, yellow and black paint.
H:21½" W:25¾" L:36¼"
#15.015, Private collection.

(top, left) **Fig.23,** Table with drawer, ca. 1875. Made by Adolph L. Waltner's father; South Dakota. Pine, original paint was removed.
H:30" W:45" L:27".
#15.011, KM 2251.34.

(bottom, right) **Fig.24,** Wash cabinet or dry sink, ca. 1880s. Made in rural Henderson, Nebraska. Pine, painted graining, oil cloth, commercial door latches.
H: 38" W:38" D:16".
#13.001, Private collection.

Fig.25, Pullout bed, pre-1874. According to family oral tradition, this bed was brought by Reverend Heinrich Epp and his wife Margaretha Wall Epp from Elisabeththal, South Russia, to Henderson, Nebraska. Together with Reverend Benjamin Ratzlaff, Heinrich Epp was the leader of the immigrant group that came in 1874. Pine, painted graining, painted decorative motifs, scalloped skirt of pullout section painted to imitate the graining of marble, turned finials, turned feet, turned trim pieces which accent the end panels and may be seen from the rest of the room.

H:37" L:72" Pulled-out width:35", closed: 24".

#17.018, Private collection.

nor warp, two problems to be prevented. The first step was to glue boards side by side to prepare one large surface. Then two accurate dovetail cuts (grooves) were sawed and chiselled across. The third step was to prepare two pieces of wood to fit the dovetail cuts precisely and push them by hammering them into place. The cool moist weather in fall and winter kept everything in place but as soon as summer set in the large table surface shrank considerably. However no boards cracked because the dovetails provided a path for sliding along.[13]

Toilet

This term and its associations derive from the French word for cloth, *toile,* in reference to the cloth used to cover one's shoulders during a haircut, or while shaving. It thus has the meaning of dressing or grooming. Only secondarily does it refer to relieving oneself, for which the term "privy" has often been used. Immigrant Mennonite homes were equipped with outhouses and at nighttime the chamber pot was used. For the comfort of the elderly and the infirm there were so-called commode chairs or chamber pot stools, some of them hand built.[14]

The furniture piece most often associated with the "toilet" ritual of daily life in the immigrant Mennonite home was the dry sink, a washstand commonly covered with an oil cloth. A fancy version has a gallery (or backsplash) with an exuberant curving line, and a base decorated with a draped skirt, often seen on dowry chests (Fig. 24).

Emerging Luxury, Special Days and Forbidden Spaces

The *Grootestow,* "big room," reflected a growing affluence and status consciousness. Having a room apart for special visitors, particularly those who came on horse or by buggy from a distance and needed accommodation for several days, provided some prestige. The *Grootestow* also served as a place for Sunday and holiday activities, as well as a showroom for silent signs of status: the dowry chest, the clock, the china cabinet, a special table (Fig. 26) and the guest bed stacked high with richly embroidered bedding. By the 1890-1900 era, when the second generation of houses began to appear in Mennonite communities on the Plains, the Anglo-American Victorian parlor, with all its connotations, began to replace the *Grootestow.*

What is striking about the *Grootestow,* in written and oral tradition, is that it is the most often described room. However, there are few references to particular events taking place there. A travel account printed in 1889 described a community meeting held in what the author called the "best room" of Abraham Reimer's house, an elder of the Alexanderwohl church near Goessel, Kansas:

> In the "best room" the meeting was in progress. The room was quite full, and the visages of all present were as immovable as the green-and-gold face of a Russian clock that ticked on the wall. These clocks are seen everywhere. They sport a long pendulum with a disk as big as a buckwheat cake, and long, heavy hanging weights of brass...there were no books in sight save a black-covered German Bible...and several Mennonite hymn-books...bound in leather and printed in Odessa.[15]

Fig.26, Parlor table, 1898.
Gift for Jakob Abrahams from the Hoffnungsau Church, rural Inman, Kansas. On the painted table top we see an open book, in which are written the German words and the date "Christlicher Haussegen, 1898" (Christian Blessing for the Home), placed on a garland of flowering leaves, held by a ribbon and encircled by a wreath of rose buds and rose leaves. Round table, wood unknown, painted graining, painted decorative motifs.
D:28" H:28½"
#15.019, Private collection.

The *Grootestow* is remembered most as a room reserved for special occasions only—Sunday afternoon visiting, special birthdays, anniversaries, Christmas and other celebrations. Might it be that all who wrote about this subject recall their childhood days and memories, times when they were forbidden from entering this hallowed room, and, consequently, cannot recall actually having done anything in it?

Helen Mierau Swisher's account of her fondness for an old pullout bed which she eventually inherited is reminiscent of the attitude toward the *Grootestow* (Figs. 25, 27). She writes:

> As a small child I was attracted to [the bed], fascinated by its structure and the fact that it was never used as a bed. My mother stored extra blankets and pillows as well as feather beds in it. They were piled high and it was always a childhood dream to sleep there. The bed stood in an attic room

(left) **Fig.27,** Reverend Heinrich Epp and Margaretha Wall Epp with his son Heinrich H. by his first wife Marie Regier Epp and Heinrich and Magaretha's son Johann. Photo taken approximately 1872 in South Russia.[10]

(facing page) **Fig.28,** Corner cabinet, ca. 1876-1900. Pine, painted graining imitates two different wood veneers, square nails. Maker unknown. From the home of Henry J. Schmidt, Goessel, Kansas. Originally mounted in Henry Schmidt's bedroom where it held books.
H:39¾" W:33" D:22".
#14.041, Private collection.

and was considered off limits for me. My mother could always tell when I had sneaked off to play there, because of course the blankets and quilts were mussed and disarranged. During my teen years and young adulthood I resolved more firmly than ever to sleep in the old Russian bed and one day to have it in my house.[16]

Spiritual and Monetary Management

Every Russian Mennonite immigrant home had a corner cupboard or *Akjschaup* where the head of the household kept his records, cash, account books, a Bible, song books, devotional books and other personal possessions (Figs. 28, 29). The exact location of the corner cupboard depended on the other room arrangements, and on the relative status of the household. Often it was located in the *Grootestow,* thus off limits to curious children.

This was the case in the memory of Jacob A. Friesen of Hague, Saskatchewan, who was in his eighties when he wrote the following account in 1990. He reflects:

> Those corner cabinets which were common in Old Colony homes were almost a "must" for a household father in the front visiting room *(Grosse Stube).* I have seen many of them—that was a private "father case" and still is for some Old Colony people of our area, contents as you will perhaps know—(out of sight corner)—a bit of money, the Bible, the *Gesangbuch,* writing paper, pen and ink, letters, important letters—these were often visible when the door was ajar or when the owner was looking for something.[17]

Don Huebert of Henderson, Nebraska, recalls that his great-grandfather Peter Huebert's *Akjschaup* was painted a buttermilk green inside.[18] It contained, among other things, mints, *Praedjer* (preacher) candy and Alpenkraeuter tonic.

(top, right) **Fig.29,** Corner cabinet, ca. 1880. From the George B. Neufeld family, Mountain Lake, Minnesota. Pine, painted graining, black paint. Cabinet features an independent swagged skirt bracket base with two legs, shaped like the bases of dowry chests and wardrobes. Standing on a wall-mounted shelf.

H:60" W:36".

#14.019, Heritage House Museum, Mountain Lake, Minnesota.

(bottom, right) **Fig.30,** Dowry Chest, ca. 1840-1849. Brought in 1874 to North America by Johann Siemens (1827-1902) from Elisabeththal, South Russia. In 1849 Johann married Maria Froese (1828-1900) of Grossweide, South Russia. Size, proportion, construction and the system of lock, key and hinges all correspond precisely to chests of Vistula Delta origin. Tinned iron hinges as elaborately tooled as those of many of the inlaid chests from the Vistula Delta. Chest may have been taken from the Vistula Delta to South Russia by the parents of either Maria Froese or of Johann Siemens.[11] Pine, painted graining, brass, tinned iron.

H:25½" W:54¼" D:26¾".

#1.013, Private collection.

(below) **Fig.31,** Back side and opened lid of Johann Siemens' dowry chest. Carved inscription identifies the chest as immigration luggage and gives name and address of the "head" of the family: *"Auswanderungsgepaeck Johann Siemens Elisabeththal Nord Amerika, Kansas, Buren [Burrton]."*

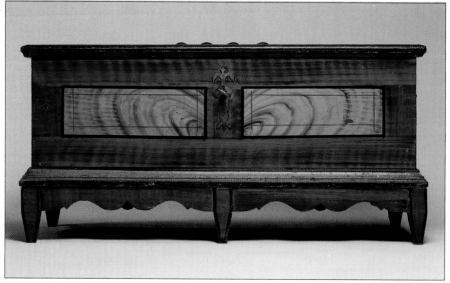

34

Generations, Inheritance and Time

Of all the household items in the immigrant Mennonite family, the dowry chest and the wall clock carried the most cherished symbolic associations. These two furnishings were by far the most frequently brought from Europe to America. The clock was relatively easy to pack. The chests were built of heavy hardwood or solid softwoods, and required several strong men to move them. The dowry chest, although it doubled as a travel packing box, also had other important connotations.

H. Worrall, whose writings were cited earlier in this chapter, had this to say about the Mennonite homes of McPherson, Marion and Harvey counties:

> Besides their farm implements they brought over their household effects, conspicuous among which are a large clock to hang upon the wall, and a huge, curiously ornamented chest to hold the household treasure; these are to be seen in almost every Mennonite home.[19]

The dowry chest represented family and household continuity, long-term planning and the projection of household resources from one generation into the foundation and well-being of the next. In this sense the dowry chest was unlike all other home furnishings. Built in anticipation of the marriage of the daughter, it became the property of the individual and held her personal belongings. The initials of the owner and the date of manufacture personalized it. The drawings and pictures inside the lid also contributed to this effect.

Many chests were also passed on to a daughter or granddaughter at the time of her marriage and the establishment of a new household. Several accounts of dowry chests follow to illustrate these points.

The back of one such chest shown here (Figs. 30, 31) bears the carved inscription in capital letters of its purpose, owner, origin and destination: "Emigration luggage, Johann Siemens, [from] Elisabeththal [to] North America, Kansas, Burton."

Constructed of softwood, either fir or pine, this chest rests on a separately assembled base with five slightly tapered legs. The skirt of the base is decorated

(left) **Fig.32,** Dowry chest, ca. 1850-1872. Brought on the ship *Vaterland* by Gerhard Dick (born 1852 Margenau) and Anna Brandt Dick (born 1853 Wernersdorf) from Nikolaidorf, South Russia; they had married in 1872. Chest willed to daughter Elisabeth Dick Dalke who in turn willed it to her daughter Agnes Dalke Bryan. Gerhard Dick wrote on the back of the chest: *"Auswanderungsgepaeck Gerhard Dick Nebraska Konty."* Chest rests on a separate bracket base with gently curved skirt. Painted graining on pine or fir imitates the color and grain of ash. Corner columns and skirt painted to imitate the grain of marble. Monochrome treatment of the floral motifs inside an interlaced border suggests inlaid decoration of dark veneer. Stencils or templates may have been used for the flowers. Left side of interior has usual till. Keyplate, bosses (bolt caps), handle and handle plates are brass; plain hinges of hand forged iron.
H:26" D:28½" W:54".
#1.034, Private collection.

(above) **Fig.33,** Detail Gerhard and Anna Dick chest.
#1.034

with a swag pattern. On the inside are the usual till to the left and a short strip of molding on the right designed to hold a narrow shelf which runs along the back of the chest at the same height of the till and which is preserved in some of the chests.

In Kansas the Siemens asked the Swiss immigrant painter Emil Kym to grain the chest in two contrasting colors to give it the illusion of a panel construction, even though the chest is a simple board chest joined, like all others, with fine dovetailing. Kym cleverly matched the graining of the double front "panel" in the fashion of symmetrical wood veneers. The pattern lends a rhythm to the resulting design of a heart. The lid is treated as one panel, and the center is further decorated with a cluster of dark blue grapes, red cherries and red strawberries, fruit grown by the immigrants.[20]

Gerhard Dick and Anna Brandt Dick left their home in South Russia in 1877 and came on the SS *Vaterland* to Philadelphia with their two small children. On the back of their chest, which "contained most of their possessions," Gerhard Dick wrote the address of his family's destination in the Henderson, Nebraska, area (Figs. 32, 33).[21]

Gerhard and Anna's daughter Elisabeth inherited the chest and she in turn willed it to her daughter Agnes, who writes:

> They settled on a farm near Henderson, Nebraska. There were nine children in the family when they moved to a farm near Hydro, Oklahoma, where grandpa Dick was instrumental in building the Bethel Mennonite Church. He was a teacher of the German Language in Russia and continued to teach in the Mennonite communities, both in Nebraska and in Oklahoma. He also served as the minister in the country church near his farm. When my grandparents left the farm and returned to Henderson, Nebraska, they left the chest in the family in Oklahoma. My family became the caretakers of it when they rented the farm...I am proud of the part it has played in my family history. It was used as a table, a desk, and a bed during the early days here in America.[22]

The chest is grained to imitate the blonde color of ash wood. On the front and the sides, painted panels imitating inlay frame the formal flowers arranged in a stemmed vase. Folded pilasters wrap the front corners of the chest, executed in monochromatic browns. This style of decorating dowry chests originated in the Vistula Delta.

Agatha Regier Janzen, having come to Elbing, Kansas, from the Heubuden community in West Prussia in 1877 as a two-year-old child, wrote the story of the dowry chest she later inherited from her mother Catherine Dyck Regier:

> As was related to me by my dear mother..., this chest comes from one or several ash trees which grew on the farm of her parents Peter and Agathe Dyck in Germany. When mother was grown up a chest was made for her (of these trees), it may have been the time of her wedding with father Abraham Regier, January 24, 1872...In the year 1877 when the parents came to America, the costs of transport were not spared. When mother's life came to a close she willed that I should inherit this piece of furniture and since now I count over 80 years and since granddaughter Doris [Janzen Longacre] shows interest in this piece I am glad that it continues, and I

Fig.34, Wall clock, ca. 1850. From Mountain Lake, Minnesota. Brought from South Russia ca. 1874. One-hand pendulum clock probably made in the David Kroeger clockmaking firm, Rosental near Chortitza, South Russia. Clock face of cut sheet metal painted green; roses and tulip in a basket decorate half circle above clock face; more roses embellish center and each corner of square clock face. Main chapter ring painted black; half-hour chapter ring painted white. One brass hand shows the hours. Brass pendulum and brass weights.
H:24" W:18".
#19.014, Private collection.

Fig.35, Chest of drawers, commode, 1899. Made by Herman J. Fast—basket weaver, farmer, teacher, church leader who lived four miles southeast of Mountain Lake, Minnesota. For his daughter Aganetha Helen Fast as a Christmas present. Pine, wainscoating, painted graining, factory-made drawer pulls, nails; nailed butt joints, rabbit joint front.
H:36¾" D:17" W:31".
#12.001, Private collection.

only wish that no one will have mis-fortune because of it. With love from grandmother Agathe Janzen.

To what misfortune was she alluding in her final sentence? This was similar to the many cautionary, moralizing stories Agatha Janzen told about accidents that had befallen relatives or acquaintances as if to remind her children and grandchildren of their mortality and God's will in their lives. Her stories echoed an entire genre in German folklore about the heavy chest lid which would fall on the unsuspecting curious child who dared to open it without adult supervision, or, even worse, the evil stepmother who would lure the innocent stepchild to the chest and drop the lid on its head, killing it, only to feign tearful sorrow to the father.[23]

In contrast, this particular chest came to symbolize a spirit of sharing of one's wealth for Doris Janzen Longacre, the granddaughter who inherited the chest. Her great-grandmother Catherine Dyck Regier had shared food stored in the chest with other travelers on a blizzard-stalled train on the way to Kansas.[24]

If the dowry chest embodied a sense of family continuity and past tradition as well as the process of planning for the future, the wall clock was essential in every immigrant Mennonite home to maintain the order of daily living (Fig. 34). The tradition of Mennonite clockmaking in Poland, Prussia and Russia may be traced back to Dutch roots and English connections. Today clocks still migrate with Mennonite emigrants from Russia.[25] Of course, Mennonites were not the only people to have wall clocks in their homes, but their ethic of stewardship and frugality certainly applied to the stewardship of time. Time-consciousness is remembered by Don Huebert:

> When the father of the house decided that it had been enough visiting, when guests should leave he would go and wind up the clock, pull up the weight, as that was the last thing you did in a day, so that sound was the sign that guests had to leave.[26]

Although the dowry chest and the wall clock were at the core of immigrant Mennonite values of family continuity and stewardship, very few chests and wall clocks were built in North America.[27] The dresser (in Low German *Komood*) (Fig. 35) and the mass-manufactured, downscaled cedar or "hope" chest replaced the handmade dowry chest. "Mennonite" clocks were easily replaced by more fashionable commercial clocks, especially the mantle clock. Family resources came to be passed on in land rather than in pieces of furniture.

Putting Loved Ones to Rest

Most Mennonite carpenters and cabinetmakers built coffins. None of the coffins made by Mennonites remain as available artifacts. Before the turn of the twentieth century when undertakers became important community figures and embalming a fashionable way to care for the deceased, the dead were prepared at home. We can imagine that coffins built by the makers of wardrobes and china cabinets also varied between plain and fancy. The family history of the Reverend Peter Unrau, who was a farmer and cabinetmaker, contains a glimpse of this activity.

In Russia the caskets for funerals were made by local cabinetmakers. The inside of the casket was lined with white material and the outside was covered with black cloth. For children the caskets were entirely white. Since the caskets had to be made after the death of the person, the time element was quite an important factor. "Often grandfather worked through the night in order to finish it. Sometimes members of the family were involved in the work of pleating strips of cloth used to complete the decoration of the casket. During the pioneer years, he also made caskets here in America."[28]

Klaas Hiebert, born in the Molotschna village of Lichtfelde, immigrated to Bingham Lake, Minnesota, in 1877. In Russia and in Minnesota he constructed a total of 340 coffins, including his wife's and his own.[29]

The Full Context of Immigrant Mennonite Homes

We have very few detailed accounts of the location of furniture and furnishings in the immigrant Mennonite home between 1875 and 1900, or of systematic uses of space in the home. Most accounts routinely repeat the stereotypic ideal layout practiced in South Russia, referring to the way it "had been" or was "supposed to be."

One very helpful exception is the unpublished description by Marie Voth of the house of her great-grandparents' Peter and Catherine Unruh Voth, which stood in the Gnadenfeld village east of present-day Goessel, Kansas, until it was razed in 1908 (Figs. 36, 37).[30] In her manuscript Voth's father Herman Voth described this house as he had known it as a boy. Marie Voth's writings are valuable, first of all, because they provide a systematic eyewitness account of *(top)* **Fig.36,** View of Peter and Catherine Unruh Voth's housebarn. Built in 1876 in Gnadenfeld village, Alexanderwohl community, a mile east of Goessel, Kansas, on the south side of the road. Demolished around 1908. Drawing by Marie Voth, their great-granddaughter.[12]

(bottom) **Fig.37,** Floorplan of Peter and Catherine Unruh Voth's housebarn.[13]

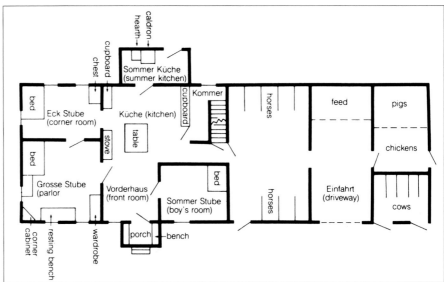

the memories of a boy in his grandparents' house. Also important is the fact that the author specifies how the Peter and Catherine Voth house differed from the "traditional" or ideal typical Mennonite house. This "atypical" and very particular example of an immigrant Mennonite home allows us to see how space and furniture were used to meet the needs created by the "rituals of domestic life."

Following long-standing European tradition the Peter Voth residence was a housebarn. The human dwelling was connected to the animal dwelling with a narrow passageway. Family oral tradition, according to Marie Voth, explained that the dark passageway between barn and house had two doors to keep the odor of the barn out of the house. Perhaps the problem with odors was one reason why the housebarn pattern did not survive more than one generation on the Plains.

The Voth house did not have the traditional massive hearth, or "black

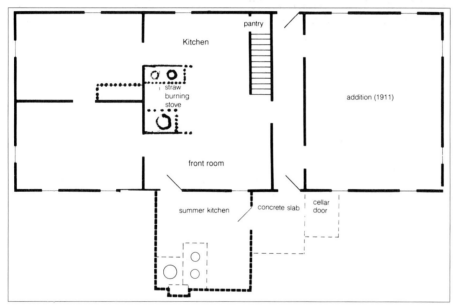

(top) **Fig.38,** Voth/Unruh/Fast House, built in 1875-6, Gnadenfeld village, Alexanderwohl community, central Kansas. Moved one mile east in 1884. Parlor added in 1911. Moved to Kauffman Museum grounds in 1974. Present state, without summer kitchen.[14]

(bottom) **Fig.39,** Floorplan of the Voth/Unruh/Fast House. Dotted lines indicate original oven and hearth location.

chimney." It is unclear whether the house originally had a hearth which was removed during remodeling or whether it was, in fact, built without one. In the place of the central hearth stood a brick stove which, family tradition held, was much appreciated in winter by those who sat there on the bench to warm themselves.

This large stove with its brick mass radiated so much heat that it was uncomfortable or unbearable in summertime. The functions of the hearth and some other aspects of year-round kitchen work, such as washing, moved to the built-on summer kitchen adjoining the house or to the smokehouse removed from the house. This may have been another reason why the conventional Mennonite housebarn style was abandoned on the prairies of North America.

With the central hearth reduced to a brick stove that could be used only when it was cold outside, the traditional Russian-style distribution of rooms—a front room and a rear room—was replaced by a large kitchen, the largest room in the

(right) **Fig.40,** Table with drawer, ca. 1876-1880. From the Isaac B.Fast family, rural Goessel community, Kansas. Pine, red-orange paint. Drawer has dovetailed joints and wooden pegs; dovetailed cleats run under the table top; horizontal molding accents the skirt, tapered legs.
H:28½" L:40½" W:29¾".
#15.010, KM 87.91.1.

(facing page) **Fig.41,** Wardrobe, ca. 1875-1880. Maker unknown. From the Isaac B. Fast family, Goessel community, Kansas. Gable constructed separately, appears to be a fragment only. Pine, with painted red-orange and black trim.
H:72" (without gable) W:23¼"
W:51½"
#11.005, KM 87.91.2.

house, where much of the daily living of the family occurred.

Sleeping arrangements in the Voth home were also different than the ideal traditional pattern, suggests Marie Voth. With three daughters and three sons the Voths needed separate bedrooms for the children. Because there was no *Kjleenestov*, the girls slept in the *Akjstow*. The parents used the *Grootestow* as their bedroom, and the boys slept in the unheated *Sommastow*. It is not clear where guests slept.

Storage needs were taken care of by numerous cupboards, wardrobes and chests. There was a *Koma* or pantry off the kitchen and a cellar provided a relatively cool place for storing apples and potatoes.

The *Grootestow,* or parlor in Americanized parlance, had all the requisite attributes: the wardrobe for the family's dress clothes; the daybed *(Ruebenkj)* for resting or sitting; a wall clock from Russia; the pullout guest bed with comforters, quilts and pillows stacked atop it; a dresser; and Peter Voth's corner cabinet where he kept his books, writing materials and, in the bottom drawer, his special pastoral papers. This room was originally heated by a brick stove in the corner. Later, an iron stove was installed in the room.

The symbols of continuity and transience, the dowry chest and the clock, respectively, both came with the family from Russia. The chest stood in the corner room, and the clock in the *Grootestow*.

From 1875 on, another smaller house without an adjoining barn stood near the Peter Voth house. This was the home of the Voths' eldest son David and his wife Marie Isaacs. It became the Voth/Unruh/Fast house that is now at the Kauffman Museum (Figs. 38, 39). Originally the house was very similar to the Mennonite house described by Worrall in McPherson County (Figs. 1-4). Interrupted floor joists suggest that this house earlier had the massive central hearth, possibly made of adobe, as well as the heating stove. It lacked the

Fig.42, Pullout bed, ca. 1875-1880. Voth/Unruh/Fast House. From the Isaac B. Fast family, Goessel community. Pine, painted orange-red. Pullout section makes this into a double bed.

H:37½" L:72½" D:28½".
#17.004, KM 87.91.3.

Kjleenestow. Little is known about the furnishings in the house at the time David and Marie Voth lived there. From the Unruh and Fast families, who lived in the house after 1884, a table (Fig. 40), cupboard (Fig. 17), wardrobe (Fig. 41), pullout bed (Fig. 42) and immigrant trunk remain.

With the breakup of the village in 1884, the house was sold and moved on rollers one mile away to a farmstead. The hearth was rebuilt of adobe brick. In 1911 the hearth was removed and a "parlor" was built on. A summer kitchen with a brick cookstove and cauldron was attached to the house.

The Peter and David Voth homes, side by side, suggest that the prairie immigrant extension of the Mennonite tradition of building and furniture making contained a considerable degree of flexibility, and that each construction expressed the perceived needs of the family. Whether large or small, with central hearth or without, what we have called "rituals and spaces of domestic life" found their expression.

In the next chapter we turn to the sources of this tradition in the Vistula Delta of Poland, and even further back, to the sixteenth century refugee Mennonites from The Netherlands and other parts of Europe.

SIGISMVNDVS AVGVSTVS
REX POLONIARVM.

2

The Sources for a
Vistula Delta Tradition

We, Wladislaw IV, by the grace of God king of Poland, grand duke of
Lithuania, Russia, Prussia, Masovia, Samogitia, Latvia, Smolensk and
Czernichow...serve notice to all concerned. All industry and effort that
serve the common good are worthy of princely grace and protection. We
are well aware of the manner in which the...Mennonite inhabitants in...
Marienburg islands were invited by the Loitzes, with the approval and
prior knowledge of the gracious Sigismund Augustus, our ancestor and
grandfather; we granted certain freedoms, rights and privileges; came to
desolate, swampy and unusable regions. Through much work and at great
expense, through clearing of bushes, building of necessary watermills to
drain the water from the flooded and swampy areas, as well as the building
of dikes to contain the waters of the Vistula, Nogat, Drausen, Haff and
Tiege...made the lands fruitful and useful. Thereby they left a remarkable
example of industry, work and expenditures for their descendants...by
virtue of our royal authority, we affirm each and every right, privilege,
freedom and exemption granted by the gracious Sigismund August our
grandfather, and confirmed by the gracious Sigismund Augustus III our
royal ancestor...[1] (Warsaw, 22 December, 1642)

The story of the domestic furnishings tradition that immigrant Mennonites
brought to the Plains in the late nineteenth century begins where the Vistula
River flows into the Baltic Sea. This region is today an integral part of Poland,
as it was in the sixteenth century when Mennonites first came to the area. For
several centuries the Delta of the Vistula River had been a very cosmopolitan
place with Slavic, Germanic, Dutch, Baltic and Italian influences.

The Mennonite culture that came to the North American Plains was largely
derived from this common culture of the Vistula Delta. The *Plautdietsch* or Low
German spoken by Mennonites was the vernacular language of the Vistula

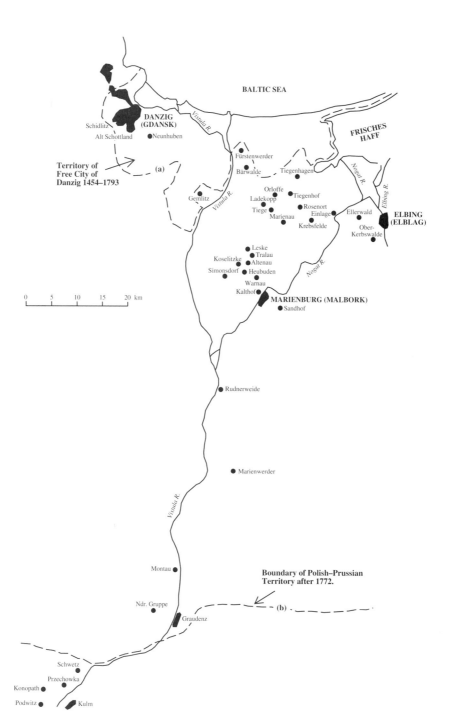

Map 4. (Detail of Map 2) Vistula Delta Mennonite settlements from 16th century on, as noted in text; territories of (a) Free City of Danzig, 1454-1793, and (b) first Prussian partition of Poland, 1772.

Delta; Mennonites learned it and made it their own. Their architecture and furnishings likewise reflected this culturally diverse setting.

This chapter sketches the background of the common culture of the Vistula Delta. The next chapter shows how the Mennonites appropriated elements of this common culture and adopted them as their own.

Rich Farmland and Cosmopolitan Centers

Opening into the Baltic Sea, the Vistula Delta landscape reminds one of The Netherlands: flat land, canals, marshy swamps, tree-lined lanes and roads, farms, villages, towns and a few cities. Through the terrain flow two mighty rivers. The Vistula River, whose headwaters begin near Czechoslovakia far to the south, continues through Cracow and Warsaw, and northward until it empties into the Baltic Sea east of Gdansk, the old port city. The Nogat flows out of the Vistula about 60 miles from the Baltic, and follows the eastern border of the flatlands, through Malbork and the imposing Marienburg Castle, past the small city of Nowy Dwor, once Tiegenhof, and on beyond Elblag, once Elbing, to the east.

A former swampland, much of which is below sea level, the Delta depends on electric pumps, which have replaced the windmills, to keep it dry. Even today eight percent of the Delta is a variety of water courses—big rivers along with major and minor canals.[2] The river outlets to the Baltic have shifted course from time to time, similar to the Nile in Egypt or the Mississippi in the United States. From the fifteenth century onward, as Poland increased its cultivation of grain, silt came down the Vistula in greater and greater volume, blocking the outlets to the sea periodically. The rivers would rise in their banks, flood the entire Delta and inundate the people who tried to live there. However, these floods and the silt made it a very fertile farming area.

After a visit in 1907 Dr. Cornelius Bergmann, whose family had a farm in the area for several centuries, wrote that from the steps of their house one could see the Marienburg Castle in all its grandeur, barely 10 kilometers distant on the high shore of the Nogat. He added, "Wherever one sees the Marienburg Castle, there the land is good."[3]

Kashubay and the Indigenous Kashubians

In prehistoric times hunters and gatherers and fisherfolk lived along these rivers, harvesting the abundant eel, salmon and flounder. Later, as cultivation developed, the Delta held much promise as agricultural land. However, rains, flooding and swampy conditions made farming too difficult much of the time. The inhabitants of the Vistula Delta developed a somewhat specialized technology for survival in the marshes. One unique feature included putting wooden shoes on horses to enable them to walk through the mud.

Today Polish people of the Vistula, and museums of the area, identify the original inhabitants of the Delta as the Kashubians, a Slavic folk with a distinctive dialect who specialized in fishing and whose riverside villages were developed on the western edge of the Vistula Delta.[4]

For hundred of years rulers of the Vistula Delta region promoted draining the swamps and developing the area for agriculture. They were eager to increase the productivity of the land over that of subsistence fishing. However, despite the construction of ever-improved dikes and levees, the region flooded more and more often. Major flood years on the Vistula and the Nogat occurred 19 times between 1376-1475, 10 times between 1476-1575, 23 times between 1576-1675, 29 times between 1676-1775 and 46 times between 1775-1900.[5]

The Mennonites who made the Vistula Delta their home must have had extensive contact with the Kashubians. Stories of Kashubian workers still circulate among Mennonites who left the region after World War II. More indicative of the centuries-old Kashubian–Mennonite connection is the presence, in today's Mennonite *Plautdietsch,* of several expressions and Kashubian language elements that date from the eighteenth century or earlier.[6]

Similarly, the cradles, which were part of the Mennonite immigrant tradition, are identical to Kashubian peasant cradles found today in Polish museum collections (Fig. 43).

The Kashubian house-styles may have contributed another major element to Mennonite building, namely, the massive central chimney and side stoves. Unfortunately, we know very little about interactions between Kashubians and Mennonites over the several centuries (1535 until after World War II) when Mennonites were permitted to settle in the marshes, to drain them and to make homes for themselves there.

The Teutonic Knights

The first efforts to drain the swamps of the Vistula were undertaken by the Teutonic Knights in the thirteenth century. These knights had been active in the Crusades. Headquartered in Venice, they were within reach of Palestine. However, the government of Venice asked them to leave. They decided to relocate to the southern and eastern Baltic perimeter, where they colonized lands about 50 miles inland by erecting up to 60 fortress-like outposts in what was to them a hostile wilderness. They built the Marienburg, the largest castle in Europe, as

Fig.43, Cradle, Kashubian, late 19th century. Ethnographic Department of the National Museum in Gdansk-Oliwa (Danzig-Oliva), Poland. Wood, polychrome paint.
96cm x 51cm x 70cm.
MNG-1004.

Fig.44, Malbork (Marienburg) Castle of the Teutonic Knights, ca. 1988. Dominating the Nogat River and the Nogat and Vistula lowlands. Post World War II reconstruction of the castle.

their headquarters.[7]

The region was already inhabited by Kashubian and other Slavic farmers who lived under nominal leadership of the kings of Poland and Lithuania. Intent on bringing their rule to these lands, the knights claimed to be there to assist the Christian kings of Poland and Lithuania in their efforts to conquer and Christianize the pagan Slavs. In their fervor the Teutonic Knights nearly exterminated the Preuthenians of the coastal area east of the Delta.[8] They then brought many colonists from central Germany to settle and build farms in the regions under their control. There resulted a synthesis of Slavic and Germanic culture that would color all subsequent societies of the area which came to be called Prussia. After dominating the area for a century, the knights were defeated by the combined allied forces of Lithuania and Poland at the battle of Tannenberg in 1410.

This history of the Teutonic Knights' presence in the Vistula Delta would be quite beside the point in this book on Mennonite furniture and furnishings, were it not for the fact that Mennonites settled on the lands of the knights, assimilating their names and other cultural features. The Marienburg Castle was within view of many Mennonite villages for centuries (Fig. 44). Colored drawings of the Marienburg appear in handmade arithmetic texts used by Mennonite students in the Vistula Delta in the 1830s.[9] Heubuden (hay sheds), one of the major Mennonite communities and congregations, was named after the site where the knights of the Marienburg once pastured and sheltered their 30,000 horses.

Hans Woede, an East Prussian historian, portrays this region as a cultural landscape with distinctive settlement forms, reflecting some of the architectural features of central Germany brought by the colonists at the time of the knights.[10] Although Dutch Mennonites brought their longhouse style to the Vistula Delta, they also lived in and built houses that incorporated some of the central German architectural forms.

Fig.45, Danzig (Gdansk) Harbor, 1765. Engraving by Matthaeus Deisch. From his "50 Prospekte von Danzig," print 34.

Mercantile Seamen and Hanseatic Cities

The similarity of streetscapes in Gdansk (Danzig), Elblag (Elbing) and Torun (Thorn) to those of Antwerp, Amsterdam, Bruges and Lubeck provide ample evidence of their common culture from ca. 1300 to 1600 (Fig. 45). All were free cities bound together in the mercantile system known as the Hanseatic League. The Hanse arose from the towns and cities of the Middle Ages as they sought to overcome political fragmentation and to promote trade between centers of specialization in natural resources and producers of crafts in the guilds.

Danzig, Thorn and Elbing emerged as Hanseatic towns—alongside older and smaller Slavic towns—and important trading centers between western European, English and even Mediterranean ports and the ports of Lithuania, Latvia and Slavic Russia on the Baltic. Poland and the hinterlands of the Baltic exported grain, flax, honey, wax, fur, wood, tar, pitch and ash in exchange for textiles, salt, fish, wine, spices and metal wares, as well as luxury goods such as art works, gold and silver wares.[11] Through this link these cities acquired a strong Netherlandish urban architectural influence, a common culture based on the rule of the city council and the guilds, as well as on seafaring merchant houses or companies. These merchants often lived in individual houses around the city square.

The Mennonites of Antwerp, Ghent and Bruges in Flanders, of Amsterdam in Holland and of the towns of Friesland were deeply involved in the craft guilds and trade centers of the Hanseatic cities. It is thus clear that they brought this culture with them to the Vistula Delta when they suffered persecution in the Low Countries and fled to Poland in the sixteenth century. They were both prominent and lowly dwellers in Danzig, Elbing and Thorn. Occupational identities of sixteenth century Anabaptist–Mennonites of the Lowlands, many of whom fled north and east, included architects, builders, merchants, farmers, craftsmen and, most commonly, weavers.[12] Indeed, Mennonite weavers were so numerous in the Vistula Delta in the sixteenth century that they essentially controlled the manufacture of lace and linen. They were not part of the guild system, however, because they had been barred from citizenship in Danzig because of their religious faith. The takeover of Muenster, itself a Hanseatic city, by fanatic Anabaptists in 1535 had so alienated the city fathers across

Europe that most Hanse cities, including Danzig, Elbing and Thorn, wanted nothing of these people, despite their skills.

However, the Polish nobility who controlled the countryside, the Polish crown and the Catholic church with its vast holdings, all taken from the Teutonic order, welcomed Mennonite refugees to settle in the swamps and flooded marshes of the Vistula Delta and invited them to use their skills of land reclamation to turn the region into a productive plain. Most Mennonite farm homes had rooms or areas where looms were used to contribute to the household's cash income. Danzig permitted Mennonite weavers to live in the suburbs of the town but not inside city limits. Elbing allowed a few Mennonite families to become citizens in the sixteenth century.

Even after the demise of the Hanseatic League in the seventeenth century, Danzig flourished as an independent city free of direct state control. One indication of its increasing economic role is the rise in grain export from the interior of Poland to western Europe, from 25,000 tons (12,800 *Last*) in 1492 to 232,000 tons (116,000 *Last*) in 1618 (Fig. 46).[13]

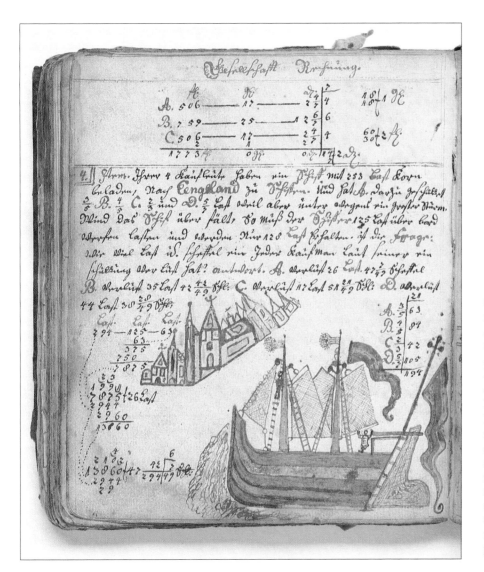

Fig.46, Ship loaded with grain from the Vistula Delta sails to England. Illumination in Gerhard Nickel's *Arithmetic Book,* 1797, Montau, West Prussia. Illustrates problem in economics *(Gesellschaft Rechnung).* "Four merchants loaded a ship with 253 *Last* grain (one *Last* is 60 *Scheffel*) to be shipped to England. A.Put in⅗ of the total amount, B.⅘. C.⅔. D.⅝. But because on the way the ship was attacked by a great wind the captain had to have 125 *Last* thrown overboard and only 128 *Last* were retained. Thus the question is: calculate, in succession, how much *Last* and *Scheffel* each merchant would have lost."[1] The teacher then also wrote the solution of the problem as well as the proof on this page.

(right) **Fig.47,** Arcaded courtyard of the Polish king's palace on the Wawel hill, Cracow, 1507-1536. Designed by Francesco Fiorentino, Benedykt von San-Domierz and Bartolomeo Berrecci.

(below) **Fig.48,** King Sigismund August of Poland (1520-1572). Engraving, artist unknown.

SIGISMVNDVS AVGVSTVS
REX POLONIARVM.

The Polish Renaissance of the Jagiellonen House

The Germanic powers of the Baltic coast waned with the defeat of the Teutonic Knights. The Peace Treaty of Thorn in 1411, and the treaty of Cracow in 1525, represented the rising prominence of the Polish crown in the area, in the form of the Jagiellonen dynasty. Political consolidation and economic prosperity, along with the pivotal mercantile role of Danzig, created a "Greater Poland" whose influence was dominant from the fifteenth century into the eighteenth century. Never before, nor since, has Poland had the territorial significance that it enjoyed during this time.

The combined forces of Jagiellonen patronage of the arts and learning as represented by the University of Cracow brought new styles and architectural structures to the Polish and Baltic region. Principal among these influences was the commissioning of Italian architects Francesco Fiorentino, Benedykt von San-Domierz and Bartolomeo Berrecci by Sigismund I of Poland to create an Italian Renaissance palace in the Wawel in Cracow.[14] The arcaded courtyard of the palace influenced new construction throughout greater Poland and Lithuania, including the facades of the buildings along the market in Marienburg and prominent country houses in the Vistula Delta and beyond (Fig. 47).

Into this setting came the Mennonites when they fled persecution in 1535-75. Under Sigismund II (Fig. 48) and for two centuries following, they were given special privileges of religious freedom and access to land in the Vistula Delta in the form of five- to thirty-year leases for block grants called *Hollandrzy,* or "Hollander settlements."

Influences of Polish national culture on life in the Delta region and on architectural and furniture styles as described above indirectly affected Mennonites. For example, the styles introduced through Italian Renaissance architecture filtered through to craftsmen and builders, most notable in the arcaded housefront style. The intricate inlay woodwork (Fig. 49) was incorporated by the guild cabinetmakers who built the finer dowry chests and wardrobes

Mennonites bought (Figs. 50a, b, c). Mennonite craftsmen also copied these designs when building their own furniture. We do not know how many Mennonite craftsmen from Flanders and Holland may have been involved in the Polish Renaissance.

However, one Mennonite family, the Uylenburgs, are known to have been very fine craftsmen. Gerard Rombout Uylenburg, who died in Cracow in 1601, was a royal cabinetmaker (joiner) for King Sigismund III. His sons were Rombert, painter in Cracow and Danzig for the king of Poland, and Hendrik, painter and art dealer. Hendrik, a close friend of Rembrandt's, was baptized in the Danzig Mennonite church in 1612 to the Waterlander Anabaptists.[15]

Fig.50 a, b,c, Dowry chest, ca. 1789-1790. Taken by the grandmother or great-grandmother of Anna Wiens Enns from Prussia to Chortitza, South Russia in 1789-90. From there Anna's mother took the chest to Bergthal, a colony of Chortitza in Ekaterinoslav Province, South Russia in the 1830s. From there Anna Wiens Enns and Diedrich Enns took the chest to Avon, South Dakota in 1876, and from there to Mountain Lake, Minnesota. Anna Wiens Enns' daughter Anna Enns (1857-1934) married Johann Harder in 1885, and inherited the chest. Her son Jacob J. Harder purchased the chest at her sale in 1930. The dowry chest is now in the seventh generation. Ash, inlaid veneers of contrasting colors form scroll and flower motifs; burr veneer covers the molding surrounding the lid. Separate five-legged bracket base with swagged skirt. Dovetailed corner joints covered with inlaid baluster motif. Brass key plate decorated with engraved ornament. Brass bosses covering the lock and hinge bolts are engraved. Handle of the cast brass key formed of countercurving scrolls, matching those of the inlay work and of the ornate hinges. Entire lock case and the corresponding lock latch plate have engraved floral motifs. Tooled metal handle plates, handles and tinned iron hinges feature ornate cut and embossed designs.[2]

    H:26" D:26" W 56".
    #1.019, Private collection.

The Prussian Connection

    The region and the people known as Prussia and Prussians enter history as the "Preuthians," a Slavic tribe occupying the area around the southeast shores of the Baltic Sea—eastward from the Vistula Delta to today's Kaliningrad, formerly Koenigsberg, in the Soviet Union. Largely exterminated by the Teutonic Knights in the thirteenth century, their region became German against a backdrop of Slavic place names. After the defeat of the knights in 1410, the area was called Polish Prussia. Although politically defeated, the knights lived on as secular dukes in the Polish kingdom and as merchants, businessmen and later industrialists. Their influence in the free cities of Danzig and Elbing was significant. Around 1600 these princes of Prussia consolidated their local power in an alliance with Brandenburg to form the state of Prussia.[16] In 1772 this ascending, economically powerful, secular, modern state took over the Vistula

Delta and with it the control of Poland's principal outlet to the sea, Danzig.

The rise of Prussia under Frederick the Great and the annexation of North Poland, including the Vistula Delta in 1772, had wide-ranging effects (Fig. 52). All residents gained individual citizenship in the new state. However, Mennonites who had enjoyed special privileges and freedom from military service—for a price—now were faced with military conscription of their youth. Whereas previously land had been negotiated by the church elders, and everyone who wished had a parcel, however small, the block leases of the Hollander system were now gone. On the other hand, private ownership of land was possible. Whereas previously the state recognized only the duly instituted leaders of the Mennonite congregations, and could in effect control this leadership by withholding land rights, now the state permitted Mennonite churches to exist as independent legal corporations.

In the next chapter we will see in more detail how the end of block leases of land quickly sharpened class divisions among Mennonites. Along with the wealthy landed, there were now growing numbers of landless persons. Many Mennonites, faced with having to be successful businessmen in a competitive capitalist economy, lost their land. They were driven, or drawn, into crafts and trades and toward emigration. At this point a "Mennonite" craft tradition emerged, which then became an emigrant tradition as the landless and poor, as well as some wealthy entrepreneurs, sought opportunities elsewhere.

Original Language Synthesis
Mirrors Cultural Synthesis

The point that the sources of a Vistula Delta culture, material and non-material, are exceedingly diverse and original has been stressed in the foregoing pages. Given the following major sources of influence— indigenous Slavic; the Germanic knights coming from the Mediterranean; the north German, English and Netherlands Hanseatic League; the Polish crown and academy filtering Italian Renaissance styles and ideas to the region; and, finally, the rationalism and state absolutism of Prussia—an original combination of forms, styles and uses developed in domestic architecture and furniture.

The originality of this synthesis in the Vistula Delta tradition that became Mennonite can perhaps best be illustrated by a brief analogy to the common language of the area, *Plautdietsch,* still spoken by some Mennonites and known to them as *Mennoniten-plaut.* The main body of the language derived from the middle and north German colonists who were brought into the region by the Teutonic Knights in the fourteenth century.[17] However, Mennonite refugees who came in large numbers in the last third of the sixteenth century, although they rarely represented a majority of the inhabitants, brought the Dutch language with them into the region. Linguists, who have studied the historical layers and sound influences of *Plautdietsch,* identify a special combination of influences from the outside: at least 150 Dutch words; possibly one Kashubian phoneme; and 50 Polish and Slavic words.[18] However, there are significant dialectal differences between the *Plautdietsch* spoken in what is known as the Old Colony community of Mennonites, who left the Vistula Delta in 1789 for Chortitza in Russia and no longer used the Dutch language but had not yet acquired High German, and the settlers of Molotschna, who did not begin leaving the Vistula

(top) **Fig.51,** Gable of a house in Gdansk, 1650. Exuberant, baroque, architectural ornament of curves, counter-curves, ovals and scrolls corresponds to the inlaid ornament of dowry chests of the late 18th century, such as the Wiens/Enns/Harder family chest in Fig. 50 a,b,c.

(bottom) **Fig.52,** Frederick II of Prussia (1712-1786). Also called "Frederick the Great." Engraving, artist unknown.

55

Delta until the 1820s. The Molotschna settlers had adopted High German as their language of worship, although they still spoke *Plautdietsch* in common discourse.

If we use language to situate material culture, we may imagine, then, that *Plautdietsch*, the common language of the Vistula Delta, was given some Dutch enrichment by Mennonites and other Netherlanders. It further reflected a Slavic ambiance.

By analogy, the domestic culture of the household form and its furnishings also reflected the multiple influences of those who built it and used it, coming from numerous origins and social classes. This is not the same as the well known and much used distinction between "folk" and "high culture," which usually suggests a country–city dichotomy. We will see that although some pieces of furniture were commissioned from professional guilds, the same patterns and styles were practiced in country workshops not allied with the guilds, producing a varied line of products for different pocketbooks. The city–country dichotomy is also not useful because it negates the constant interaction we know existed between the two realms, both within and without Mennonite circles. Class distinctions in the furniture tended instead to reflect the distinction between the landed, rural elite, just as there were urban elite, and the rural poor, just as there were urban poor.

3
Making the
Tradition Mennonite

Whereas the previous chapter sketched the sources and synthesis of the common culture of the Vistula Delta, the setting within which northern European Mennonite culture flourished, this chapter looks at Mennonite life from the inside, asking what was the basis of the distinctive Mennonite material culture, and how did it draw from its diverse sources?

Anabaptist-Mennonite Identity in the Vistula Delta

Mennonites, as a result of sixteenth century Reformation radicalism, emphasized separation of church and state, non-participation in war and a believers' church based on adult baptism. In the diaspora resulting from severe persecution in the Holy Roman Empire, Mennonites from all over western Europe found refuge in the Vistula Delta under the protection of the Polish kings. The dominant cultural identity of these Mennonites was Flemish, Dutch and Frisian. Although early church polity was unified under a bishop at Danzig, later differences emerged between Flemish and Frisian factions.

The language of worship for the first two centuries of the Polish period remained Dutch. Danzig Mennonites retained the Dutch language into the eighteenth century, whereas Mennonites in other parts of Poland had begun by this time to worship in the vernacular, *Plautdietsch*. Only in the Prussian period, that is around 1790, did High German become the language of worship among Mennonites, replacing Dutch where it was still used, and the vernacular where it had come to be used.

Architecture and the Mennonite Role in Vistula Delta Culture

As with the analogy of language, so in architecture and other areas of material

(facing, page) **Fig.53,** Wardrobe made in 1878 by Klaas Hiebert, Cottonwood County, Minnesota, for Jacob and Susanna Klassen Harder on the occasion of their marriage. Wood, painted graining, flower decals. Center for Mennonite Brethren Studies, Fresno, California.[1]
H:90" W:57" D:24".
#11.031.

(left) **Fig.54,** Four houses in Danzig (Gdansk), 16th-18th centuries, Sw. Ducha (Heiliggeistgasse). Note similarity of form between pediments of Mennonite wardrobes and pediments of townhouses in Northern Europe.

culture the Netherlandish influence was strong in Danzig, Elbing and Thorn. The facades of the prominent streets were identical to those in Antwerp, Bruges and Amsterdam. Furniture forms often mirrored these architectural forms and decorative devices. As we saw in chapter two (Figs. 50, 51), the baroque scroll and counterscroll of the townhouse gable was stylistically similar to the inlaid scroll design of the dowry chest, both having been shaped by common style themes. Similarly, the pediments atop many wardrobes reflected the townhouse gables (compare the wardrobe pediments in Fig. 53 and elsewhere in this book with house gables in Fig. 54).

The Mennonite furniture tradition that emerged was historically tied to the urban architecture of the Vistula Delta region, especially the highly sophisticated inlaid hardwood work which was controlled by furniture-making guilds.

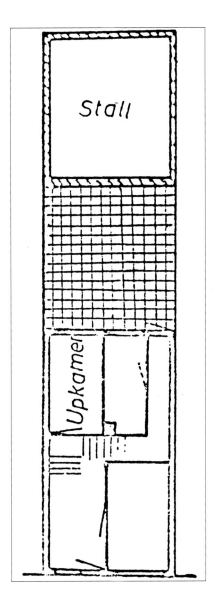

We know that Mennonites were not permitted access to burgher status in Danzig prior to 1772. However, many of them lived and worked just outside the city limits in the suburbs of Schidlitz, Langfuhr and Alt Schottland. There and in the Vistula Delta countryside—most notably, the Mennonite craft center of Tiegenhof—they skillfully copied the patterns and decorative styles of the guilds. Some of the influential architects and builders, such as Van Obbergens of Antwerp (*Stadtbaumeister* 1572-74), who worked on the old City Hall, the Van den Blocks and the engineer Adam Wiebe, who helped change the face of the city to that of a Netherlands Renaissance style, may have been Mennonite, although there are no documents to substantiate this fully.[1]

The possibility that Mennonites contributed to life in the city of Elbing during the sixteenth century was greater because we know the decree by the city council in 1571 ordering them to leave was not upheld. As early as 1585 Jost van Kampen and Hans van Koeln had received burgher status and were living in

(right) **Fig.55,** House at Prinzess-strasse, Friedrichstadt, North Germany. Built in the early 17th century by refugees from The Netherlands among whom were numerous Mennonites.[2]

(above) **Fig.56,** Floorplan of the house at Prinzessstrasse, Friedrichstadt. The urban housebarn—ancestral form of both later townhouses and country long-houses—as seen in Vistula Delta Mennonite settings.[3]

Elbing.[2] By 1610 there were 16 Mennonite families living in the city. In any event the presence of Mennonites around Danzig and in Elbing, the continued arrival of Netherlandish Mennonites in the late sixteenth and early seventeenth centuries and their return to The Netherlands for baptism and education, in the context of active sea trade with The Netherlands, assured a strong cultural continuity in matters of domestic culture.

This Netherlandish influence must be related to the presence of active guilds in Danzig and Elbing for all of the building and craft trades with the exception of fine weaving, which Mennonites brought from Flanders and which they succeeded in controlling throughout Polish rule of the Vistula Delta.[3] In areas such as urban house building and the production of ceramic tiles, the guilds were especially active, and there are fine examples of their work in museums in Gdansk, Elblag and Torun. We know that middle class Mennonites used ceramic stoves in this regional style and Elbing inlaid-type chests and wardrobes.[4]

The Netherlands Renaissance house form and the longhouse had grown out of similar ancestral forms in which the house facade faced the street, and the household, including the barn and shed for livestock, extended back from it. In Friedrichstadt in northern Germany, where the ravages of the world wars were less severe and where excellent records were kept, examples of such houses built by Mennonites and other sixteenth and seventeenth century refugees from Flanders are either still standing (Fig. 55) or have been documented in the city records (Fig. 56).[5]

In addition, the square courtyard with separate buildings around it, as represented by middle German and Slavic peasant farms, and the southern Renaissance courtyard were used by Mennonites in the Vistula Delta. When we speak therefore of "making the Vistula tradition Mennonite" we mean that Mennonites both brought their architectural styles to the region, mainly the longhouse (Fig. 57) and the urban Renaissance house, and they also adopted other already-existing forms in the area, such as the square farm (Fig. 58).

Fig.57, Elevation and plan of a longhouse, Vistula Delta, 19th century. Houseplan brought to the Vistula Delta from The Netherlands.[4]

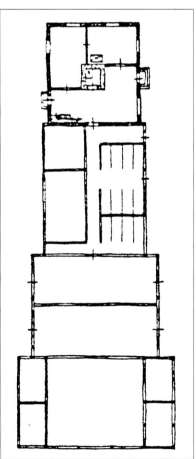

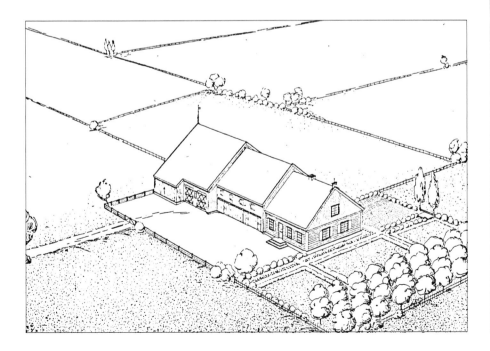

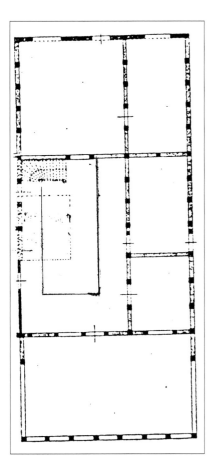

Fig.58, Elevation and plan of an arcaded farmhouse and square farm in the Vistula Delta. Form derives from German colonists under Teutonic Knights.[5]

Mennonite church architecture is the most original contribution of Mennonites to Vistula Delta culture. We have identified two reasons for this: 1) Anabaptist theology professed distinctive concepts of the congregation and of worship; 2) Mennonites were not allowed to build their own worship centers for almost two centuries after their arrival in the Vistula Delta. During this time they worshipped in homes and barns. Consequently, a distinctive Mennonite religious architecture emerged in the mid-eighteenth century.

These particular origins of the architecture, and the fact that the buildings in question were called prayerhouses *(Bethaeuser),* help to explain its distinctiveness from Catholic, Lutheran and Reformed church architecture.

Mennonite Prayerhouses

Mennonite prayerhouse architecture offers an important glimpse into a distinctively Mennonite approach to building, one with a close proximity to the domestic realm. The first Elbing Mennonite prayerhouse is an example of a Renaissance building (Fig. 59), built in the late sixteenth century, at the time the first Mennonites were admitted as burghers to Elbing.[6] It is really a "house-church," founded by 1590, in a patrician-style house at the address of Jost van Kampen, one of the 16 early Mennonites admitted to burgher status in Elbing.[7]

By the seventeenth century there are records of two small Mennonite schools that doubled as local places of worship.[8] The five prayerhouses constructed in the eighteenth century represent the first full architectural expression by Mennonites in the Vistula Delta. This expression subsequently shaped and influenced several centuries of Mennonite prayerhouse building in Russia and in North America. The Rosenort prayerhouse, built in 1750, and those built at Fuerstenwerder (Fig. 60), Heubuden (Fig. 61), Ladekopp and Tiegenhagen in 1768 were constructed following the consent of the Polish king through the bishop of Kulm.

Even so, certain restrictions and conditions affected the outcome, suggesting

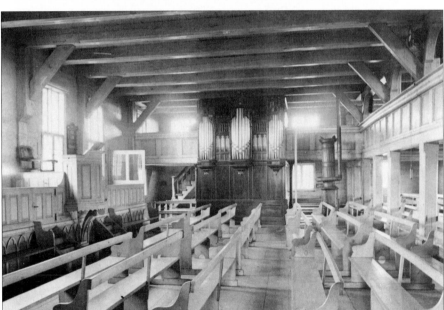

(above) **Fig.59,** Mennonite house and prayerhouse in Elbing (Elblag), built ca. 1590 in the patrician style of Hanseatic cities of northern Europe. Second oldest Mennonite church in Europe (after Pingjum in Friesland, 1575).[6]

(top, left) **Fig.60,** Mennonite prayerhouse, Fuerstenwerder, Vistula Delta, Poland. Built in 1768; photo from 1947.[7]

(bottom, left) **Fig.61,** Interior of the Heubuden Mennonite prayerhouse, Vistula Delta, Poland. Built in 1768; photo from ca. 1890s.[8]

that we cannot be sure what these buildings, which were very similar, would have looked like had no conditions been imposed. First, before building their own meetinghouses, Mennonites were required to construct a Roman Catholic chapel. Second, their prayerhouses were not permitted to resemble "churches." These conditions corresponded with the restriction placed on Mennonites not to proselytize for their faith.

Still, the construction of five of their own major buildings represented a florescence of Mennonite religious distinctiveness in Poland as well as a unique architectural style. These buildings have been called "Gothic" by at least one contemporary student of Mennonite culture in Poland.[9] They were massive wooden log structures dovetailed at the corners. The steep roofs gave the buildings clean almost severe lines in keeping with the Mennonite ethos of plainness. Windows were consistently plain. There was no marked front or entrance, nor a marked sanctuary space. Most had a main entrance at one end with a secondary entrance on one side. On the inside there was an entrance to side rooms, one of which was used for meetings of elders and ministers. Seating separated the men from the women. Benches were arranged in a U-shape around the slightly raised chancel where the elder and ministers sat. A balcony at the back reached from one end to the other (Fig. 61).

Where did this architectural form and its interior use of space originate, since it is unlike those of the Catholic and Protestant churches? Jeremy Bangs, who has studied the origin of this distinctive Anabaptist–Mennonite architecture in The Netherlands, traces it to the Vistula Delta.[10] Its central source is the

Fig.62, Entry hall with second floor balcony, Vistula Delta farm house, photographed ca. 1920.[9]

64

face-to-face meetings favored by Anabaptist–Mennonites of prior centuries which were held in homes, barns, sheds or even outdoors. In architectural terms, Bangs identifies the large two-story halls of the Polish Renaissance houses (with their arcaded fronts) as the likely interior spaces after which these meeting-houses were modeled (Fig. 62). These houses usually have a balcony that wraps around the large central room, connected to the ground floor by a formal stairway. On one side of the room is the massive chimney and hearth that provides the heat for the entire house.

Bangs suggests that this distinctive Mennonite architecture was brought to The Netherlands from the Vistula Delta in the eighteenth century, and was influential in the construction of the remodeled Singelkerk in Amsterdam. The similarities between Anabaptist meetingplace architecture and the architecture of Dutch synagogues suggests a common face-to-face ethos of the congregation; the idea that the sacred presence is in the congregation, rather than in the building or in the altar.

The Danzig church (1818-19), built in the early Prussian period, reflects the late baroque influence seen also in Netherlands and German Mennonite churches of the time.

Mid-nineteenth century Mennonite brick churches in Elbing and Marienburg are similar to other brick buildings of the era and the dominant neo-Gothic style

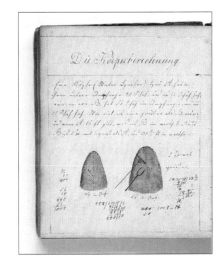

(above) **Fig.63,** Calculation of the volume of a hay stack *(Koerperberech-nung):* "Calculate the volume of two hay stacks of different sizes and calculate the market value of the larger one based on the value of 16 florin for the smaller one." From Peter Penner's *Arithmetic Book,* 1838, Ober Kerbswald, West Prussia.[11] Pen and ink, watercolor.

(left) **Fig.64,** Calculation of land *(Landrechnung),* 1797. From Gerhard Nickel's *Arithmetic Book,* Montau, West Prussia.[10]

8" x 6½".

Pen and ink, watercolor.

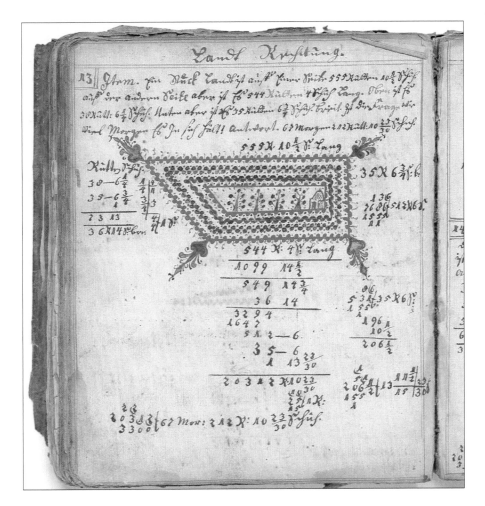

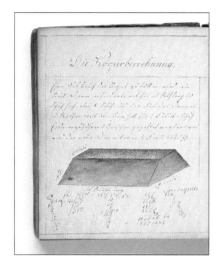

(above) **Fig.65,** The Calculation of Volume *(Koerperberechnung):* "How to calculate the costs for filling a break on the dike on the Nogat River with dirt. Two cubic feet dirt cost 1 *Groschen.* From Peter Penner's *Arithmetic Book,* 1838, Ober Kerbswald, West Prussia.[12]

(right) **Fig.66,** How to Calculate a Well (Brunnenberechnung): "Someone is hired to dig a well which is to be 10 *Ruthen* deep and which is to cost 10 *florin.* But when he had dug 6 *Ruthen* deep he found already enough water. Now the question is, how much does he need to be paid?" From Peter Penner's *Arithmetic Book,* 1838, Ober Kerbswald, West Prussia.[13]

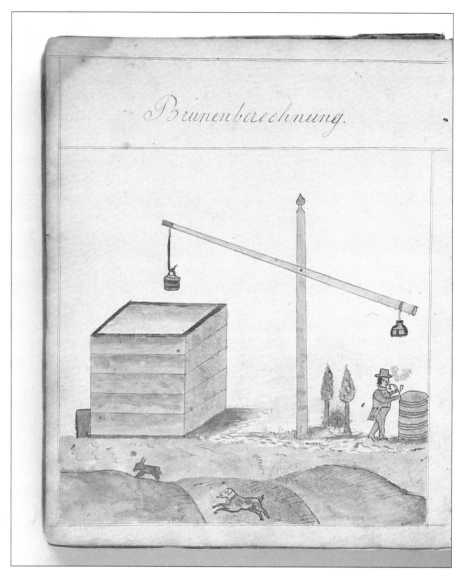

used by architects for churches at that time. These churches also reflect the independence of congregations as corporations under the Prussian state, thus a different legal system that allowed greater local autonomy and variety in building. The nineteenth and twentieth century neo-Gothic churches built by Mennonites show complete acculturation to the dominant cultural forms.

Mennonite Domestic Architecture

The environment and its dictates shaped the architecture of both urban and rural Mennonite domestic architecture. In the cities this included building customs and codes, material uses and space constraints; in the country it included the whole matter of living in and adapting to the lowlands along with the legal issue of land tenure. (Figs. 63-67 show drawings by Mennonite teachers Gerhard Nickel and Peter Penner of scenes from this setting.)

Several Mennonite authors have identified the rural house form of Vistula Mennonites with a distinctive type of village[11]—the *Marschhufendorf*[12]—

(top, left) **Fig.67,** Housebarn or longhouse, 1838, Ober Kerbswald, Vistula Delta. From Peter Penner's *Arithmetic Book.* Following this page are a series of problems on land measurements (*Landberechnung*). Pen and ink, watercolors, 8" x 6¾".[14]

(bottom, left) **Fig.68,** Farm of Elder Johann Kaethler, Vistula Delta. Artist Marie Birckholtz-Bestvater, ca. 1930. Oil on canvas, 86cm. x 113cm.[15]

which featured longhouses along an elevated dike street—house facing street, then connected barn for animals, then connected shed, then long fields stretching back to canal or river. Remnants of the longhouse form built up against canals, or even on polder-like rises in the lowlands near Elbing, are still visible, but no examples of full villages survive. This form was taken to South Russia in the 1790s-1820s, and continued as the basis of Mennonite village architecture until the late twentieth century.

The *Hollanderdorf* (Polish, *Oledrey*) system, based within the larger structure of Polish feudalism, was initially both an architectural and a legal institution, often but not exclusively involving Mennonites. Legally it referred to the communal "block lease" by a land-owning nobleman or the Catholic bishop to a group of farmers for a duration from as few as five to as many as thirty years.[13] Later, in the eighteenth century, non-Mennonites entered into this arrangement with the Polish noble or ecclesiastical landowners. Although the lease could be inherited by the lessee, the landlord could at any time reject the lease holder in favor of another lessee. There was some risk involved in the system, but it offered the incentive to keep the land, dikes and canals in good condition so the lord would renew the lease, hopefully, without raising the rents exorbitantly. The earliest Mennonite leases in the sixteenth century had been in the Danzig lowlands where the city of Danzig was the Mennonites' landlord. City fathers soon reduced the timespan of the leases to five years and doubled the rents at every renewal. Most Mennonites abandoned the Danzig lands for even swampier lowlands where the lease basis was more favorable. In the region around Kulm, "Kulmish law" came under the control of the Catholic bishop, the Mennonites' landlord in these areas. In the Elbing lowlands and the region around Heubuden, northwest of Marienburg, Polish nobility were the landlords.

Mennonite domestic architecture in the Vistula Delta followed two basic forms, each of which had certain variations.[14] The longhouse or housebarn

Fig.69, Central chimney in a dismantled home in Fuerstenwerder, Poland. Photographed summer 1990.[16]

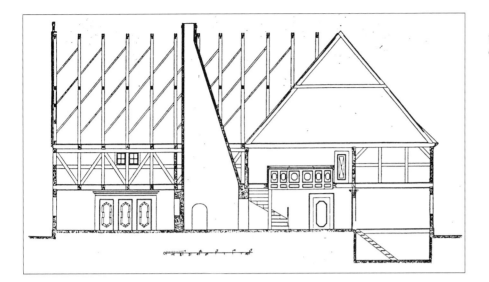

Fig.70, Cross section of an 18th century house with massive central chimney over the central kitchen.[17]

originated in The Netherlands and has already been discussed (Figs. 55, 56,57, 67). The other type arranged detached buildings around a square yard (Fig. 58). The cultural history that separates these two types of architecture appears to go deeper than mere building arrangements.

Bernhard Schmidt, who has studied language, legal and architectural correspondence, notes that the first type—the longhouse, with house, barn and shed built together (straight or L-shape)—was found most often in group-lease or lease-rent settlements and accompanied small or middle-range landholdings and the use of the *Plautdietsch* language. The other type, a farm with buildings surrounding a square, was found primarily in the villages laid out during the Teutonic Knight era under Kulmish law. These villages had large holdings and the primary language was Middle German. Houses were usually of the arcaded type (Fig. 68).

The post World War II Polish scholar Jerzy Stankiewicz, who surveyed the Vistula Delta countryside, identifies in these two different systems, often found side by side in farms and villages, patterns for expanding the farmstead and its buildings. The longhouse could be extended in three ways as space and means permitted. The entrance, usually on the long side, faced the yard and road. The ground floor plan included a "room with built-in cupboards, one with the kitchen, a chimney over a hearth, and a large entrance; and a utility room that abuts and enters the barn." Expansion usually occurred by adding an L-shaped barn to the longhouse barn. It could also be expanded into a huge T-shaped building by adding two L-shaped extensions onto the barn, one in each direction.[15] Occasionally the longhouse of this expanded type appeared with an arcaded front.

The square yard with separate buildings could also be expanded from its basic formula of a house, a barn and several sheds. This usually occurred by adding rooms onto one or both sides of the house and running the roof perpendicular to the arcaded front facing the street. Of course, where the house was more elaborate, the barns also increased in size.[16]

Mennonites lived in and, at least from the eighteenth century, constructed both types of homes. Although they apparently had a greater affinity for the

Fig.71, Ceramic tile stove, 1792. From the home of the Mennonite farmer, T. Goossen, Vistula Delta. Museum of Kwidzin (Marienwerder).[18]

longhouse and were, undoubtedly, the major players in bringing this household form to the Delta, Mennonites also began purchasing farms of the square yard type soon after their arrival. They repaired, reconstructed and eventually also built in that style. There were also long-time Vistula Delta inhabitants among the Slavic peoples of the area and the Germanic colonists who became Mennonite, thus also bringing into the Mennonite community their diverse styles of homes.

Many of the surviving homes of both types, built by Mennonites, have inscriptions on the lintels above the doors. These are often scriptural or moralistic verses in addition to the names of builders or patrons, and the date of construction.

The Role of the Chimney

Stankiewicz points out that the massive black kitchen chimney, accessible from the entrance room or the hall, was a basic feature in many Delta houses (Fig. 69). It was more vast in the large-hall house (Fig. 70), often arcaded, than in the longhouse. Stankiewicz also notes that the massive chimney occurred not only in the Vistula Delta, but also southward to Torun and Mazovia near Warsaw, eastward to Prussia, Ucker and Neumark and westward to Braunschweig and Posen.

Scholars puzzle over this distribution, considering that many rural house traditions in western Europe—e.g., the Saxon and the Frankish houses of Germany and the housebarns of Flanders and Friesland—had open hearths until the late nineteenth or even early twentieth century.[17] It is possible there may have been houses with open hearths in the Vistula Delta very early on—e.g., fifteenth century—but there is no documentation of it. All suggestions of the indigenous building structures, such as among the Kashubians, display the massive chimneys. The uniqueness of the massive chimney in all levels of Delta society is even more pronounced because, as Schmidt notes, in much of central Europe—the Kurland, the Black Forest, Austria and the Alps—peasant houses, even at the turn of the twentieth century, still had no chimneys.

A plausible explanation for the presence of massive chimneys in Vistula Delta and adjoining peasant homes and farmhouses is that the form must have been developed well before the sixteenth century. Thus, Mennonites, who brought the longhouse style with its open hearth to the Delta, adopted the chimney construction from their neighbors. Mennonites then took the massive chimney and its adaptations along to the Ukraine. The separate room heater became the "Russian oven" attached to the chimney.

The Interior Furnishings of Mennonite Homes in the Vistula Delta

A glimpse back in time to Mennonite home interiors prior to the Prussian era, and prior to the migrations to South Russia, is necessary for our discussion.

The early eighteenth century household of Heinrich Bartz of Kossowo, recorded at the time of his death in 1748, reveals the basic set of furnishings. His well-to-do farm had 12 horses, 17 cows, two bulls, numerous calves, 33 pigs, seven sheep, geese, ducks and chickens. Land holdings were 2 *Huben,* 29 *Morgen* and 139 *Ruthen.* Furnishings included "a table and all benches found in the large room; the wall clock, the large wardrobe and the corner wall cabinet."

Fig.72, "Children's Room in the Danzig Mennonite Dwelling Place." Artist Marie Birckholtz-Bestvater, ca. 1935. Oil on canvas, 81.5cm. x 99cm.[19]

The record also mentions a key or hook board, wooden shelf, table, chest, bed, chairs, and again table, chest, bed and chair valued at 60 *Gulden* and 39 *Groschen*.[18]

A house in Neunhuben, built in 1753 by Peter Rosenfeld, was studied in the 1930s by Herbert Wiebe. It had been changed in recent years, but the original outline and interior could be discerned.

> [The house] consists of one large room and two or three smaller rooms. In the center of the house there used to be the so-called black kitchen...A room which is preserved in the style of the 18th century features a Dutch tile stove [see Fig. 71], ceilings and walls painted with old patterns of birds, the pullout bed piled high with pillows and featherbeds *(Himmelbett)*, the corner cupboards and the built-in wall cabinets. This room is similar to the furnishings of living rooms in Danzig [Gdansk] of the same period.[19]

These two accounts from the mid-eighteenth century may be matched with a painting of a "corner room" (Fig. 72) and a 1907 description of the interior of a Mennonite farmhome in the Heubuden community, between Marienburg and Dirschau, farm No. 43. This farm and house had been in the family since 1743.[20]

> There was the large hall with a cloakroom, with wardrobes and with a window in the interior wall which lights the enclosed kitchen. To the right a small room for the children or for the retired parents, to the left a not-so-large study for the owner of the farm. Then one continues to the *Grosse Stube,* which has three or four windows. Ivy vines frame the windows and along the cornice across the whole room. On the walls were hung—or hang still today—engravings of well-known paintings: the *Deposition of Christ* by Rubens, the *Portrait of Christ* by Guido Reni or other religious images which appealed to pietism; also landscapes of the

Rhine, such as the Loreley or similar scenes.

The Biedermeier-canape [sofa] has been replaced by a plush sofa of the Victorian era, but the curved chairs and tables have endured and witness to the taste of those years when the art of the country craftsmen was equal to that of the craftsmen of the city. And many a commode [chest of drawers] of the last quarter of the 18th century had a right to take the first place as room decoration. Here in the center room also stood, still, the furniture of great-grandmother which had been part of the dowry she had brought to the home. The large ash wardrobe of 1770 in a moderate Danzig-baroque style sufficiently adhered to horizontal and vertical lines so that it complemented the unpretentiousness of a farm home [compare with setting of Fig. 73]. One door bore the burn scars of a pine torch which Napoleon's soldiers had negligently fastened there in 1812. Also the 1783 clock from Amsterdam had found its space in this room and had guided the fates of people through time. A graceful sitting bench, probably the precursor of the later canape, made of cherry wood, had a well made comfortable seat which served as the lid for a chest and a most decorative, low backrest. In a Biedermeier *secretaire* old documents were safely kept, the first deed of 1742, the division of the estate of the grandfather of my grandfather in 1799, signed by Abraham Harder, Agatha Harderin, Abraham Enss, Klas Enss, Anna Enssen, Johann von Riesen, all names of relatives of the family whose descendants had their homes and were known here as well as in the daughter colonies in Russia.

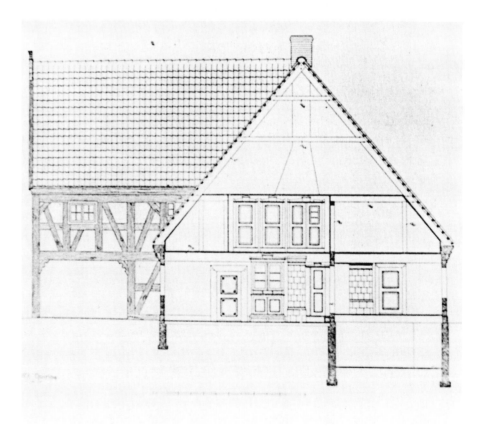

Fig.73, Cross section of the Quiring House in Ladekopp, West Prussia. Built in 1749. Note the massive central chimney. This drawing is also the most convincing document for establishing the Vistula Delta origin of the cabinet and wardrobe styles of the Mennonite immigrants to the Plains. Note the cabinet with glass doors, cabinets on either side of the prominent tile stove, and notice three wardrobes standing side by side on the second floor.[20]

The Emergence of the Mennonite Furniture-Making Tradition

Important reasons for the gradual emergence of a Mennonite tradition of domestic furniture, and its continued reproduction for 120-150 years, revolve around household inheritance practices, landowning laws and practices, and the forces that led to emigration.

Unlike their Slavic and some Germanic neighbors, who, if they were not serfs, practiced the patrilineal stem-family type of household whereby the farm or business was inherited by a single descendant, Mennonites divided their estates equally among their children, a form of inheritance that has been called "partible inheritance." This inheritance pattern emphasized the household of the newly married couple, that is the "neolocal residence," thereby bringing together a share of the parental property of both spouses at the time of marriage. The dowry chest symbolized this process.

Mennonites had originally obtained communal rights to land through the patronage of the Polish kings. Households tended to be of similar size and status; a common pasture and village provided access to basic resources.

In 1772 the rising state of Prussia took control from Poland of the Vistula Delta lands that had been occupied by Mennonites for two centuries. Prussia abolished the block lease system and introduced universal citizenship, including the buying and selling of land. To develop a middle class of farmers, they, like the Russian state, instituted the "minimal farm size." The Prussian imposition of military conscription, which went against Mennonite scruples and convictions, was suspended for Mennonites only against monetary payments and other types of tribute.

The threat of conscription and, for some, economic hardship became very real reasons for Mennonites to think of emigration. With the advent of commercial buying and selling of land, many small farmers lost their land as the emerging middle class consolidated its holdings. This led quickly to a landless class of poor Mennonites, and to a corresponding class of wealthy landowners. The former found themselves of necessity drawn into a range of other occupations and crafts, including furniture building, carpentry and painting.

At the close of the Polish era, as revealed in the 1776 Prussian census of Mennonites in the Vistula Delta, out of 3,366 households, or about 12,000 individuals, only seven were engaged full-time as carpenters, three as cabinetmakers and six as painters. Textile-related occupations were more numerous, with 112 weavers, 25 tailors, eight linen weavers and three lacemakers.[21] Undoubtedly, many of the Mennonite farmers, who constituted the majority, built their own furniture, as they grew their own food and raised their own animals.

A noteworthy development in late eighteenth century Mennonite communities was the emergence of an occupational group who built what came to be known as "Mennonite furniture." The growing gap between landless and landed Mennonites spawned the first of many emigrations, including these craftsmen, to settlements in central Poland and South Russia (1789-1830), and later, by the 1870s, to the United States. Migrations and new settlements created a need for furniture in the settlements of South Russia and North America. The Mennonite tradition evolved as new homes acquired furniture built by Mennonite carpenters, joiners and skilled cabinetmakers. By 1850 the Ukrainian Molotschna Mennonite Colony alone had 50 registered master carpenters and 14 painters.[22]

The Jakob Adrian family illustrates the pressures on Mennonites after the Prussian annexation, and how a furnishings tradition became Mennonite. Jakob Adrian (1758-1837) and Eva Konert (1765-1835) of Neu Marsau were farmers. Their status, according to the census, was bad *(schlecht)* even though they had their own farm.[23] Their son Jacob (1801-1866) did not become a farmer, but apprenticed in 1819 as a cabinetmaker with a Heinrich Foth. In a diary entry in 1822 he writes, "I moved away with my plane from Peter Schroeder—he still owes me money...to Kommerau."[24] In 1828 Jacob married Anna Foth and in 1836 he took on his own apprentice, Peter Lau, who was to receive half of his allowance at the beginning, the other half at the end of his apprenticeship. In 1839 the Adrians immigrated to the Molotschna Colony in South Russia with many other Mennonites of the Vistula Delta.

We see in this family vignette how the loss of land as held in the block lease system led to learning a craft and, eventually, emigration. In later chapters we shall return to the Adrians and follow them from South Russia to Kansas.

Placing a Distinctive Mennonite Material Culture in Time and Space

The sources of the Mennonite material tradition were pluralistic, with elements from Slavic and Germanic traditions—both upper class and common cultures—and with legal conventions in the southern Baltic region from the sixteenth to the eighteenth centuries. Further, in its formal and stylistic characteristics this new "Mennonite furniture" reflected a blend of folk and sophisticated traditions. It embraced European architectural and artistic periods from the seventeenth to the nineteenth centuries (elements of so-called baroque, rococo and empire-derived Biedermeier).[25] This unique synthesis of style became the hallmark of Mennonite craftsmen as they began to build their own churches and homes as well as their furnishings. When Mennonites lost their land in the Vistula Delta and began their migrations to central Poland and South Russia, many became craftsmen. These Mennonite craftsmen took up the template of this unique synthesis of style which became the norm where they settled and which was lovingly brought to the American Plains in the 1870s.

Thus transplanted, the tradition continued to be identified as "Mennonite" by Mennonites and others, and continued to be reproduced by three generations of craftsmen for the Mennonite populace which patronized their shops. In central Poland and South Russia it remained a part of the self-contained cultural world with little evidence of copying or borrowing from the outside. In effect, it was a middle class Mennonite tradition suspended in a 150-year transition from feudalism to agrarianism to industrial capitalism in three distinct settings.[26]

4
Furnishing a New Home

Marie, en dem Garden,
dar ga wi alleen,
dar ward ons nich Vader
nich Mutterken sehn.
Witt bleejen de Kiarshen,
de fleeder es green,
dar soett wi em Schatten,
wi beid alleen.
On bawer ons singt di
en Baleken scheen,
dat ward nich vertelen,
wat kunn et uk sehn.
De Broder es buten,
de Soester to kleen;
Marie, en dem Garden,
dar ga wi alleen.[1]

Marie, in the garden,
we can be alone.
There neither father
nor mother will see us.
The cherries blossom white,
the lilac is green.
We will sit in the shade,
we two alone.
Those who sing above us beautifully
will not tell what they see.
Your brother is elsewhere,
your sister still small.
Marie, in the garden,
we will be alone.

Let us imagine for a moment that Marie in the above verse resembled the young Vistula Delta Mennonite woman whose portrait was painted by an unknown artist in the 1820s (Fig. 74). Let us also imagine that the poem's author resembled the young Mennonite man featured by Polish artist Daniel Chodowiecki in his 1782 series on marriage proposals (Fig. 75). Ideally we would also have a diary written by the unknown woman, or the man, to learn of their perceptions at the time they undertook marriage and founded a new household. It would further help to have an understanding of their families' ideas about the creation of such a new home. Indeed, there are some things we do know.

The very future of the society was seen to depend on the successful launching

Fig.74, Portrait of a young Mennonite woman, ca. 1820. Brought from the Vistula Delta to North America by Abraham Ensz, ca. 1876. Tempera on paper.
H:12¾" W:11¾" (including frame).
KM 2710.

Fig.75, "Mennonite Marriage Proposal," 1782, Danzig (Gdansk). Etching by Daniel Chodowiecki.[1]

of new households and families. The aspirations of the parents were translated into the symbolic energies of artists and craftsmen. Some of the finest work in this Mennonite setting therefore grew out of the preparation of the dowry.

The dowry in Vistula Delta Mennonite society around 1800 often featured new furniture and furnishings. The furniture from this era is of particular importance to our story of the North American Plains Mennonite furniture because it became the prototype for most of the migrant offshoots of the tradition.

This chapter examines the origins of several pieces of furniture brought to the North American Plains in family migrations. We assume that these pieces, to have warranted transport over land and sea to new homes, were cherished personal household items of more than mere utilitarian worth. By studying the stories of particular pieces of dowry furniture and furnishings in the Plains inventory with origins in the late eighteenth and early nineteenth century Vistula Delta setting, we may better understand the ideas and forms that inspired this material tradition.

The set that constitutes this glimpse of the new household as dowry furniture includes several dowry chests representing significant varieties of the Vistula Delta type; a range of textiles, including an 1818 dated and initialed bedcover;

wardrobes from the beginning and into the second half of the nineteenth century; a 1766 spinning chair; an 1800 wall clock; an 1820s portrait of a woman; a sewing box; and a fraktur painting.

The Economic Status, Inheritance Patterns and Dowries of Vistula Mennonites

In the first 25 years of Prussian rule in the Vistula Delta, from 1774 to 1798, an average of 131 marriages per year were performed among the Mennonites.[2] Some of these marriages were arranged through the services of a matchmaker. Arranged marriages were not only commonly practiced, but they were also an important way for Mennonite families to maintain their standing in the community and, above all, their continued access to land. Cousins often married each other as a way of perpetuating the estates of families while still adhering to the principle of equitable inheritance.

The Vistula Delta Mennonites, many with a distant background in The Netherlands, stressed the previously mentioned "partible inheritance" type of household transmission of property. In this system household goods were divided among offspring in every generation.[3] Each new household was established as the newly married spouses brought their property together, including new furniture commissioned or built for the occasion.

The residence form that accompanied this property transmission has been called "neolocal." Upon marriage, a new couple lived in their own house or apartment, rather than under the same roof as the parents, as was common in some other surrounding communities in Europe.

The bride's dowry of linens, silver and other household items was often kept in a dowry chest that had either been newly built for her or had been inherited from her mother or grandmother. Men's dowries consisted of clothing such as linen shirts, tools and, sometimes, even farm animals. Wardrobes, chairs, clocks and other pieces of furniture were also given as dowry.

The place of land in inheritance was complicated by the nature of land tenure laws and practices. As long as Mennonites had lived under Polish jurisdiction, the block grant from a nobleman or the Catholic church, in contract with Mennonite church leaders, determined access to land. This usually resulted in the land within the block grants being divided into ever smaller farms as generation after generation divided and subdivided its holdings. In the Prussian era, a complex set of laws specifically negotiated between Mennonites and the Prussian state authorities governed who could have access to new land. Special taxes for military support, support of Protestant churches and public services were some of the conditions placed upon Mennonite land ownership.[4]

The Prussian census of *1776* sheds light on the economic conditions of Vistula Mennonites. We do not know the criteria used by Prussian census takers, but we may examine the size of the categories among Mennonites and what occupations were in each category. Only two percent were of good standing (*gut*), among whom were merchants, distillers, brewers and shopkeepers; 18 percent were ranked as *mittelmaessig,* middle class, among whom were farmers, guesthouse keepers, distillers, millers and shopkeepers; a 78 percent majority were ranked schlecht or poor, among whom were most of the farmers, as well as many free workers, weavers and other craftsmen; one percent was *sehr arm,*

(above, right) **Fig.76,** "Of a Large Dowry." Woodcut by the Petrarca Meister, 1532. Note the till with a lid on the inside of the dowry chest and the ornate fittings. 16th century woodcuts and paintings illustrating interiors and domestic scenes usually include chests.[2]

(above, left) **Fig.77,** Portrait of Catherine Ensz Claassen (1819-1890), Marienburg–Caldowe, Vistula Delta, pre-1874.[3]

very poor or destitute, of whom many were also "very old" people residing in the church hospices.[5]

Emigration to central Poland, Volhynia, South Russia and, eventually, America was seen by an increasing number as the only way to be free of onerous economic burdens without compromising their faith. The first emigres had left the area in the 1780s for Chortitza in South Russia. By 1800 there were 3,183 Mennonite families registered in all the Prussian territories. In 1805, following the emigration of a further 342 families, the number declined to 2,987, and to 2,408 families by 1809.[6]

The household artifacts shown in this chapter reflect the early Prussian period in Vistula Delta Mennonite society, as well as the pressures of emigration taking the artifacts to distant lands. Undoubtedly, they also reflect more prosperous households because those people could afford to take their cherished belongings with them.

Some Examples of Dowry Objects

Dowry Chests

From the Middle Ages on, the chest was the most important piece of furniture in almost every European home (Fig. 76). In rural households it continued to hold an important place well into the twentieth century. The chest was used for storing the supply of bed linens, table linens, bedclothes, under garments and the linen shroud for burial, as well as supplies of unworked linen. More or less, all of these linen items were part of the dowry of a young woman or man, prepared long before marriage and intended to last a lifetime.

All of the Vistula Delta chests feature a till, called *Bijlaad* or *Beilade,* on the left side, sometimes fitted with one and even two secret compartments or small hidden drawers for valuables such as jewelry or money. Across the back of the chest a narrow board usually held kerchiefs and other small items for frequent use, still called a *doekbord* in Low German.

Among the general Vistula Delta chest forms one can distinguish at least five

(above) **Fig.78a,** Dowry chest, ca. 1819. From Caldowe, Vistula Delta. Written on bottom of the chest in black paint are a date, the name of the owner of the chest at that time and the place name: "C.Claassen Ww [meaning widow] Anno 1819 No. 2. Caldowe." Ash, veneer inlay decoration, six brass bosses, brass key, brass key plate and ornately cut and engraved tinned iron hinges and lock plate. Separately constructed bracket base with straight skirt. Dovetailed joints hidden by the inlaid veneer pilaster motif folded around the corner. Joints of the sides with the back of the chest camouflaged by the same pilaster motif only on the side view of the chest. Three small drawers are fitted under the till on the left side of the chest, marked No.1, No.2, No.3.[4] Flowers in framed fields with Greek key borders decorate the front. Lid features a rose and tulip bouquet tied with a ribbon bordered by an inlaid zigzag pattern. The chest has seen many repairs, including several butterfly key joints to keep the boards from separating.

H:26½" W:54" D:28".
#1.038, Private collection.

(left) **Fig.78b,** Lid of Widow Claassen's dowry chest.
#1.038.

variations which pertain to technique and style of surface decoration, choice of wood and style of decorative hardware, but not to construction and general form. The first type is made of hardwood, usually ash, with inlaid decorations of darker veneer. The second is the plain chest made of hardwood, usually ash, without the inlaid decorative fields, but with pilaster or baluster of veneer covering the two front corners to disguise the dovetailed joints. The third type is made of softwood, fir or pine, painted to simulate the grain, color and decoration of the inlaid chests. The fourth is a painted chest type that simulates not the blonde color of ash, but the red of mahogany. These carry a painted panel decoration that is a mix of late baroque and Biedermeier ornament. A fifth type is the plain variation of the mahogany imitation grain-painted chest, without the floral decorative fields on the front or the architectural motifs covering the corner joints.

The following four dowry chests represent a cross section of types that originated in Mennonite dowries in the Vistula Delta in the first half of the nineteenth century and were in every case handed down to succeeding generations.

Widow Catharine Claassen Dowry Chest, 1819

The Widow Claassen (Fig. 77) to whom the painted name, date and residence on the dowry chest in Fig. 78 refer is Catharine Ensz Claassen (1819-1890) born to Aron and Anna Ensz. She married Johann Claassen in 1849, and became a widow in 1874, when she was living in Caldowe (Kalthof), a suburb of Marienburg. She was a member of the Heubuden Mennonite congregation. With her two sons Aaron and Jacob and one daughter, Catherine, she immigrated to Beatrice, Nebraska, in 1876.

The exact age of the chest is not known, nor is it clear why Catharine's birth date, 1819, would be painted on the chest at the time of emigration. The chest dates at least to 1849, the year of her marriage. The fact that the inlaid design of the lid is of a later style—a formal Biedermeier bouquet—than that of the main body—asymmetrical rococo floral motifs—suggests that this replacement was a repair of a much older chest. The markings "Widow Claassen" may have

Fig.79, Dowry chest, ca. 1850. First owned by Agathe Regier Harder (1830-1861), Heubuden Mennonite community, Vistula Delta. Second wife of Bernhard Harder who brought the chest to the Whitewater community, Kansas, in 1876 with Agathe's two sons and his third wife. Ash, inlaid floral and geometric motifs, separately constructed bracket base with five feet. (The front center foot is missing.) Till on the inside left side, brass key plate, cast brass key, brass handle plates and handle, six brass bosses, tooled hinges of tinned iron. Tinned iron lock case is also tooled with a floral design.

H:28" D:28½" W:55½".
#1.033, Private collection.

been added later. This may be the earliest chest of its type known to us.

Widow Claassen's granddaughter Catharine Claassen Andreas inherited the chest in 1880. Thus it must have been given by Widow Claassen to her daughter and then to her granddaughter, or, perhaps, directly to her granddaughter Catherine Claassen Andreas, whose daughter Catherine inherited the chest in turn. It stood upstairs in the old stone house on the farm where Catherine Andreas Claassen lived with her husband Albert Claassen. She passed the chest on to her daughter, and it is now in the home of a great-great-granddaughter of the Widow Catharine Claassen, that is, the sixth generation of direct female descendants from the woman who brought her dowry chest from the Vistula Delta to North America.

Agathe Regier Harder Dowry Chest, ca. 1850

This chest (Fig. 79) and the previous one are excellent examples of the inlaid form of cabinet work built in specialized shops in Danzig or Elbing, most likely by guild craftsmen. It was originally made for Agathe Regier Harder (1830-1861), daughter of Elias Regier and Ida Wall, in Altenau, Vistula Delta. She was the second wife of Bernhard Harder (born 1811 in Marienau, died 1900 in the Emmaus community near Whitewater, Kansas), whom she married in 1853.

They also belonged to the Heubuden Mennonite Church. Only two of Agathe's six children survived childhood: Johann, or John, and Gustav, who immigrated with their father and his third wife Justina Bergman in 1876 to the Whitewater community in Kansas, bringing Agathe's chest along.

Since there were no daughters in the family, John, the oldest son and full-time farmer on the home place, inherited his mother's chest. It has been passed from father to son now for five generations along an uninterrupted line of male heirs. This pattern, contrasting to the more common inheritance pattern along the female line—mother to daughter or granddaughter, exhibited by the previously introduced chest—indicates that once the chest was made, family circumstances dictated how it would be transmitted to the next generation.

The size, form, construction (by a skilled cabinetmaker or joiner), type of wood, surface decoration and hardware (tooled and tinned iron hinges and brass escutcheons, handle plates and handles) of this chest are characteristic of all inlaid chests of this type brought to the Plains states in the 1870-80s migration (Fig. 80). It represents the sophisticated tradition in dowry chest, the best money could buy in the first half of the nineteenth century from cabinetmakers in Danzig, Elbing and Marienburg, as well as south along the Vistula River, including the area of Torun. Inlaid furniture in this region was first produced for the homes of urban patricians and was adopted by Mennonites as their means and their social ambition allowed.

Polish museum curators identify this style of chest in terms of the region in which it was produced—Zulawy or the Vistula Delta.[7] Many similar chests may still be found in museums and historical buildings in the Vistula Delta today.[8] The curator of furniture at the National Museum of Gdansk, Krystyna Mellin, related that no documentation about the exact origin of these chests exists. Historically the cabinetmakers' guilds, from which Mennonites were officially excluded, controlled the production of inlaid work at least throughout the seventeenth century.[9]

Fig.80, Detail of the Agathe Regier Harder chest. Note the folded pilasters, the Greek key frame, the Grecian urn-shaped handle plates and the massive cast brass handle.

(right) **Fig.81,** Sara Schulz and Gerhard Claassen, 1885, engagement photo.[5]

(below) **Fig.82,** Dowry chest, 1866. From Krebsfelde, Vistula Delta. The initials SS probably stand for Sara Schulz (born, 1844, Vistula Delta, died 1908, Newton, Kansas). According to the inscription on the back of the chest, this is the 69th chest painted in Krebsfelde, Vistula Delta, by painter Schuetz. It stands on a separate five-footed bracket base with scalloped skirt. The painted graining on pine imitates the color and grain of ash, and the painted flower bouquets and zigzag border imitate similar chests of inlaid hardwood. Brass keyplate and key, ornate tinned iron handle plate, cast iron handle, plain hand forged iron hinges.

H:28" D:27½" W:55".
#1.024, Private collection.

Sara Schulz Dowry Chest, 1866

Sara Schulz (1844-1908) was the second wife of Gerhard Claassen, whom she married in 1885 in Beatrice, Nebraska (Fig. 81), where her family settled after emigration from West Prussia.[10] Sara brought to this marriage her dowry chest, initialled "SS" and dated 1866 (Figs. 82, 83, 84). A puzzle surrounds the significance of the date 1866, the year when Sara was 22 years old. Was she married for the first time then? Was she a widow when she married into the Claassen family? If this was her first marriage, then what was the occasion in 1866 upon which she received her chest? Could it have been the year of her baptism? Some sources connect dowry gifts with the rite of passage of adult baptism in the church.

Furniture received upon the establishment of a new home at the time of marriage was often personalized with the marriage date or another significant date and with the owner's initials. Personalization symbolized ownership of and pride in one's dowry furniture. This is one of very few chests in the Plains Mennonite immigrant furniture inventory which bears initials and date on its front. However, in Polish museum collections of Vistula Delta chests—inlaid or painted—dates and initials marked a number of dowry chests. The backs of the dowry chests were never decorated. Often, at the time of emigration the head of the household, the new address and, sometimes, the place of origin were identified there.

Among all the Vistula chests studied on the Plains and in the Polish museums, this is one of few that bears the signature of its painter and the location of manufacture on the back: "Schuetz - Krebsfelde Maler #69."[11] This is the 69th chest decorated by the painter Schuetz at Krebsfelde.[12] The painted decoration

(above) **Fig.83,** Detail of the side of Sara Schulz's dowry chest. Note how the painted architectural baluster motif "wraps" around the corner. The back corner joint is camouflaged with the same architectural motif, but it does not "wrap" around to the back side of the chest which is made—as are all chests—of rough, unfinished boards.
#1.024.

(below) **Fig.84,** "No. 69 Schuetz-Krebsfelde Maler." Signature of the painter of Sara Schulz's dowry chest.
#1.024.

Fig.85, Linen towel detail. First monogrammed "AB" and dated "1818;" a generation later monogrammed "CJ" (Cornelius Jansen) and dated "1848." Linen damask.
L:60" W:27½".
KM 6517.3.

of this Krebsfelde style reproduces very closely its inlaid prototype (see the Agathe Regier chest).

Anna Claassen Regier Dowry Chest, ca. 1875

Anna Claassen was 16 in 1878 when she, with her parents Peter Claassen and Anna Regier of Sandhof, came to join the many families that had settled in the Kansas communities of Newton, Whitewater and Elbing, as well as in the Beatrice, Nebraska, region. Young Anna's dowry chest, modestly finished with a plain mahogany red stain, accompanied her on the ship where she met young John Regier. They were married six years later in 1884. The chest remained in their home for two generations until John and Anna's unmarried daughters died.

A Dowry's Textiles

Both women's and men's dowries included textiles, in particular linens such as shirts or vests, frocks, nightshirts, napkins, tablecloths, bedspreads and knitted stockings, as well as the burial shroud. It was not uncommon in nineteenth century middle class Mennonite homes in the Vistula Delta for a dowry to include up to 25 shirts, enough for an entire lifetime. These items were commonly numbered in a series, dated and monogrammed with the initials of the individual for whom they were intended (Fig. 85).

Unfortunately, no complete textile inventories have been found in this particular Mennonite dowry tradition.[13] However, one interesting laundry list has survived which allows us to approximate the textiles in such a dowry in the Vistula Delta in the nineteenth century. Ernest Claassen translated the list his grandmother made in 1868 of her entire linen inventory.[14] In the Vistula Delta laundry day did not occur weekly as it would later in Kansas, but perhaps only twice or three times per year, because of the large inventory of linens and clothing. The list in full:

- 8 shirts too small for John, tied in a bundle in the *Kammer*
- 12 of John's, 8 marked J.C.
- 20 of Helena's, 12 marked H6; the others are old
- 19 of Anna's, of which 15 are marked A6, the other 4 are marked H
- 31 men's shirts, marked AK, numbered 1-31
- 6 men's shirts, marked AC, numbered 1-6
- 4 men's shirts, marked AC4
- 2 men's shirts, marked AxC
- 15 old shirts, marked AK or GB
- 1 muslin shirt, marked AK

[total 59 men's shirts]

- 15 old women's shirts, marked HR, JR, or LB
- 18 women's shirts, marked AB 1855
- 12 women's shirts, marked AB 1854
- 6 women's shirts, marked AB 1853
- 5 women's shirts, marked AxB 1845 No.16
- 1 woman's shirt, marked AxB 1844 No. 7
- 6 women's shirts, marked AxC, numbered 1-6
- 10 women's shirts, marked JK or HR

[total 73 women's shirts]

- 75 child's shirts on March 28, 1868
- 11 1½ width sheets
- 3 coarse 1½ width sheets
- 10 double width sheets
- 2 double width sheets
- 7 white bed spreads
- 2 red figured bed spreads
- 14 ticking table cloths
- 7 ribbed table cloths
- 7 ticking towels
- 6 white linen towels
- 8 checked ticking towels
- 3 blue towels

An inventory of this size certainly required a large wardrobe or at least one ample chest.

The Epp Spinning Chair

The oldest known piece of Mennonite furniture of Vistula Delta origin in a North American collection is a chair (Fig. 86).[15] The owners of the Epp spinning chair took it along when they migrated to South Russia sometime in the early nineteenth century. From South Russia the Epp family brought the chair to Canada in 1923, and donated it to the Kauffman Museum in 1951. The family's oral history speaks of this chair as having been used for spinning. It bears a carved date on the lower back slat, 1766, centered between an heraldic arrangement of horses and flowers.

Just as they continued building the previously mentioned Vistula Delta chest forms in South Russia, Mennonite craftsmen also built this Vistula Delta chair form, which actually had Dutch origins (Fig. 87), in the new settlements in South

Fig.88, Living room in a South Russian Mennonite home, ca. 1920. Note the pair of slat back chairs, which would have been brought from the Vistula Delta.[7]

Russia. A rare photograph of the interior of a Mennonite *Grootestow* in South Russia shows two such Vistula Delta chairs (Fig. 88).

Another chair in this style built by Heinrich Epp as a wedding gift for Katharina (Boese) Epp in 1862 in Neuhof, South Russia, testifies to the persistence of this chair form for more than a century after the craft tradition was transplanted from the Vistula Delta to South Russia by Mennonites. "It was one of the few belongings rescued when Katharina and her family fled from Neuhof. When emigrating from Russia to Canada, Katharina took it along to sit on on the ship."[16]

The practice of presenting a pair of chairs as a wedding gift continued in North America. For example, in 1905 Dietrich B. Neufeldt and Sara Balzer Neufeldt were given two chairs in the Lake Valley community near Inman, Kansas.[17]

The Wardrobes from Koselitzke and Caldowe

In the city societies the chest was supplanted as status furniture by the wardrobe in the seventeenth and eighteenth centuries. As early as 1800 patrician furniture could be seen in some of the commodious homes of well-to-do Vistula Delta Mennonite farmers, such as the Schulz estate in Fuerstenwerder (Fig. 89).

Some families could afford to ship a wardrobe along with their household goods when they emigrated from the Vistula Delta to the Plains states. The oldest such wardrobe, dating to the first quarter of the nineteenth century, came from Koselitzke. Constructed of ash with a simple inlaid decoration of thin ebony veneer, it featured a keyplate carved from a piece of animal horn. The wardrobe stood on five turned ball feet (Fig. 90), a pattern based on Dutch baroque prototypes.[18]

In 1869 Aaron Claassen of Caldowe (near Marienburg) built a wardrobe as a wedding present for his half-brother Johann Claassen who brought it to rural Beatrice, Nebraska, in 1875 (Fig. 91).[19] The style of this wardrobe follows very closely the main style characteristics of Biedermeier furniture with carefully

(left) **Fig.89,** Wardrobe, ca. 1790. Photographed by Kurt Kauenhoven in the farm home of the Mennonite family Schulz, Fuerstenwerder, Vistula Delta, July 1937.[8] Wood unknown, inlay designs in contrasting wood veneers.

(above) **Fig.90,** Wardrobe, ca. 1820. From Koselitzke, Vistula Delta, oldest confirmed wardrobe brought to the Plains by Mennonite immigrants, donated by P.M. Claassen. Ash, inlaid ebony veneer, animal horn key plate, iron key. Wardrobe disassembles into ten separate components. Five ball feet fitted with pegs.

H:92½" W:65" D:26".
#11.008, KM 2066.

matched grain patterns of blonde fruitwood veneers, in this case applewood. Sparse use of ebonized moldings underscores the proportion, color and grain pattern of this imposing furniture form. This wardrobe demonstrates the close cultural linkage between Vistula Delta and South Russian Mennonite communities, since Mennonite immigrant cabinetmakers from South Russia continued to build wardrobes in this style after their arrival in North America.

No wardrobes are known to have come with immigrant families directly from South Russia, but trained carpenters from these South Russian communities built wardrobes in North America according to patterns that had already existed

Fig.91, Wardrobe, 1869. Made by Aaron Claassen (1850-1929) as a wedding present for his half-brother Johannes Claassen, Alt Muensterbergerfelde, West Prussia. Black stain trim pine, applewood veneer. Disassembles into 16 separate components.

H:86" W:64" D:26".

#11.032, Private collection.

in the Vistula Delta at the time of the earlier migration to South Russia. The form or structure of the wardrobes remained consistent in the Plains states inventory, just as the form and the decoration of the chests remained essentially consistent. We will show that chests and wardrobes share particular structural and decorative elements.

The Rempel Clock

Wall clocks were also a part of the furnishings of a new home. Some were purchased from manufacturers in Amsterdam or London; others were made by local clockmakers, some of whom, such as the Kroeger brothers, were Mennonite.[20]

The original owners of the clock of our study are not known, but its construction and decorative style suggest that it dates to 1800, perhaps earlier (Fig. 92).

The oral tradition of this clock begins in 1876 with Isbrand and Justina

Fig.92, Pendulum clock, ca. 1800. Probably made by Johann Kroeger, Vistula Delta. Brought to Beatrice, Nebraska, in 1876. Biblical story painted on the clock face based on 2 Kings 19:9-14. Cut sheet metal, one brass hour hand, brass pendulum, two brass weights.

Diameter: 18" x 15".

#19.021, Private collection.

Rempel's decision to immigrate to North America, leaving their home near Marienburg, West Prussia, and traveling to a new home in Beatrice, Nebraska. With them came their 11-year-old foster son and nephew, Henry Dyck.

Among the belongings which they packed to take with them across the ocean was this round-faced clock of metal, with one shiny brass hand to show the hour, a long pendulum and two weights. In the center of the clock several figures tell a story. They are painted within the chapter ring with its 48 spaces representing the quarter hours, which is encircled in turn by the main chapter ring with its large Roman numerals on the hour and the clover leaves representing the half hour marks.

The clock was most likely made by a Johann Kroeger (1754-1823), son of one of two brothers by the name Krueger or Kroeger who were registered as clockmakers in the Vistula Delta in 1727-1729.[21]

Johann Kroeger emigrated from Reimerswalde in 1803 to settle in Rosenthal, South Russia, where he continued the clockmaking business as did his sons and grandsons after him. Clocks of exactly the same style and material were brought from South Russia in the 1870s migration to North America.[22] Since this clock was brought directly from the Vistula Delta by a Mennonite family, it is likely that it was made by Johann Kroeger before he left for South Russia in 1803.

Earlier we wrote of the importance of the dowry chest and the clock as symbols of time in the Mennonite home: the chest as a mark of the continuity of the family, as the heartbeat of the home; the clock as a reminder of fleeting time, of human mortality. One can think of the clock as the first machine to enter the home other than the spinning wheel, as a mechanical device by which people

Figs. 93-95, Sewing box, ca. 1870. From the Marienburg area in the Vistula Delta to Beatrice, Nebraska, in 1876. Wood, roll-top, dovetailed joints, three drawers. Red grained painting to imitate mahogany. The painted motifs—rosebuds, tulips and Grecian urn—occur frequently as painted, inlaid or metal ornaments on dowry chests, in fraktur and in embroidery throughout the 19th century. The urn is also a favorite motif in album pages of the Biedermeier era.

H:7¼" W:11¼" D:9".

#4.008, Private collection.

ordered their lives, especially with the coming of the Industrial Revolution in the mid-nineteenth century. Equally important, if not more so, the clock was a symbol, a moral device, admonishing people to live their finite days righteously.

This is the point of the Old Testament King Hezekiah story which is depicted on the clock's face. That story and other biblical stories appearing on dowry furniture will be evaluated in greater detail later in this chapter.

The Visual Language of Dowry Objects

The objects in a Vistula Delta Mennonite dowry all bore a symbolic and narrative charge reflected in their decoration. The carved back slats of the 1766 spinning chair portray the creation, showing Adam and Eve with horses, birds and flowers. The painted face of the Rempel family clock features an Old Testament scene. Biblical scenes are expressions of life regulated by moral ideals derived from scripture. Architectural themes in furniture conveyed a vernacular rendering of academic ideas and prototypes. Thus, the dowry's objects transmitted basic beliefs and cultural forms within the community.

Floral and Other Natural Motifs

Not only does the set of home furnishings in our study show the functional connectedness of the individual items, but it also shows them aligned symbolically through the floral motif to various rites of passage such as betrothal, marriage and founding a new home. The etching by Polish artist Daniel Chodowiecki, from his 1782 collection on marriage proposals (see Fig. 75), shows the groom wearing a sprig of flowers on his lapel and the room furnished with two chairs of the same style as the 1766 Epp family chair (see Fig. 88), a type known to have been given as wedding presents.

The dominant ornaments on the decorated chests are flowers, a universal symbol of validating significant events in the human life cycle. We mark important rites of passage with flowers; baptism, betrothal, marriage and burial. We express affection, love and gratitude, and we honor achievement with flowers. Special holy days of the church year—Easter, Pentecost and Christmas—are celebrated with flowers. Since flowers are life forms, they are especially appropriate images on furniture and furnishings; specifically, textiles and sewing boxes with which they are most closely related (Figs. 93, 94, 95).

Bedcovers richly embroidered with a flowering garland and called *Vorstecksel* (literally "pinned in-front-of") were often displayed on the show-bed in the Grosse Stube to demonstrate the embroidery skills of the *Hausfrau*. A very fine example of this type of linen, dated 1818, comes from a Mennonite home in Tralau, part of the Heubuden congregation (Fig. 96). The oldest documented Vorstecksel is dated 1799.[23]

Additional evidence of the important symbolic role of flowers may be seen in a bouquet of flowers painted in 1839 by Franz Dueck as a special Christmas present (Fig. 97); a multitude of fraktur paintings with flowers as principal motifs, executed as part of penmanship instruction in Mennonite schools in the Vistula Delta and in South Russia (Fig. 98); floral decorations on a sewing box (Figs. 93, 94, 95); and an embroidered linen pillow case (Fig. 99).[24]

The bouquets on the dowry chests, whether inlaid or painted, were often similar to those found on other heirlooms—roses and tulips tied tightly with a

Fig.96, Bedcover, 1818. From Tralau, Vistula Delta, to the Whitewater community, Kansas.[9] Embroidered in white, featuring flowering vines growing from a basket and ending in a circle with a crown. Initials "AF," name of place and date. Cotton embroidery floss on cotton. Eight different embroidery techniques were used: outline or stem stitch, French knots, buttonhole stitch, satin stitch, drawn work with 10 different motifs, faggoting with herringbone stitch, eyelet work and sawtooth edging.

L:53¾" W:78¾".

KM 5657.

ribbon bow.[25] Tulips became enormously popular and a major item of trade in the seventeenth century. They were exported by sea from Holland to Danzig and Elbing and are symptomatic of the influence of Dutch trade and culture in the cities of Danzig and Elbing.[26]

In 1989 an elderly Polish acquaintance of the authors, known to her friends as "Tante Anna," who served as a maid on a Fast family farm in the Vistula Delta until World War II, remembered both the chests decorated with flowers, as well as the Mennonite fondness for flowers in their gardens and homes.[27]

Another Vistula Delta woman, Anna Loewens von Bockelmann, chronicled a childhood memory from around 1869. She remembered visiting a baptismal service in the Mennonite prayerhouse at Ellerwald: "The church was decorated with thick wreaths of fresh flowers...the girls wore plain black dresses and held tight bouquets of flowers next to the folded handkerchief."[28]

Biblical Motifs

Biblical motifs are presented both as visual and as narrative themes.

On the upper slat of the Epp family chair Adam and Eve stand on either side of the Tree of Knowledge of Good and Evil in which two birds are sitting. The snake, coiled around a branch, whispers into Eve's ear, while she reaches up to pluck the apple (Fig. 100). This motif is also found in Mennonite embroidery

Fig.97, Flower bouquet, December 20, 1839. Franz Dueck, ink and tempera on paper.
  6½" x 6¾".
  KM 3132.

(top) **Fig.98,** A moralizing poem introduces lessons on subtraction *(Subtrahieren).* Gerhard Nickel's *Arithmetic Book,* Montau, West Prussia, March 1, 1797. Note the roses tied with a ribbon, a motif which occurs frequently in fraktur paintings, until the 1870s.[10]

8" x 6½".

Mein lieber Schüler,
nach Anleitung dieser Regel
gebe ich dir diese Lehre und
Vermahnung.
Die Lust des Fleisches subtrahier,
und Dein Leben gar wohl regier,
damit du bestehest gar eben,
In diesem und jenem Leben;
Vermeide Boeses und Gutes stifte,
dass dich nicht wuerg des Satans List,
und zeug ab all Untuegend fein
so kannst du desto sicherer sein,
fur der ewigen Hoellenqual,
wenn dich Gott zeugt aus diesem
Jammerthal.

My dear pupil,
according to this rule
I give you this teaching and admonition.
Subtract all fleshly lust
and conduct your life well,
so that you will carry forth,
in this life and the next.
Avoid evil and do good,
so that Satan's tricks do not choke you;
Deter all untowardness,
so that you can be secure
from eternal tortures of hell
when God calls you from this woeful vale.

(Authors' translation)

(bottom) **Fig.99,** *Glueckliche Reise* (Happy Journey), ca. 1875-1900. From the Vistula Delta. Note how the interlaced corners of the "frame" for the central motif echo the framing motif found on the Sara Schulz dowry chest—a variation on the Greek key corners found on inlaid chests. Unbleached linen, turkey red and white cotton embroidery floss, stem stitch and satin stitch, seven handmade button holes, seven metal buttons covered in cotton *(Waescheknoepfe).*

H:23½" W:20½".
KM 2982.

(top) **Fig.100,** Adam and Eve and the snake. The moment of temptation or "The Fall." Detail of carved slat on spinning chair.
KM 3474.

(bottom) **Fig.101,** Calculating the diameter of the earth from Gerhard Nickel's *Arithmetic Book*, 1797, Montau, West Prussia.[11] Note Adam and Eve at the moment of temptation under the tree with the snake. The same motif is carved on the spinning chair in Fig. 100.

(facing page) **Fig.102,** Pendulum clock, ca. 1800. The story of Hezekiah, 2 Kings 19:9-14.

#19.021, Private collection.

samplers and hand-illuminated arithmetic books from the Vistula Delta (Fig. 101). The moment of original sin is depicted, and thus the image serves as a constant reminder of humankind's need for God's grace. The large flowers on either side of Adam and Eve are carnations, an old symbol of love, as are the two large doves. These symbolic images, as well as the date and the initials, suggest that this chair was intended as a wedding present.[29]

A particular genre of clock, represented by the Rempel family clock, features the most fully developed visual rendering of biblical themes in the Vistula Delta Mennonite dowry. Not many of these are known, but we believe they must have been common around 1800, and they were made by Mennonite clockmakers.

The Rempel family clock shows a king seated on an elevated throne in an open portico of a palace. The artist makes it very clear that this man is a king by giving him attributes of royalty: a golden crown on his turban and a scepter in his right hand. Confronting the king is a bearded man reading from a large piece of paper covered with letter-like figures. Two other men are standing between the king and the man reading the letter or scroll. Their dress is simple, they are bareheaded and they stand on a platform below the throne, so it is clear they are of lesser rank. Behind this scene, in the distance, we see a turban-clad man holding a horse by its bridle. On the horse we see a rider holding a scepter and wearing a crown on his turban. This man, therefore, is most likely also a king (Fig. 102).

The horse-riding king and his groom are confronted by a figure which directs them away from the enthroned king with his right arm and extended index finger. In the distance on the horizon the artist painted the unmistakable silhouette of a pyramid next to that of a stately building.

If we assume that the source of the story is biblical, then the setting with two kings, an audience and a pyramid takes us to the Old Testament. Since the artist placed the letter in the very center of the image, which is also the center of the clock, this letter must be of special significance. The question is, in which Old Testament story does a letter play a special role?

We conclude this must be the story of King Hezekiah, seated on his throne, listening to a threatening letter brought by the Assyrian King Sennacherib's messengers (2 Kings 19:9-14). This is the letter, or scroll, which Hezekiah "spreads before the Lord" (verse 14) and which causes him to pray for deliverance from the king of Assyria.

The horseman with scepter probably represents King Sennacherib of Assyria whom the Lord, in answer to Hezekiah's prayer, promises to turn back on the way he came (2 Kings 19:28 and 33). "Because you have raged against me and your arrogance has come to my ears, I will put my hook in your nose and my bit in your mouth; I will turn you back on the way by which you came." The figure confronting the King of Assyria and pointing him back in the direction from which he came demonstrates the promise of the Lord pictorially.

The artist, therefore, joins several episodes of the story in one image for the sake of brevity and completeness of content. Between the antagonists, the letter, or scroll, acts as a catalyst in the conflict, bringing about a turning point in the story. The scroll was understood as a symbol of prophecy. The whole scene reads like a shorthand version of Hezekiah, with the density of meaning one finds in emblems and the didactic urgency of popular preaching.

It is a story about faith, about the power of prayer, about a God who gives potent signs of power and who saves people from the enemy. God's condition for peace and prosperity is faithfulness to the covenant.

King Hezekiah's faithfulness to the Lord, expressed through fervent prayer, also reveals God as the master of time. The Lord promised to add 15 years to the king's life in addition to restoring his health and providing deliverance from his enemies (2 Kings 20:5-6). In order to prove faithfulness to Hezekiah, the Lord "brought the shadows back ten intervals by which the sun had declined on the dial of Ahaz" (2 Kings 20:11). Anyone who knew the story of Hezekiah would have known this passage as well.

This story had special relevance for Mennonites in the Vistula Delta, under new Prussian rule in the last quarter of the eighteenth century. Their rights and privileges, their religious freedom, their freedom not to bear arms, upheld by the Polish crown from the sixteenth century, were now threatened and needed to be newly negotiated, not only with the Prussian crown, but also with the Protestant state church. For Mennonites in this political situation—one that threatened the continuity of their way of life as an autonomous community of believers—the story of Hezekiah's faithfulness and God's rewards for this faithfulness must have been a source of strength and comfort in the struggle to remain faithful in the face of opposition.

The style of the painting points to a date before 1800. The composition reflects standard baroque devices: a grandiose architectural setting for the main protagonist and sudden, deep vistas. Though executed by a hand not academically trained, it is quick and sure, and highlights are placed effectively. The red color areas appear very flat in contrast to those treated with blue and may have been painted over more recently, since red colors are rather unstable and fade with time.[30] The question arises whether the painter of the clock worked from a prototype such as a popular print or ceramic tile painted with biblical narratives, or whether the composition was his or her own unique invention. The former is more likely, especially if one considers the enormous repertory of biblical scenes painted on Dutch tiles in the seventeenth and eighteenth centuries, which were found in many Mennonite homes in the Vistula Delta.[31]

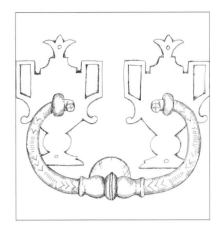

(above) **Fig.104,** Detail of Greek urn-shaped handle plates and handle from the dowry chest #1.033, (see Fig. 80).

Other biblical scenes were also painted on such round sheet-iron clockfaces. According to David H. Epp in his biography of Peter Lepp (1817-1871), the story of Israel's military hero Jephtha being greeted by his daughter upon his return home after defeating the Ammonites (Judges 11:29-40) was a fairly common image on such clocks. Epp writes about Peter Lepp's apprenticeship to his brother-in-law, a clockmaker named Janzen in Prussia. Lepp returned to Chortitza in 1836 and was called the "father of German factory industry in our colonies."[32]

> On the round clock face one usually saw King Jephtha high on a horse, joyfully received by his daughter and her friends, but the King, bound by a rash vow, has to greet her with the words "Oh, my daughter, you make me sad (you fill my heart with sorrow)."

One such clock is known in North America, brought by a Mennonite immigrant family in the 1870s to Henderson, Nebraska (Fig. 103).[33] Its painted image matches David H. Epp's description of these clocks perfectly. The Jephtha story contains several lessons: obedience to God is more important than anything treasured here on earth, and the virtuous daughter gladly obeys both her father and God.

The stories of Hezekiah and Jephtha were popular in the period around 1800 not only as visual images, but also as music. For example, Johann Kunau wrote an organ work on the theme of Hezekiah and Handel composed a choral work on the story of Jephtha. Another clock in this style from 1795 features the scenes of Epiphany—the three wise men meeting the Christ child with Mary and Joseph. It is known to have been made in Tiegenhof, the Mennonite craft center.[34]

(below) **Fig.105,** Arcaded entrance of the Janson House in Tiege, ca. 1920, Vistula Delta.[12]

Apparently it was fairly common for clocks to serve as reminders of the brevity of life which ought to be lived in the fear of God. At the beginning of the twentieth century, in the living rooms of the well-to-do Vistula Delta farmers one could see clocks whose cases were decorated with rhyming, moralizing verses *(Sinnsprueche)* such as "I run quickly, oh man, think of the end" *("Ich lauf behende, o Mensch, bedenk das Ende!")* and "Here goes time, there comes death, o man, act justly and fear God!" *("Hin geht die Zeit, her kommt der Tod, o Mensch, tu recht und fuerchte Gott!")*[35]

Architectural Motifs

Folded around the front corners of many of the dowry chests are pilasters on high bases, executed with inlaid veneer or paint. These creative allusions to architectural pilasters hold up, as it were, the corners of the projecting molding on the heavy lid, acting as if they were actual structural elements supporting the cornice of a building. These pilasters are also intended to hide the dovetailed corner joints. As ornament they are derived from fanciful adaptations of Renaissance motifs by sixteenth and seventeenth century Italian, French, German and Flemish Mannerist designers of pattern books, such as those of Hans Vredeman de Vries, who worked for the city of Danzig in the last decade of the sixteenth century.[36]

Using the column or pilaster as a decorative device had its origins in classical architecture and decorative arts. It can be traced in furniture styles to the Renaissance, is revived in the furniture of the neo-classical style called Empire and is, in its popular derivation, Biedermeier, which dominated northeastern European furniture styles during the first half of the nineteenth century, especially in German speaking regions. Furthermore, the chests' decorative double frames with the Greek key or fret corners and the Greek urn-shaped brass plates for handles are all elements which constitute a late revival of classical decorative vocabulary borrowed from "high" art (Fig. 104).

Chests, as well as wardrobes, speak an architectural language and one can certainly see parallels between architectural motifs on houses in the Vistula Delta and the furniture produced there. Many of the farmhouses with arcaded entries feature columns on high square pedestals, with ornate capitals reminiscent of the classical orders.[37] The columned entry of the Janson House in Tiege,

(right) **Fig.106,** An arcaded entrance to a farm home in the Vistula Delta, *Haus Seedat in Gemlitz.* Echoes the scalloped skirting of bases of dowry chests and wardrobes, and the motif of the column or pilaster found on the chests.[13]

built in 1802, is a fine example of this type of Vistula Delta vernacular architecture (Fig. 105).[38]

An oral tradition recorded by architectural historian Bernhard Schmidt, and restated by Arkadiusz Rybak, maintained that the number of posts, which were later changed to columns on some farms, indicated the number of Hufe or the amount of land owned by the particular farmer.[39]

The separately constructed base on which many of the chests rest is decorated with a scallop or swag motif which, like the columns, finds a parallel in some of the arcaded houses. The spaces between the columns are sometimes decorated with a drapery swag motif also echoed in the bases of many furniture pieces (Fig. 106).[40]

The Personalizing of the Object

One of the primary symbolic functions of the chest was as display furniture. Thus, it declared the material status, aspirations and aesthetic orientation of the home to the community. The chest also functioned as a keeper of personal memories.

While the exterior form speaks a generally understood, public architectural language, a symbolic language is spoken by the imagery of inlaid or painted motifs on the front, top and sides. A more private symbolic language is spoken by the images fastened to the inside of the lids in many of the chests. Since the chest belonged primarily to an individual rather than to the entire family, it is on the inside of the chest that most personal documents, such as frakturs, Christmas and New Year's greetings, religious mottos and any other pictures or notes valued for aesthetic or sentimental reasons, were kept or displayed.

The oldest such decorations are frakturs—handwritten and decorated moralizing or religious passages from the 1840s—often done in penmanship classes and later preserved by pasting them on the inside of a dowry chest's lid.[41] In a number of chests some or all of these have been removed, leaving evidence of their presence with small fragments of paper and traces of glue.

The practice of decorating the inside of chests with *Bilderbogen* or popular prints was very common in the nineteenth century. It served as the main storage, often the only storage for a man's or a woman's entire property of clothing, as well as special objects including the Bible and secular and religious mementos. Portraits of European nobility, at once expression of and stimulus for personality cults, were traded internationally, and were available from itinerant salesmen and from stores.

Political loyalties were thus sometimes expressed. In a chest built by Heinrich Schroeder the inside of the lid reveals lithographed portrait reproductions of Frederick the Great of Prussia; Grossfuerst Alexander, heir to the throne of Russia, with his spouse Alexandrowna; and Czar Nicolai of Russia and King of Poland, with his spouse Alexandra Feodorowna.[42] In Manitoba one Mennonite family pasted a newspaper photo of the early 1950s, featuring the British Queen Elizabeth and her Consort Prince Philip, on the inside of the door of their corner cupboard.[43]

One of the most complete personal statements inside a dowry chest lid is that of Anna Franz, who was married in South Russia sometime before 1867 to Johannes Voth of the Alexanderwohl community (Fig. 107a, 107b).[44] Themes

Fig.107a, Popular prints and fraktur drawings on the inside of the lid of Anna Franz's dowry chest, ca. 1860s. Brought from the Molotschna Colony, South Russia.
H:27" W:27" L:53"
#1.059, Private collection.

of romance, marriage, royal families of Prussia and Russia with an emphasis on the royal couple, religious devotion, baptism, motherhood and children are expressed by fraktur drawings and commercial prints. Five small fraktur paintings by Anna Franz, one with her name, feature stylized flower bouquets, some tied with a ribbon bow. The overall configuration of images, their placement and their size reveal the owner's values. Viewing or "reading" the images from left to right, as in a picture book, the sequence follows a young woman's life course from romance to marriage. To the left is a "soap opera" of discovered, forbidden romance in which a father discovers his daughter behind a curtain in the arms of a young man and exclaims, "So here you are!" With the exception of this Russian print, dated 1867, all prints in this chest have German writing. Then follows a color print and poem about the sanctity of marriage; a newlywed couple leaves the church. In the center of the lid, rather prominently displayed, is a color newsprint of Prince Friedrich Wilhelm of Prussia being shown his newborn son by his wife. This is followed by a color print with a German account of the coronation of Alexander II in Moscow, where much is said about Alexander crowning his wife. On the lower register there are smaller prints of a woman administering medicine to her sick baby and of children's summer games. One small color print depicts Christ's baptism, another one Christ's transfiguration. These pictures reveal the private thoughts of a young woman poised for adult life.

Other chests feature popular prints of the young Queen Victoria of the British

Empire, princesses of Sweden and of Norway, but most often Prussian and Russian royalty. Sometimes these private decorations on the interiors of the chest lids compose veritable chronologies of the history of the chest.

In one case the commercial color reproductions reflect the story of migration from South Russia to Canada and on to Mexico, while the form of the chest itself is based on the Vistula Delta prototype. The chest's stay in Russia is marked by the now mutilated picture of a Russian aristocratic lady, by German devotional poems, religious mottos and Bible verses. Its stay in Canada is marked by English language product advertisements, which can be dated to the 1920s and 1930s on the basis of their design.[45]

Direct expression of historical consciousness is very rare. In 1944, aware of her chest's centennial, one woman wrote a brief history of her chest, outlining the path of inheritance over five generations on a small piece of paper, and pasted it between the other keepsake mementos inside the lid of her chest.[46]

Conclusion

In this chapter we sought to identify some of the bases for a Mennonite furniture tradition in the Vistula Delta dowries of the late eighteenth and early nineteenth centuries. For several reasons these dowries are of significance to an understanding of the immigrant Mennonite furniture tradition. They represent the tradition at its source. The historical branches of the tradition diverge from this common source into migrations to other parts of Poland, South Russia and North America. The dowry also represents the point at which a new household's furnishings are put together, either through inheritance or through the construction of new pieces. At this time, due to the high regard for a new family in the

Fig.107b, Detail of Anna Franz dowry chest lid. #1.059.

renewal of the society, the furniture reflects central values about home and household. Ideas and decorative symbols come from nature (such as flowers), from biblical stories, from architecture and from personal fancies to give meaning to the dowry's furnishings. In comprehending this set of forms and meanings, we may "read" the essence of the tradition, seeing the society and the people who lived it and passed it on to later generations.

5

The Migration
of the Tradition

The later Polish and early South Russian chapters in Mennonite history are very distant to Mennonite recollections today. To most non-Mennonites they are obscure and esoteric. The localities with which this story is concerned carry place names like Wymysle, Kazun, Wola-Orscynska, Ostrog, Vignanka-Futtor, Novograd-Volynsk, Kotosuvka, and somewhat more familiar, Chortitza and Molotschna (see Maps 4,5,6). This Mennonite story must be seen against the backdrop of large-scale political events that included the partition of Poland after 1763 by Frederick the Great of Prussia, Catherine the Great of Russia and Maria Theresa of Austria-Hungary and the rising tide of unrest against European monarchies that created the French Revolution in 1789.

Mennonites were like pawns in a giant chess game, trying to retain their fragile privileges, to escape conditions that had become onerous for them or to make their arrangements with new patrons. Some Mennonites in the Vistula Delta welcomed the rigorous rationalism of Prussian citizenship, even with its demands of militarization. Others hoped for continued privileges and opportunities and turned to Polish counts and princes who had lands to develop and were offering religious freedom in which to raise children and worship in the manner Mennonites had known. This is what attracted some to Volhynia, a borderland between Warsaw and Kiev. Beyond Poland lay the new lands on the shores of the Black Sea that Russia had taken from the Ottoman Empire. Here, too, promises of religious freedom and opportunities for economic prosperity held out hope for continuation of the familiar and cherished Mennonite way of life.

For many these changes meant migration and resettlement, sometimes many times. Therefore, the documentation of furniture and furnishings from the Polish Mennonite settlements is very sketchy. Perhaps the hard work of making a living in a new place left little time or energy for writing diaries. Very few pieces of furniture accompanied these communities to the New World in 1874-75.

A few records associated with particular pieces of furniture allow us to bring the story of Mennonite domestic furnishings and home life up-to-date. Often these pieces and stories are identified with particular actors, whose family names, for North American Plains Mennonites, are as familiar as the place names are strange: Cornelius Wedel and Peter Fry of Wymysle, Jacob and Franz Adrian of Molotschna, Jakob and Elizabeth Schmidt, Gerhard Thiessen, Peter Friesen and his wife Eva Abrahams, Heinrich Schmidt, Benjamin Schmidt and his wife Catharina Siebert, Cornelius Jansen and his wife Helene van Riesen, Peter Unrau, Heinrich Friesen and others. We also meet the Swiss Mennonite emigrants from Alsace and the Palatinate in Volhynia, people with names like Stucky, Schrag, Krehbiel, Goering and Albrecht.

Mennonites in Central Poland

In 1762 six years before Prussia annexed the lower Vistula Delta, a small group of Mennonite families from the Old Flemish congregation at Przechovka, near Schwetz south of Marienburg, moved south up the Vistula and settled in Wymysle near Warsaw (see Map 2).

Many other Mennonites left the Vistula Delta area after 1772 when Prussian annexation brought burdensome taxes and land restrictions. In 1776, from the Kulm–Graudenz area south of Marienburg, Mennonites migrated to Kazun, just north of Warsaw on the Vistula (Map 2).

Mennonites were attracted to settlements in central Poland for the same reasons they had come to coastal Poland in the first place: lower taxes and a degree of religious liberty. Through its nobility, the Polish government continued to utilize the concept of the *Hollander* block lease to bring into its society particularly productive farmers. This was the case with the Wymysle Mennonite settlement north of Warsaw in Mazovia.[1] These Mennonites from the Vistula Delta used horses for plowing rather than oxen like the Polish peasants. The Mazovian gentry wanted agricultural modernization without changing the feudal system. Thus, colonists such as the Mennonites provided them with improved productivity without threatening their social order.[2]

Whereas earlier in the Vistula Delta the block lease system primarily benefited Mennonites, in Wymysle this arrangement accommodated not only Mennonites, but also Jews, Herrnhuters, Lutherans, Evangelical Baptists and other groups who sought religious freedom but who remained outside of Polish society. For some reason these groups were often seen as one group by the Poles. According to the Polish historian Samuel Myovich, they all favored the longhouse architecture, they were freeholders and they ate Dutch cheese which was not used by Polish peasants.[3] In contrast, the Polish peasants were tied to a particular nobility or gentry and a community at the center of which was a Catholic church. Their architecture was based on the square farm with separate buildings.

As if mirroring the different types of architecture, the overall setting in Polish feudal society was compartmentalized, with each segment having direct contractual, even personal, ties to a patron or lord.

The Cornelius Wedel Estate, Wymysle, Poland

Recent research by Polish ethnographer Wojciech Marchlewski affords a glimpse of one of the Mennonite households of the Wymysle settlement north of Warsaw, and an impression of the kind of furnishings it held.[4] When Cornelius Wedel died in 1830, an inventory of his estate was made by Peter Fry. It was then witnessed before a notary by Fry and Wedel's eldest son. The list and monetary value in Polish *Zloties* of this typical Mennonite household included:

The household and farm:
- the house, 2,000 *Zloties* [this would have been a typical longhouse with 2 bedrooms and a kitchen facing a common room]
- land, 2,300 *Zl.*
- farm equipment for horse and farm
- 15 cows, 2 horses
- 5 boxes flour
- boxes for wheat storage
- sauerkraut making barrel and 2 barrels to sit on
- 5 wooden shovels

The wardrobe:
- pillows, clothes and towels
- 30 *elle* long new woolen material
- 4 towels
- 28 new men's shirts
- one suit
- old woolen cloth worth 2 *Zl.*
- 3 irons, 3 *Zl.*

Furniture and household goods:
- 4 wooden beds, 12 *Zl.* 6 gr.
- 3 ordinary tables, 6 *Zl.*
- 6 ordinary sitting benches, 1 *Zl.* 6 gr.
- 4 chairs
- 1 child's seat, 4 *Zl.*
- 1 "Credence" (china cabinet or cupboard) 4 *Zl.*
- 17 spoons, 17 *Zl.*
- 1 candle holder
- 33 wooden sour milk/cheese bowls, 4 *Zl.*
- 60 Hollander cheeses, 60 *Zl.*
- 2 cabbage cutters, 15 gr.
- 2 old, 1 new saws, 15 gr.

Debts:
- to Catherine Buller, 2,986 *Zl.*
- to Michele Luther, 900 *Zl.*
- interest [owed] on rent money 180 *Zl.*

Although there was little migration from the Wymysle and Kazun Mennonite Polish settlements north of Warsaw to the Plains of North America, the household furnishings of Cornelius Wedel were probably very much like those of the few Mennonites who came directly from these Polish settlements to the Plains.

Fig.108a, Dowry chest. From Karolswalde, Polish Volhynia. Brought by Benjamin P. Schmidt and his wife Catharina A. Siebert in 1874 on the SS *Kenilworth*. The Schmidts settled in Pawnee Rock, Kansas.[1] Pine or fir, dovetailed joints, plain key plate, handle plates, handle, hand forged iron hinges, four brass bosses. Till on the left hand side. Originally this chest may have had a bracket base.

W:47" D:25" H:18¼".
#1.049, Private collection.

Vistula Dutch and Swiss Mennonite Traditions Meet in Polish Volhynia

Volhynia is a flat plateau region between Warsaw and Kiev that was once part of greater Poland. As has been noted, Polish and Russian counts and princes in the late 1700s and early 1800s sought to develop their lands with the help of western European colonists, among whom the Mennonites figured prominently because they were industrious farmers who usually agreed not to spread their nominally radical faith.

In 1785 about 38 Mennonite families left the Graudenz area in the Vistula Delta for the estate of Polish Count Potocki near Michalin (Map 5). Within a few years (1793) some had gone on to the lands of Prince Eduard Lubanirsky near Ostrog, and others (ca. 1821-28) to Karolswalde. In 1811 another group of families left the Schwetz–Graudenz region for Count Olisarov's land in Zabara and Waldheim near Novograd Volynski (New Volhynia). The group that settled in Ostrog, although mostly farmers, reportedly included persons who were also smiths, carpenters, wagonmakers, cabinetmakers, weavers, millers, stonemasons and bricklayers.[5]

Another group of 21 Mennonite families came from Neumark in Brandenburg in 1811 and settled on the lands of Polish nobleman Waclav Borejko, in the village of Zofyovka near Wysock, and in 1828 moved to Ostrova and Jozefin.

Most of these people came to Kansas in 1874-75. The Karolswalde group is represented by two plain chests (Fig. 108a, 108b) which belonged to descendants of two families who migrated from the Delta to central Poland. After living there for nearly 60 years, both families moved on to North America on the SS *Kenilworth*. The chests resemble a type attributed to Polish folk traditions, and may well date to the early 1800s, having come with the families to central Poland at the time of emigration from the Vistula Delta. Unfortunately, the original painted finishes which would yield stylistic and historic clues have been lost to overpainting and radical stripping. Several fraktur drawings (Figs. 109, 110), of the type that would have been kept inside the lid of a dowry chest, from the Michalin group feature floral motifs and show the continuing connection in furniture and the decorative arts with the Vistula tradition.

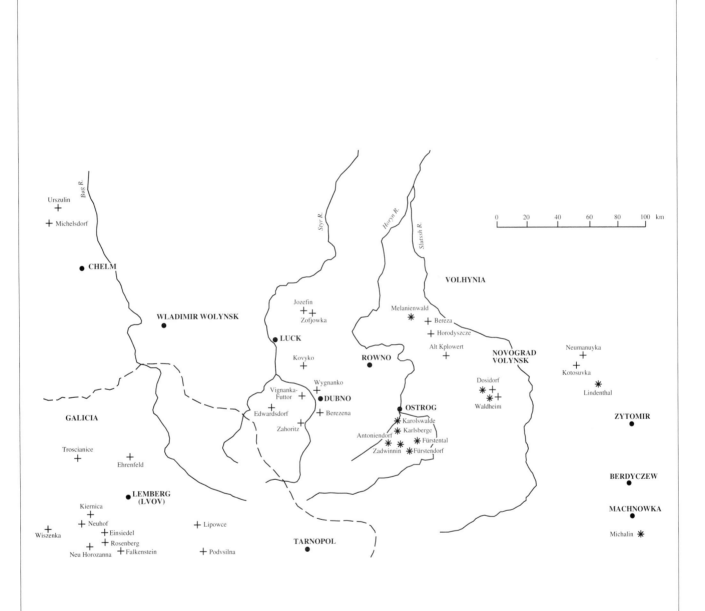

Map 5. (Detail of Map 2) Mennonite settlements in Galicia and Volhynia, eighteenth to nineteenth centuries (after *Mennonitisches Lexicon,* Vol. 4, p. 559); settlements of Vistula Delta origin (*), Swiss-Alsatian-Palatinate origin (+). This region was culturally and politically Polish until 1772, the first partition of Poland, at which time the area southwest of the line came under Austro-Hungarian rule, and the rest under Russian rule.

111

(top) **Fig.108b,** Dowry chest, not later than 1869—the year of Abraham and Eva Schultz's marriage. From Karolswalde, Polish Volhynia. Brought by Abraham D. and Eva Decker Schultz to the Friedensthal community near Moundridge, Kansas, in 1874. Pine, dovetailed joints, hand forged iron fittings, lock and key. Original painted finish has been stripped. Bracket base attached with wooden pegs. Till on left side. Narrow shelf with ledge along the back.
  H:25½" W:47½" D:24½".
  #1.074, KM 91.29.

(bottom) **Fig.109,** "Spiritual Wonder Clock," fraktur, 1846. For each of the twelve hours of the day the poem relates a passage from scripture, admonishing faithfulness. Unknown artist, Michalin, Polish Russia. Paper, ink, tempera paint.
  14" x 16".
  Private collection.

Other Mennonites of Alsatian and Palatinate origins, living in the Austro-Hungarian empire, also sought refuge and prosperity in this immediate area. They too were beneficiaries of Poland's open-door policy toward religious dissenters from Catholic and state church Europe, a policy that benefited not only Mennonites, but also other groups such as the Jews.

The numerous small Mennonite settlements in Volhynia, on the lands of Polish and Russian nobility, communicated with one another.[6] However, there are only scant records of home furnishings among the groups from the Palatinate and Galicia and the Swiss-Alsatian Volhynians. The absence of evidence regarding home furnishings from these groups leaves us with little basis for saying either that they retained their own distinctive furnishings tradition or that they assimilated the one around them.

Harley Stucky suggests that the Palatinate-Galician and the Swiss-Alsatian Mennonite communities in Volhynia became a single socio-economic-religious culture (Map 5 shows joint settlements),[7] in spite of the fact that they were required by law to remain isolated, that is not take in outsiders, especially not by religious conversion.[8] Some of the Swiss-Volhynian settlers from the Alsace were followers of Jacob Amman, and thus brought the Amish way of life to Volhynia.[9] The Alsatian and Amish migrants to Volhynia had been stock and milk producers. In Volhynia they became grain farmers. In Switzerland and the Alsace many of them had lived in massive housebarns on large farms. The Palatinate group settled with other Germans in land and buildings that had belonged to Catholic monasteries. A 1786 letter from a Mennonite in this settlement reported with amazement that the local inhabitants had no tables, benches or beds in their homes, and that their livestock and buildings were in very poor condition. In contrast, the Mennonite homes were constructed on uniformly lain-out farm plots, often with a housebarn and shed constructed of wood with clay brick walls and with a thatched roof. The house consisted of a kitchen, three larger rooms and a utility room.[10]

Because of their many moves and consequent exposure to other people,

Fig.110, Four-drawer dresser or *Kommode,* 1846. Drawing for a New Year's Wish. Unknown artist, Michalin, Polish Russia. Paper, ink, tempera paint.
17" x 14".
Private collection.[2]

Fig.111, Travel trunk, pre-1874. "Brought by Mother Kauffman's father" (Jacob Kauffman's father-in-law) to Marion, South Dakota. Wood, paint, hand forged fittings and lock.
H:18.5" W:36.5" D:20".
#2.025, KM 2251.36.[3]

including the Vistula Mennonites, the Swiss-Volhynians developed a culture that was a synthesis of numerous regional and national elements, including Russian–Polish food and clothing. Furthermore, various words from different languages became part of this particular Swiss-German dialect.[11]

Several sources offer some details of the merged Palatinate and Alsatian immigrant way of life. Few families owned their land; rather, they lived on block lease areas characteristic of Polish and Russian feudalism. Family land use was usually assigned by the church elders so there was a considerable degree of equality in the community, at a poverty level.[12] Clothing was homespun and woven out of homegrown flax and hemp. Farming was done with horse-drawn implements and handheld sickles, scythes, forks and rakes.[13] The housebarn was the predominant form of dwelling, with a hallway between the house and the barn. In later years (sometime before 1874) some houses and barns were built under separate roofs. All buildings were of wood, the materials having been cut by the farmers. While some homes had wooden floors, many had dirt floors. Most homes had two or three rooms with a central stove built into the wall, extending into each room. All furniture was homemade.[14]

When the Swiss Volhynians migrated to Kansas and South Dakota, they either bought travel trunks or built their own shipping boxes. Several trunks have survived (Fig. 111). The pullout bed built by Johannes Albrecht in South Dakota (Fig. 10) and the Waltner table (Fig. 23) are also from this tradition.

Mennonites in South Russia

The emigration of Mennonites from the lower Vistula Delta continued. From 1789 until 1802 about 460 families immigrated to the south Russian region of Ekaterinoslav and formed the first Mennonite colony in the Ukraine at Chortitza. Beginning in 1804 and continuing until 1835, another 1,200 families immigrated to a nearby colony in the province of Taurida named Molotschna after the river

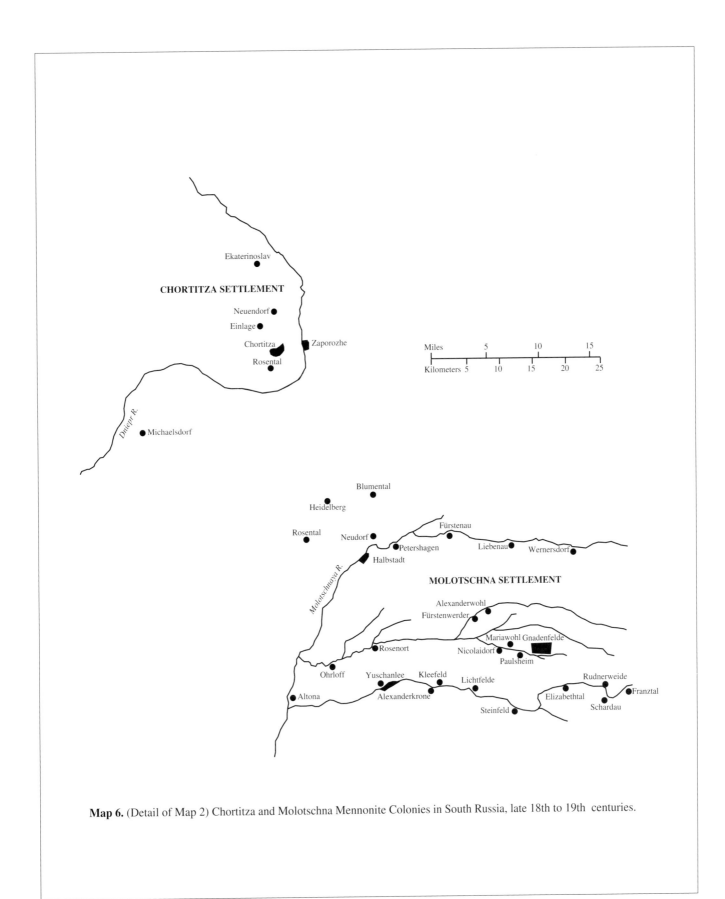

Map 6. (Detail of Map 2) Chortitza and Molotschna Mennonite Colonies in South Russia, late 18th to 19th centuries.

on which it was located. Most of the Mennonite immigrants to the American Plains in the 1870s came from these two Mennonite colonies in South Russia. The Mennonite settlements of Chortitza and Molotschna were culturally more homogeneous than those in Volhynia, but there was a greater class division between rich and poor. The opportunity to expand holdings and to hire non-Mennonite workers and landless Mennonites soon led to a class of large landowners with estates that compared to the Russian nobility. These divisions are reflected in the household structures and pieces of furniture depicted in this section.

In the Molotschna Colony the economy supported large groups of craftsmen. Among these were Jacob Adrian, introduced in chapter three, who arrived in the Molotschna as a landless carpenter in 1839; Gerhard Thiessen, a wealthy estate owner; Jakob and Elizabeth Schmidt of the Old Flemish congregation in Alexanderwohl; and Cornelius Jansen and his wife Helene van Riesen, who moved from Schidlitz near Danzig to the Black Sea port city of Berdjansk, where he became a businessman and a politician.

Craftsman and Householder

Indicating a variety of skills around furniture and household furnishings, the Russian Mennonite colony of Molotschna had the following craftsmen in 1854:[15]

- 22 masons
- 65 linen weavers
- 96 blacksmiths
- 50 master carpenters (*Zimmermeister*)
- 51 cabinetmakers (*Tischler*)
- 13 turners (*Dreschler*)
- 61 wheelrights (*Stellmacher u. Radmacher*)
- 9 clockmakers
- 44 tailors
- 25 glassblowers (*Glaser*)
- 4 locksmiths
- 50 shoemakers
- 12 harness and saddlemakers (*Sattler*)
- 8 *Maschinenbauer*
- 8 coopers, or stovemakers
- 2 bookbinders
- 14 painters
- 2 tanners
- 1 each of ropemaker, baker, pewtersmith, coppersmith, canvasmaker

Jacob Adrian was one of the 51 cabinetmakers in Molotschna. Adrian (1801-1866) had come to Molotschna in 1839 with his wife Anna and family, documenting the account of their emigration from the Vistula Delta in a notebook.[16] An historical treasure-trove, his notebook also includes the tale and drawing of an imaginary wild animal, marriage vows, dates of births and deaths of close family members, occasional drafts of letters, a verse from a hymn, days worked on a job, and a series of recipes (given in Appendix C) on polishing and staining wood with different shades of red, light red, yellow, blue, green and black. This part of the diary also includes recipes on how to imitate the stain of

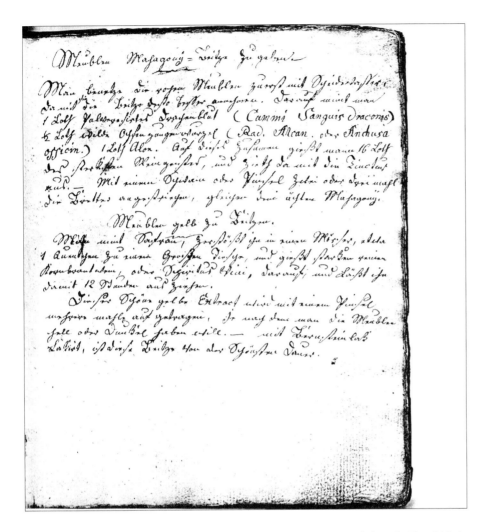

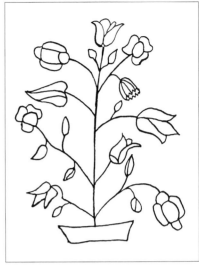

(above) **Fig.112,** Floral motif, ca. 1836. Drawing actual size from Jacob Adrian's notebook.[4]

(left) **Fig.112a,** Page from Jacob Adrian's notebook: "To stain furniture [the color of] mahogany" and "To stain furniture yellow." Collection of Walter Adrian.

mahogany on furniture and how to paint gun shafts a brownish red (Fig. 112a). Here is the recipe for one type of mahogany stain:

> First moisten the raw furniture wood with nitric acid so it will accept the stain more easily. Then take one lot of powdered dragon blood (*cummis sanguis draconi*), 1/2 lot ox-tongue roots (*rad. alcan or anchuso officin*) 1 lot alum. Mix this together and pour 16 lots of the strongest ethyl alcohol in to pull out the red color. Take a sponge and brush the stain two or three times. When the boards have been painted with this, they will look like genuine mahogany.[17]

A faint sketch in the diary of a floral motif (Fig. 112) of the kind found so often on dowry chests suggests that Adrian may have painted floral designs on his furniture as well.

Jacob Adrian's family of five first settled as landless renters (*Anwohner*) at the edge of the village of Schardau in the Molotschna. There Jacob supplied the local demand for spinning wheels and wooden plow wheels. In the spring of 1840 Jacob, together with other newly arrived craftsmen, was asked to register at Johann Cornies' model farm at Jushanlee. Plans were discussed to establish a permanent village of craftsmen. Jacob also was asked to appear at Orloff where an extensive questionnaire was now required of each craftsman, covering in great detail his personal and professional life. In the fall of 1841 Jacob and Anna Adrian's family moved to the village of Rudnerweide.

Jacob's son Franz Adrian continued to make entries in his father's journal, beginning with a note on Jacob's death in 1866. However, none of Franz's jottings relate to his work as a builder and cabinetmaker. According to the writings of Franz Adrian and those of his grandson Walter Adrian, the story of Franz and Katherina Adrian begins as follows:

In 1860 Franz married Katharina Janzen (1837-1905) in the home of the bride's parents, Peter and Anna Nachtigal Janzen, in Franztal, Molotschna Colony. The young couple made their first home at the west end of the neighboring village of Rudnerweide.

Franz, like his father, became a cabinetmaker and carpenter, making spinning wheels, furniture and other necessary household items. He also made all the cogwheels and shafts from oak timbers for the Cornelson mill located at the east end of Rudnerweide. We will pick up the story of Franz Adrian's furniture building business in the next chapter following his move to Kansas.

Although no records remain of the Adrians' cabinetwork in Russia, we may

Fig.113, Dowry chest. Brought in 1874 from Paulsheim, South Russia, to the Bruderthal community, rural Hillsboro, Kansas, by the Cornelius Funk family. Pine, painted graining, brass key plate, hand forged hinges, five-footed separate base with scalloped skirt.

H:26¼" W:53" D:27½".
#1.022, Private collection.[5]

assume that they built furniture much like the many plain, mahogany red dowry chests built by Heinrich Schmidt and other cabinetmakers of the nearby Alexanderwohl community (Fig. 113).[18]

Jakob and Elisabeth Schmidt, of Mariawohl village in the Molotschna Colony, had a very similar chest in their home. The Schmidts were members of the Alexanderwohl congregation, which included many people who had emigrated from Prezchovka, between Marienburg and Graudenz, in the Vistula

(top, left) **Fig.114,** Dowry chest, made prior to 1857. Brought by Jakob Schmidt from Mariawohl, South Russia, to the Goessel community, Kansas. Pine, painted graining to imitate mahogany, painted floral bouquets of roses and a tulip tied with a ribbon. Lid decorated with the same motifs. Brass bosses, brass key plate, key and hand forged iron hinges. Separate five-footed base with straight skirt.[6]
   H:27" D:28" W:54".
   #1.020, Private collection.

(above) **Fig.115,** *S*ide view of the Jakob Schmidt dowry chest.
   #1.020.

(bottom, left) **Fig.116,** Lid and back of the Jakob Schmidt chest. Note the floral motif and the inscription on the back: "Jakob Schmidt, Mariawohl."

(right) **Fig.117,** Detail of fraktur pasted inside the lid of Jakob Schmidt's dowry chest, Alexanderwohl, January 1, 1842. New Year's wish by Jakob Schmidt to his parents.
#1.020.

(facing page) **Fig.118,** Helene van Riesen, Schidlitz-Gdansk, 1843. At age 21, three years before her marriage to Cornelius Jansen. Watercolor portrait by an unknown artist.[7]

Delta to the Molotschna in 1820.

The Alexanderwohl group belonged to the conservative "Old Flemish" Conference that discouraged its members from dressing fancily and from having bright and colorful household interiors.

An experience with their plain dowry chest nearly got the Schmidts into trouble with the elders of the congregation. The story is told within the Schmidt family of a tramp who was taken in when he came half frozen to their house in the dead of winter.[19] When spring came, he wanted to repay them. His only currency was his painting skill, so he offered to decorate their plain chest. The unknown painter sought to create a background over the solid red paint that would imitate the color and graining of mahogany. Over that, he painted multicolored bouquets of flowers, imitating dyed veneers used in inlaid furniture (Figs. 114, 115).

When word reached the congregational leaders regarding the repainted and brightly decorated chest, the Schmidts were almost put into the ban. Although plain red chests were perhaps the norm, painters were available who could decorate them on demand.

Helena v: Biron 1845

(above, right) **Fig.119,** Dowry chest, ca. 1800. Probably made in Gdansk, owned by Helene van Riesen who married Cornelius Jansen in Schidlitz-Gdansk in 1846. Brought from Berdjansk, South Russia, in 1873. Oak, six solid boards, dovetailed joints. Inlaid veneer ornament of flowers within interlaced borders. Till on the left inside and mounts for the kerchief board across the back. Embossed ornate tinned iron hinges and handle plates, tooled cast-iron handles, brass key plate. Bottom board was replaced. Independent five-legged bracket base may be later replacement. Key and lock are missing.

W:55¾" H:27¼" D:27¼".

#1.010, Mennonite Library and Archives, Bethel College, North Newton, Kansas.

(above, left) **Fig.120,** Cornelius and Helene van Riesen Jansen and their children. Left to right across back: Peter, Anna van Riesen (sister of Helene van Riesen Jansen), Carrel(?), Helene van Riesen Jansen, Cornelius Jansen, Margarethe. Front row: Anna, Johannes, Helene. On the entrance steps of their home in Berdjansk, South Russia, in 1870—three years before they left for North America.[8]

The Jakob and Elisabeth Schmidt chest was later brought to Kansas in the Alexanderwohl migration of 1874. On the back of the chest (Fig. 116) the name, place and date were painted in white fraktur letters: "Jakob Schmidt, Mariawohl, 1857." On the inside of the lid in the upper right-hand corner was written in ballpoint pen, and quite small, "To Abraham" and "To Aron."

A German fraktur New Year's greeting addressed, "*Vielgeliebte Eltern...*" (Much loved parents), dated January 1, 1842 and signed by Jakob Schmidt at Alexanderwohl (Fig. 117), was pasted to the inside of the lid. Somewhere along the way, a second fraktur was torn out; only fragments of border decorations and the date 1845 remain. [20]

Inlaid Chests in City and Country

The Mennonite movement to Russia was so massive and diverse that we may not imply that all came as landless craftsmen. Nor did they all settle in agrarian villages. The arrival of those who brought top-of-the-line inlaid chests in the Vistula Delta style may be marked by two families who came to Russia in the 1850s.

Cornelius Jansen, originally of Tiegenhof in the Vistula Delta and of the Heubuden congregation, was trained by his uncle as a businessman. In 1850 following his marriage to Helene von Riesen (Fig. 118) of Schidlitz near Danzig, who brought into the marriage, as her dowry, a fine inlaid chest (Fig. 119), Cornelius and his new wife moved to Berdjansk on the Black Sea coast, where Cornelius became the founder and representative of the Prussian and Mecklenburg consulate (Fig. 120).

We may infer the contents of the Jansen dowry by studying another account of a similar inlaid chest brought to Russia in 1855 when Cornelius Harder and his wife Margarethe emigrated from a farm near Schoensee in the Vistula Delta.

> From this house came the large chest of ash wood with its brass fittings, the dark star and its framing motif in inlaid work, which grandfather had taken along on his emigration and which [he] had given to his eldest daughter as her inheritance. It stored the heirlooms of old linens, silk kerchiefs. The large tablecloth lay in there, with the woven patterns of twelve stags in the wreath of leaves which signified the place setting.

Great-grandmother had woven it herself still before the time of the French [Napoleonic wars and occupation]. The little gold ring which had been inherited by the sister who stayed behind [in Prussia], was kept in the chest, and passed on, engraved with the date of the emigration, so that it should belong to the eldest daughter who bore the same name as her grandmother, Agathe. But the beautiful cigarholder of amber with the carved fox was equal in the eyes of the boy to the heirloom ring which in any case had to become his sister's inheritance.[21]

We do not know the fate of this chest and its owners. The Jansen chest, however, left Berdjansk in 1873 when Cornelius, who had actively promoted emigration of Mennonites and been an outspoken advocate against military conscription, was banned by the Czar. The Jansens immigrated to Beatrice, Nebraska, where Cornelius became a legislator in the Nebraska State House.

Furnishing the Estate

By the late nineteenth century and into the early twentieth century well-to-do Mennonites in Russia were accustomed to ordering their new furniture from Mennonite craftsmen. Two accounts will demonstrate the relationship of furniture buyer to craftsman in the South Russian Mennonite colonies.

Even though Gerhard Thiessen, an estate owner, made some of his own furniture, he had the means to commission new products from other Mennonite craftsmen and also to buy from non-Mennonite craftsmen in the surrounding towns. The owner of the Krutojarowka Estate in the Ukraine, he ordered a wardrobe made of cherry wood out of his orchard from a Herman Sawatzky. His diary entry reads:[22]

> March 1, 1912. Morning -1 frost, sunny till noon and lightly overcast in the afternoon. I went and got the clothes wardrobe from Herman Sawatzky that he made for us from cherry tree wood. With transport it cost us 69 Rubel and 18 Kopek; very expensive and not made accordingly. The scoundrel used our wood for it too. Our Wallachian horse was sick all day, could not urinate, got better in the evening.[23]

The relative value of this wardrobe may be ascertained from Thiessen's mention of the cost of some other items: the service of a maid for five months was 23 rubles; a basket cost 20 kopeks; an everyday suit made by the "Jewish tailors" cost 6 rubles; lining a fur coat with cloth, 6 rubles; and a jacket, 4 rubles and 50 kopeks.[24]

Thiessen may have been disgruntled with Mennonite craftsmen, or perhaps he simply decided to shop commercially outside of the community. Thus, he records another shopping trip for furniture in the provincial town:

> Feb. 17, 1907. Morning tem. -4. In the morning I drove to Ekatarinoslaw and deposited 5100 Rubel in the Petersburger Bank. I also bought a big mirror and six chairs and came home in the evening. The mirror was 15 Rubel, the chairs 18 Rubel.

Despite his affluence and ability to afford purchased furniture, Thiessen still made some of his own furnishings:

Fig.121, Housebarn in Margenau, Molotschna, South Russia. "One of the few that had survived for nearly a century." 1914 photo.[9]

> Dec. 11, 1907. Morning -9 frost and -12 in the evening, windy all day. I put some verses under glass and frame.[25]

He also built Christmas gifts for the program that presumably included the Russian estate workers:

> Dec. 24, 1907. Morning -7 , evening -4 frost. Light winds and blowing snow. Have finished three toy wagons for our boys for Christmas. We all went to the school to our Christmas program. All the estate people gathered with their offspring around the tree. The children sang songs and recited poems.[26]

Peter Jansen remembers that, "Practically every farmer kept a special room in which repair work could be done. There he patched and sewed the horses' harnesses, made his own furniture and, perhaps, did some simple metal work.

"The most common wooden benches without a back could be found in every home. The more elaborate sleeping bench (*Schlafbank*) had a lid which covered the bedding during the day and provided a place to sit. Every household had at least one sleeping bench where the youngsters were bedded down.

"Clothes closets were not built into the wall, but a simple wardrobe was used for extra clothes. A large chest was used for packing winter clothes. This piece was usually made by a professional because it had to be made airtight to keep the moths out.

"A chiffonier-type drawer chest was often built to hold linen. It was called a commode and usually had been decorated."[27]

The relationship between building for oneself and hiring a specialized craftsman in the Mennonite colonies of Russia is further demonstrated in the writings of Heinrich Friesen, a farmer (Fig.121) whose brother Gerhard became a cabinetmaker. In 1857 Heinrich Friesen wrote:

> My brother Gerhard [Friesen] was apprenticed with a cabinetmaker the first years. After we finished threshing, Father built a sheep barn on the yard and on one end of this barn a nice workshop for Gerhard where he could work at his trade in winter. [28]

The Friesens' encounter with the furniture painting trade in Molotschna is evident in this brief entry:

124

During February [1857], the painter master, Johann Martens, asked father to go along with him to Chortitza in the old colony. He had a paint mixing machine that was out of order which he had bought at the Loepp factory there and wanted to have it repaired...at Einlage Martens bought a barrel of linseed oil.[29]

A Visit in a South Russian Mennonite Home

The goal of the craftsman was, of course, the fully furnished home—the setting of family life. Alexander Petzholdt, writer and traveler, published a description of the interior furnishings of a Mennonite farm home in South Russia in 1855, after having traveled about in western and southern Russia. He renders a picture of the "classical" interior of the *Grosse Stube* in Molotschna.[30]

Finally I ask the reader to cast a sympathetic glance in the interior of a Mennonite living room, where the *Biedermann* with his brave wife rests from his work, smoking his pipe with tobacco he grew himself. In the background, between the two doors which lead to the bedroom and to the utility room (*Wirtschaftszimmer*), hangs a Black Forest clock (which is however produced here in the colonies)[more than likely, this resembled the clock in figure 122, not a cuckoo clock]. In the corner of the room, opposite the windows, stands the huge *Himmelbett* with colorful curtains where the store of featherbeds is piled high like a tower. Nobody sleeps here, the bed just stands here for show. In the other corner, behind the stove, is the big chimney (*Hoelle*), and a built-in utility cupboard, which is also accessible from the other side, from the utility room. Next to the large tile stove, on the side of the entry door, is also a built-in cabinet in the upper part of which porcelain things are stored for use on festive occasions. On the wall across from the entry, which usually has windows with a view towards the garden, the mirror finds its place, and under the mirror is the chest (*Truhe*), in which the mistress of the house keeps her belongings and her valuables; three gleaming large brass knobs decorate this piece of furniture, often colorfully painted. Along the fourth wall with two windows looking to the farmyard stands a sofa with a table placed in front of it. Such furnishing of the living room one finds in every Mennonite home; everywhere the clock, the *Himmelbett*, the chest, the built-in cabinet, and everything in Dutch cleanliness. (Authors' translation)

This scene is idealized—a mixture of what Petzholdt had been told and what he saw in this well-to-do home. Its static photographic description comes to life in samples from the many South Russian Mennonite diaries which describe scenes of daily life in the home.

Scenes of Daily Life in the Russian Mennonite Home

Many diaries and books recount with fondness experiences in the lives of South Russian Mennonites, where it must truly be said that they experienced a sort of "golden age." These experiences often occur in the homes, and offer an excellent profile of the use of rooms, spaces and furniture; a combined theme that in chapter one we identify as "rituals and spaces of domestic life." The

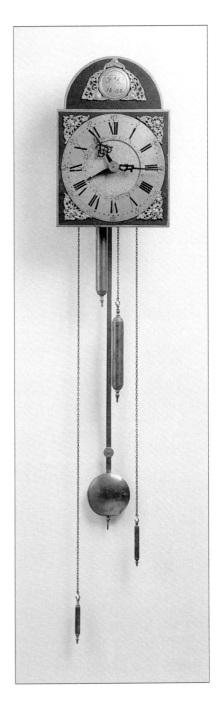

Fig.122, Pendulum clock, 1858. Made by the Kroeger clock manufacturing firm, Rosental, South Russia. Hour and minute hands, calendar hand, chimes, cut sheet iron, brass, gilt relief ornament of angels (one in each corner, one in the half-circle above the clock face). Initials "TK."
H:20" W:14".
#19.011, Adobe House Museum, Hillsboro, Kansas.

(top, left) **Fig.123,** Mennonite family's living room *(Grosse Stube)* in the Chortitza Colony, South Russia, ca. 1910-1920. Note the guest bed piled high with extra bedding and its richly embroidered cover, the cradle at the foot of the bed and the religious wall mottos.[10]

(bottom, left) **Fig.124,** The Abram H. Friesens, Schoenau, South Russia in their *Grosse Stube* (livingroom), ca. 1900-1920.[11] Note the guest bed piled high with embroidered linens. The embroidered bedcover *(Vorstecksel)* is reminiscent of the 1818 bedcover from Tralau, Vistula Delta (see Fig. 96).

(right) **Fig.125,** *Kleine Stube,* Mennonite Kitchen," ca. 1930. John Peter Klassen, (1888-1975). The artist depicts a childhood memory from South Russia. A mother rocks her infant in the cradle while she knits a stocking and keeps watch over the bake oven built into the kitchen wall. Rockers fashioned from sections of wagon wheels were a common alternative to solid wooden rockers on Mennonite cradles.[12] Bronze relief. 12¾" x 13¾".

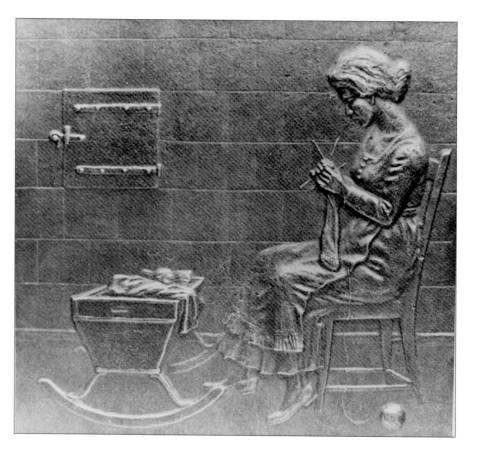

following entries from various writings provide us with the South Russian version of this idea.

Grosse Stube

- "Father placed delicacies such as sweets, peppernuts, nuts in the bottom of the wardrobe in the *Grosse Stube* (living room, Figs. 123,124.)"[31]
- "Father took his nap on the *Ruhebank* in the *Grosse Stube*."[32]
- "The village alcoholic slept off his drunk on the resting bench."[33]
- "They placed the resting bench—on which father then was to die—in the middle of the *Grosse Stube* when he lay dying."[34]
- "The resting bench on which father died was inherited by my favorite brother Gerhard. It is placed under the window of his *Grosse Stube*."[35]
- "When there was hogbutchering the brown resting bench in the *Grosse Stube* was used for the breakfast meal."[36]

Kleine Stube

"The *Schlafbank* was in the *Kleine Stube*, which was used as a dining room for the family. The *Schlafbank* served as a bench at the table, then as the bed for the youngest son (Fig, 125,126).

"It was my habit to always have something to nibble on in little bags (such as dried fruit) in the sleeping bench (*Schlafbank*) when Gerhard's or Abraham's or Tienke's children came to visit.

"To the right of the door which led to the kitchen was the milk bench (*Milch und Schuesselbank*). On the lowest shelf was the small box with shoe polish and two shoe brushes, one for applying the polish, the other to polish the shoe. Next to it was the box with David's toys...wood horses and blocks.

"Other than this milk bench there was a table, a few chairs, and two sleeping benches. A small one for our David was placed under the only window. The larger one, on the wall of the corner room (*Eckstube*). In this one Tienke and I slept. The *Kleine Stube* also served as dining room and my father's two blacksmith apprentices sat on this bench when they ate here. But when my sister emigrated to America this sleeping bench was sold and I asked my brother Gerhard to buy it for me. Then, when Tienke came back from America after a year, impoverished, I gave her this bench in which we had slept together as children. It stands in her *Grosse Stube* where other people place their upholstered resting bench (*Ruhbank*)."[37]

Dowry

In about 1870, before the beginning of emigration, one South Russian Mennonite woman wrote about preparations for her own dowry and the construction of dowry chests:[38]

> This fall we received our entire customary dowry, especially linen (*Waesche*) and furniture. Already my father had prepared for this for several years. Each time he went to Halbstadt or Takmak to get wood he selected the best boards, let them dry well in the sun or in winter in the *Grosse Stube* next to the stove, so that there was always such a fine scent of warm fir in our house, and then he put the boards in the loft of his workshop. Now he took them down, one after another...After several weeks father showed me two new chests, complete except for the hinges, handles, lock and paint...Father saved the most beautiful of the wood shavings to place into the coffins which he built for all the dead of the village.
>
> Such chests were then part of the dowry of the grown-up girls just as chests of drawers are today. The hinges on the lid of the chest were fastened with thick screws which had large shiny brass knobs. Two at each end of the lid. As large as a silver ruble. Also on the front of the lid there were such knobs. The triple lock requires that the key needs to be turned three times. At each turn there is a sound like that of a beautiful bell.
>
> My sister's and my chest were painted with light brown paint and were placed into the attic since there was no room for them in the house. The linen dowry was started already when my mother was still alive. The cloth (fabric) was purchased by our parents in a large store in Takmak...As soon as our chests were finished, father began with work on the wardrobes for our brothers, for the youngest one as well as for the two older ones. (Authors' translation)

On April 2, 1866 the cabinetmaker and farmer Jacob J. Friesen of the village of Schoenfeld in the Molotschna Colony wrote detailed measurements for a wardrobe, which may have gone into someone's dowry, in his notebook (Fig. 127):

Fig.126, Table. Possibly built prior to immigration in 1877 by Peter Unrau. Initialed "P.U." under the table top in red stain. According to family oral history, Peter Unrau was a popular cabinetmaker in South Russia and made many items—resting benches, bedsteads, tables and chairs, as well as caskets. He had three to five men working for him.[13] Pine, original red "milk" paint. Cleated top, tongue and groove joints, no nails, removable legs for ease in packing.

H:29½" W:28½" L:36¼".
#15.022, Private collection.

Fig.127, Page from Jacob Friesen's notebook, 1866, Schoenfeld, South Russia. Measurements for a wardrobe and a verse from a hymn are written on the same page. The realms of the sacred and the profane were closely connected for Jacob.[14]

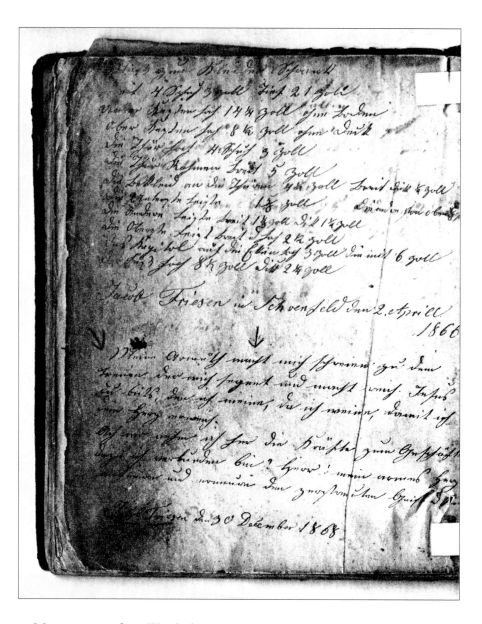

Measurements for a Wardrobe
> Width 4 feet 3 inches Depth 21 inches
> Lower cabinet 14 1/4 inches high without the drawer
> Upper cabinet 8 1/2 inches high without the deck [cornice]
> The door 4 feet 3 inches high
> The door frame 5 inches wide
> The casings on the doors 4 1/4 inches wide, 1/4 inch thick
> The bottom moulding 1 5/8 inches
> The other moulding 1 1/8 inches wide, 1 1/4 inches thick
> The upper moulding 2 1/2 inches wide and high
> The crown [top decoration] on the corners 3 inches high diameter 6 inches
> The foot 8 1/2 inches high 2 1/2 inches thick
> —Jacob Friesen in Schoenfeld, April 2, 1866

Two years later, on December 30, 1868, he wrote a hymn on the bottom of the same page. In the absence of wardrobes known to have been brought from

South Russia during emigration, this notebook entry constitutes a unique and valuable document.[39]

Marriage

Marriage proposals in South Russia were usually made sitting around a table, as described by Heinrich Friesen. In the winter of 1859 he went to the house of his future parents-in-law, the Cornelius Duerksens, in order to ask for their daughter Helene's hand in marriage.

> I went into the parlor (*Grosse Stube*), was greeted heartily, and was asked to sit down behind the table. The school teacher, Cornelius Dueck, was visiting there and they were talking about smoking tobacco...they must have had something to discuss outside for it took a while before the old uncle came back in. After he sat down I at once made known my desire...after everything had been fully discussed, both parents gave their consent. Then Helena (Lenchen) had to come into the parlor also and the engagement day was planned by us all.[40]

Beds and the Cycle of Life

Diaries from South Russia reveal glimpses of sibling squabbles. In one household the boys' beds were made by their sister, and she tried to find their hidden and forbidden playing cards.

> At this time, a rag dealer was staying at our house. He taught us how to play cards which we learned to enjoy greatly...Netke (Aganetha) was very much upset by this. She came into our room every day to make our beds and she was very punctual with this and while she was in our room, tried

Fig.128, Cradle. Brought by Mr. and Mrs. Aaron Fedrau in 1879 from South Russia.[15] Woven wicker, removable wooden rockers, wooden base.
H:16" L:32½" W:23".
#18.026, KM 5634.

to find the cards but we hid them well so she couldn't.[41]

Beds figured in transactions. In the following instance Gerhard Friesen offered to build a bed for his brother Heinrich in exchange for some work Heinrich had done for him:

> After the wedding it was so wet that the road became almost impassable. Since I had helped brother Gerhard in his cabinet shop during the winter, he offered to make a bedstead for the work. I helped him with that also. We got this ready before the spring sowing.[42]

The bed figured in the creation of a metaphor of plenty, as H.B. Friesen wrote in his diary, "...but never have we had to go to bed hungry...this causes us to praise and thank Him."[43]

The bed was also the setting of the most momentous experiences—birth and death—and was often mentioned in association with important or memorable events.

> When Mamma had been in bed for about a week [following son David's birth on April 23, 1879] a rather strange incident happened late one evening. Mamma was lying in bed, I on a bench and was asleep when suddenly there was a crash as if everything was falling over. The Russian maid who was lying on the porch cried and shouted and I myself could not think clearly for a moment... somebody had thrown an unbaked brick with such force that it struck on the opposite wall breaking glass and frame of the window and scattering glass over the bed and cradle. Thank God no one was injured...Later on we heard who the culprit had been...he probably had had too much whiskey.[44]

Johann Siemens describes the last illness of his son John in Fuerstenwerder, South Russia, October 1856.[45] He and his wife lost four children within four days.

> When I came in, [John] had lain down on the bench where my wife had made a couch for him. When I asked him what was wrong, I received the answer, "I am sick." As I talked with him further, I noticed that he called me *Du* [You, familiar address used only by young children] which he no longer did otherwise. From this we concluded that his illness was serious. Then I went to the wardrobe and brought him an apple (which he usually was especially fond of). He took it, but soon returned it with the words "I don't want it." So we put the third sick child to bed. Anna, who was sickest, we took into our own bed.

In approximately 1865 Heinrich Friesen wrote extensively in his diary about sickness and death, first about his neighbors, the Duerksens, then about his own home.[46]

> Brother and sister Duerksen's youngest daughter, Marie, about two years old, died suddenly. I was there and had played with her. Then when I looked at her I noticed that she had foam in her mouth and rolled her eyes. I took her and laid her into the cradle where she also died. That was a great shock for the parents [Fig. 128].

The disease [dysentery] also came into our home. At first little Anna got sick. She lay in her bed near the window and close by was her nursery chair on which she could sit comfortably...the next day Heinrich also got sick. It seemed as if the sickness was more severe with him. Gerhard usually sat at his cradle ready to rock him. Then he was absent one day and when Henry saw him the next day he cried immediately, "Gerhard, rock me." When we heard that we hoped it was a sign of improvement but it lasted only a moment. When Gerhard sat at the cradle and noticed the great pain Henry had to endure, he sobbed and cried...Henry was sick only three days when toward evening he died.[47]

Preparations for Emigration

Some carpenters and cabinetmakers who had emigrated from the Vistula Delta to South Russia lived long enough to participate with their craft in the preparations for the next emigration.

At my sister's sale my husband bought several things, which came from my parental home: a sleeping bench (in which my sister and I and then my three brothers had slept and at which our apprentices sat when they came to eat at the long table) and an old wooden pullout bed (in which my parents had slept).

In his workshop my brother Gerhard built the travel trunks in which everything was to be packed.

Fig.129, Immigrant trunk of Heinrich Regier, 1876. Brought from Alexander-krone, South Russia, to Mountain Lake, Minnesota. Pine, red stain, carved and painted name and address, dovetailed joints, two dovetailed cleats on lid, wrought iron hinges. Original fittings for the lock are missing.
H:24½" W:57½" D:29".
#2.013, KM 6498.

The trunks, the baskets and the chest which my father had made yet stood piled up in the *Vorhaus* [Fig. 129].[48]

Conclusion

The furniture tradition that emerged as Mennonites left the Vistula Delta flourished in central Poland and in South Russia. For these migrating people, the new settlements offered the opportunity to build their own lives and cultures. In Volhynia most craftsmen were also farmers. In the colonies of South Russia the sustainers of the tradition achieved a degree of professionalism they had not had before, and would not maintain after their arrival on the North American prairies. However, the strength and mastery they knew stayed with them.

It is fitting in this chapter devoted to Mennonite migrations to Russia to briefly note the fate of the Mennonite furniture tradition in the Soviet Union in the 120 years following the first migrations to America. Within several decades after 1874 the manufacture of Mennonite furniture became industrialized, as did agriculture and other activities. By the time of the Russian Revolution in 1917 numerous Mennonite firms were manufacturing commodes, benches, beds and tables in large plants in Chortitza and Molotschna.

Elsewhere, migrations had taken Mennonites from the Ukraine to other settlements in Russia. By the time of the Revolution there were over 40 Mennonite colonies in greater Russia, comprising 380 villages.

In a visit to the Mennonite settlements of Pleshanov (New Samara) and Deyevka in Orenburg Oblast in June of 1991, we discoverd cabinetmakers and carpenters still practicing longhouse architecture and the canon of Mennonite furniture, as described in this book. Despite the ordeals of labor camp exile, collectivization and religious persecution, Mennonite culture and religious life had survived and, in fact, experienced a renewal in recent decades.

6

The Tradition Comes to America in Shipping Crates and in the Minds and Hands of Immigrant Craftsmen

Yesterday we took our baggage to the train station [in Marienburg]. We took four chests, the largest contained the parents' wardrobe and weighed 480 kilos. I also sent my own wardrobe in a separate chest and it cost me 10.50 marks. I also included my saddle.[1] —Herman Janzen, on the eve of his family's departure from Sandhof in West Prussia.

We began this work with the question, "What is Mennonite immigrant furniture?" In chapter one we presented the canon of this furniture, as we have identified the tradition, in terms of functional types and representative pieces used in typical ways in the early Plains Mennonite immigrant homes.

Through a study of the historical origins of the forms and styles of the furnishings built and placed in Mennonite homes in the Vistula Delta, in Poland and in South Russia, we have come full circle. Before this tradition was carried to the Plains, it had become a synthetic tradition among Mennonites because ideas were frequently shared and exchanged among craftsmen in these several locations.

Until at least the beginning of the twentieth century, it was customary for the sons of farmers in the Vistula Delta to apprentice in one of the craft trades, such as cabinetmaking, harness making or saddlery, sometimes even going to South Russia to serve the apprenticeship.[2]

For example, Aaron Claassen (1850-1929) from Caldowe, West Prussia, went to Russia in 1869, on a deferment from the Prussian military, to practice the cabinetmaker's trade. He returned to West Prussia shortly before Christmas in 1872.[3] In 1876, with his widowed mother Catharine Claassen, his brother Jacob, who had been apprenticed to the shoemaker's trade, and his sister Catharine, he immigrated to Beatrice, Nebraska.

Only one other immigrant cabinetmaker who came directly to the central Plains from the Vistula Delta, not by way of South Russia, has been found. Jacob

(top, right) **Fig.130,** Travel trunk, pre-1875. Used by Susanna (Loewen) Fehdrau Richert and Jakob Richert, Alexanderwohl, South Russia. Brought through Antwerp and Philadelphia to rural Hillsboro, Kansas. Wood, metal, green stain, painted flowers.
　H:20"　W:40¾"　D:22".
　#2.002, Private collection.[1]

(bottom, right) **Fig.131,** Dowry chest of Anna Wiens Vogt and Peter Vogt. Wedding gift from Anna's parents John and Aganetha Wiens in 1882, Pastwa, South Russia. The young couple immigrated to rural Inman, Kansas, that same year. Anna had monogrammed and dated 32 linen shirts with cross-stitch embroidery for her husband-to-be.
　H:28"　D:26¾"　W:53½".
　#1.052, Private collection.

Harder (1849-1937) of Whitewater, Kansas, reportedly made the furniture for his home, "beds, wardrobe, table, benches and more."[4] Unfortunately, we were unable to trace any of the Jacob Harder works.

　This chapter presents the continued migration of the tradition to the Plains of North America through the lives of several immigrant craftsmen who built furniture in the style of the canon of Mennonite furniture. 1) Franz Adrian from Rudnerweide, Molotschna Colony in South Russia, whose father Jakob we have already met in earlier chapters. Franz Adrian settled in the Hoffnungsau community east of Buhler, Kansas. 2) Heinrich Schroeder of Alexanderwohl, Molotschna Colony in South Russia, who settled in the Alexanderwohl community near Goessel, also in central Kansas. 3) Heinrich Rempel who came most likely from Lichtfelde, Molotschna Colony in South Russia, who lived and worked in the Henderson, Nebraska, community. Many more Mennonite craftsmen are known by name and by at least one work and are listed in Appendix A.

The Tradition Comes as Luggage

Chests and clocks were the two pieces of this Mennonite furniture tradition most frequently brought along to the Plains. One fairly common type of travel trunk found among the immigrants' luggage, featuring a rounded lid, diamond-patterned metal bands and boldly painted red flower sprays on a green ground, seems to have been mass-manufactured in South Russia (Fig. 130). Many of the migration diaries of the 18,000 or so Mennonite travelers reveal a concern for the safety of their luggage, especially for the dowry chests (Fig. 131). The following entries are typical.

About their arrival, Maria Janzen wrote in a letter to relatives in Prussia, "...the men went to get our chests from the depot at Peabody [Kansas] today. Our large clothes chest was undamaged in shipping. Only two saucers in it were broken."[5]

Fig.132, Katharina Janzen Adrian and Franz Adrian. Photographed shortly before they left South Russia in the fall of 1874.[2]

135

(right) **Fig.133,** Corner cabinet, 1879, Franz Adrian. Date painted in the center of the pediment around a sunburst motif and laurel leaves, which also frame the painted name of the maker–owner written the length of the pediment. Pine, painted graining, trim molding strips painted black, varnish. Separately constructed gable and three-footed base with tapered straight legs. Built-in triangular wall shelf which was originally placed under these feet is missing. This form with double glass doors for display represents a deviation from the "classical" corner cabinet type with a single solid door (see figs. 28, 29).
H:36" W:32" D:17".
#14.014, KM 5893.

(above) **Fig.134,** Detail of Franz Adrian's 1879 corner cabinet.

Abraham Claassen wrote, "Until now most of the chests had stood up quite well, but here every worker had an iron hook with a wooden handle, and the chests were thrown end over end. Our chests arrived in pretty good shape. On my wife's chest the bottom was jarred loose somewhat. On mine the strip on top got a mighty jar, and the ornamental plates on top are dented, although it was bound in a horse blanket and the blue robe and a double canvas cover. The two freight chests show the least damage."[6]

The chest of Helene van Riesen Jansen, introduced in chapter five, was part of 47 pieces of baggage with which her family landed at Quebec in August 1873 on their migration from Berdjansk, South Russia. Peter Jansen, Helene's oldest son, remembered:

> We had been used to servants doing the manual labor, but here everybody waited on himself. How well do I remember going after our numerous trunks and baggage to the station, they were all piled on the platform, to which a dray had backed up. The station agent came out while I was looking for the usual baggage carriers seen at European railway stations to load the trunks. The station master looked at me for a minute and then said: "Look here, young fellow, you seem pretty husky, take hold with me and be quick about it." That was my first introduction to American independence, and it seemed very strange to me, in the first place that an official should perform manual labor and also that he should have the temerity to command me to help him. Well, I soon got over my ideas regarding labor.[7]

A Century of Adrian Carpentry

The skills, perspectives and building ideas Franz Adrian brought to Kansas from Molotschna, South Russia, represented a century of craft tradition, beginning with his father Jacob Adrian, a craftsman-cabinetmaker in the Vistula Delta (Fig. 132).

In Kansas Franz struggled like everyone else with the demands of frontier living. But he also carried on his furniture building with a passion. The remaining tangible evidence of his life's work, built for his family's adobe home in Kansas between the years 1876 and 1882, are a corner cabinet (Figs. 133, 134), a chimney support cabinet (Figs. 135, 136), two wardrobes (Figs. 137, 138) and a china cabinet (Figs. 139, 140). Franz Adrian's furniture endured far longer than the two homes he built for his family. In the family's oral history there is talk of another wardrobe, considered his best, in the home of his daughter Anna Adrian Buller, which burned with her house in 1924. There is also a memory of a round gateleg table with drop leaves, "to place a lamp on," which originally stood near a sleeping bench in the *Grosse Stube* or south living room of the Adrian's adobe home.[8]

Several storage chests, which are remembered by his granddaughter Martha Buller, seem not to have survived. A dowry chest which Franz and his wife brought from their home in South Russia is still in the family. According to family oral tradition, this chest was made by Franz and repainted by the Swiss immigrant painter Emil Kym ("*Maler* Kym") in the early 1900s. In the late 1970s it was stripped of its original painted floral decoration to the bare pine.[9]

Franz Adrian was born in 1836 in the village of Kommerau on the Vistula River, not far from the city of Graudenz (Map 4). He spent his formative years in Rudnerweide in the Molotschna Colony, in a landless *Anwohner* family at the end of the village. Franz learned his craft from his father, Jacob Adrian, while growing up in South Russia. He married Katharina Janzen (1837-1905) of Franztal and had a family. He died in 1910 in the home of his daughter Anna Adrian Buller in the Hoffnungsau Mennonite community near Buhler, Kansas. The following account is based on the writings of Franz Adrian's son, Franz J. Adrian.

By 1874 six children had been born to Franz and Katharina of whom four lived to accompany their parents in the great migration to America—Franz 13,

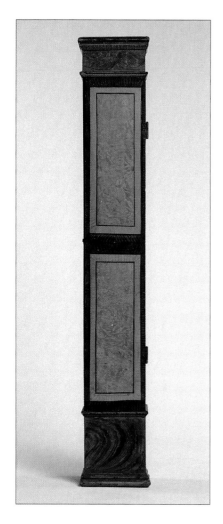

(above) **Fig.135,** Chimney base cabinet, ca. 1876, Franz Adrian. For his new adobe brick house. Pine, painted graining, flowers painted later (1885-1890) by daughter Anna Adrian Buller. Painted graining simulates burl and regular grain of two different woods and gives the effect of inset and recessed panels. The interior with five shelves features bold painted graining in red.
H:68" W:11⅜" D:10".
#10.010, KM 86.375.1.

(right) **Fig.136,** Chimney base cabinet, open.

Jacob 12, Katherine 6, Anna 4. In late July this family left Franztal and boarded the train at Hochstadt going via Berlin to Hamburg. They embarked on the *Teutonia* along with the Dietrich Gaeddert group of 203 adults and 114 children. The Atlantic crossing lasted eighteen days. The group landed at Castle Garden in the New York harbor where they were greeted by David Goerz and Wilhelm Ewert. Here they were registered as immigrants and exchanged their Russian currency.

The next major stop was Topeka, Kansas, where they lodged in a vacant factory for three weeks. They could purchase farm animals, machinery and household goods which would be shipped free by the Santa Fe Railroad to their destinations.

It was October 4, 1874 when the Adrian family reached their 80 acres, four miles east of present-day Buhler, driving a yoke of oxen and followed by a milk

(above) **Fig.137,** Wardrobe, ca. 1878, Franz Adrian. Pine, painted graining, painted white roses and laurel leaves, *trompe l'oeil* keyhole painted on the drawer in the lower cabinet. Five-footed base with straight skirt and pediment constructed separately. The case does not "knock down." It is built as one piece. The interior has one shelf with four hand-carved hooks along the front side and five hooks placed along the back side (three are missing).
H:86" W:42" D:19".
#11.006, KM 6255.1.

(left) **Fig.138,** Wardrobe, 1882, Franz Adrian. This is said to be the last piece built by Adrian. "1882" is marked on the back of the wardrobe. Painted motifs of roses and a bird may have been added around 1900 by Anna Adrian Buller or by Emil Kym. Pine, painted graining, bottom drawer has commercial metal pull, double row of hand-carved wooden pegs to hang clothing.
H:86½" W:48" D:19".
#11.015, KM 27.1.

(right) **Fig.139,** China cabinet, ca. 1879, Franz Adrian. For the south room in his adobe house. Pine, narrow red strip of molding around the cornice, separately constructed five-footed base and pediment. Two glass doors and five drawers. Back is commercial wainscoting. Painted graining, painted white wild rose blossom with five buds, garland of leaves and stylized white flowers along the gable. Painted graining on the facade imitates burl grain of bird's eye maple. Sides show very bold graining in large swirls. Drawer fronts outlined with a narrow red painted line.
H:85" W:34½".
#14.004, KM 5894.

(above) **Fig.140,** Detail of the china cabinet, side view with painted graining.
#14.004.

Fig.141, Floorplan of Franz Adrian's sod housebarn, built in 1875-76. Sketched from memory by his son Franz Adrian (1860-1946). This house was demolished after the new adobe house was built next to it.

cow purchased in Topeka for 22 dollars. Neither farm buildings nor any shelter greeted them, only a heavy growth of tall blue-stem grass. Their first home was a small board shack. Cooking was done outdoors. They soon began to build a more substantial home using pieces of sod four inches thick and from 12 to 18 inches long. The sod walls were 18 inches thick and seven feet high. The finished structure was 18 feet by 44 feet with a board roof, not always waterproof. The north end was partitioned for the livestock and farm machinery (Fig. 141). Fortunately, the winter was mild.

In 1876 sons Franz and Jacob made 11,000 adobe bricks with a form 5½ inches wide, 11 inches long and three inches thick. The resulting adobe house was to stand for nearly 55 years. This structure was divided into three rooms. The north room served as the bedroom for the boys, the middle part as a large kitchen, dining and living area, and the south room as the bedroom for the parents and smaller children. The inside walls were plastered and whitewashed; the outside was covered with siding to preserve the adobe brick walls (Fig. 142).[10]

The barn was now built separately. It was for this second house (Fig. 143), torn down in 1928, that Franz Adrian built and painted furniture. What remains of that furniture is illustrated in these pages. One of the first pieces he built was the chimney support cabinet (Figs. 135, 136). A grandson of Franz Adrian remembers that "odds and ends" like garden seeds and shoe polish were kept in this cabinet. According to family oral history, Franz Adrian's daughter Anna painted the flowering vine on this cabinet.

Anna Adrian Buller (1869-1927) showed an affinity for painting even as a child. The family remembers, "Anna always messed around with paint." She is remembered as fastidious, as dressing "just so," as loving pretty things. After she painted the flower garland on the inside door panel of the chimney support cabinet (Fig. 136), her father evidently suggested, "If you are going to do it

Fig.142, Floorplan of the second Adrian house, built 1876 of adobe. Drawn from memory by Franz's grandson Walter Adrian, 1991. Note the placement of furniture Franz Adrian built for this house. It was torn down in 1928.

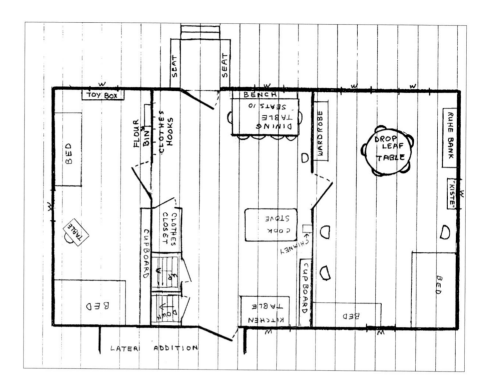

[painting], get some training." She had a reputation for very fine sewing and embroidery work.

In 1898 the Swiss immigrant painter Emil Kym and his family had settled in the Hoffnungsau Mennonite community and become members of that church. Anna's stepdaughter Martha Buller remembers that Kym became a good friend of the Buller family—Anna had married the widower Jacob Buller in 1903. Martha also remembers Kym coming to the house with his paints to give Anna painting lessons.[11] Anna grain-painted much of the woodwork in her house, the facade of the kitchen cabinet, the walls and ceilings in the living and dining rooms and the doors. Therefore, it is likely that Anna painted the floral decorations on most of her father's furniture.[12] What was considered Franz's "best" wardrobe was in Anna's house.[13] It burned with her house in 1924.

The two wardrobes (Figs. 137, 138) are said to have been used in the bedrooms, one in the bed-sitting room of the parents (the south room) where the corner cabinet (Fig. 133) was also placed. According to Franz's grandson Walter Adrian, Franz did all the painted graining of his furniture. However, as we have already noted, the painting of roses and other motifs over the painted graining was evidently done by daughter Anna.

A step-granddaughter of Franz Adrian, Martha Buller, remembers his home and his character.

> Grandpa built his own adobe home, Russian style. The walls were more than a foot deep which made the window sills also deep—this gave Grandma Adrian plenty of space to fill all of them with potted plants. She used geraniums and always had beautiful red blooms to cheer all those who came to call on them. Grandpa also built the barn which had a large spacious front room. Here he built pigeon cotes where the birds came and laid their eggs. Every so often he would "rob" the nests of the baby birds.

Grandma would make a delicious meal in what we call a casserole—yum, yum! In this large room [in the barn] were built-in cupboards where he kept the tools, and other equipment. Everything was in apple pie order. This also applied to the flower and vegetable gardens which yielded abundantly under his tender care.

Grandpa pined for his homeland Russia, so he lived Russian style in every possible way. Grandma made his trousers with home-spun cloth, [with] a very full back that went far below the "seat" and swayed back and forth as he walked. He also drove something we would call a cart with two huge wheels [that] needed only one horse.

Grandpa was a devout Christian and taught us to love Jesus who could save us from sin. He also admonished us children to always say our *Tischgebete* [table grace] before we eat—also to say our short bedtime prayer kneeling at our father's knee.

When Grandpa became ill and it was quite evident he would soon be with the Lord, our parents took him home with them. All the family was called and the next morning they were assembled. After the devotions they started to eat, about 9 or 10.

I was standing at the far end of the room and watched them when Grandpa became ill [worse]. So Uncle Klassen, his son-in-law, grabbed Grandpa's long night shirt in back tightly and with Grandpa hobbling uneasily led him to the bed next door. Grandpa immediately died.[14]

Martha Buller emphasized how her grandfather "pined and pined" for Russia, how he would not wear conventional clothes but dress in his full pants of grey homespun linen, big collared blousy plain shirts and "funny" caps. He only came to North America because his wife wanted to join her brothers and sisters who all emigrated together. Martha exclaimed that his gardens were very pretty, that he taught the grandchildren to love animals because they were all made by the Lord and that he was always busy, but that he let the farming of the land to his sons. "Franz was not a farmer. Eighty acres did not allow you to be in the ballgame."[15]

Fig.143, Franz Adrian with wife Katharina Janzen Adrian and children Katharine, Anna, Henry and Jacob, ca. 1880. In front of their adobe house and barn near Buhler, Kansas.[3]

143

Maldwyn Allen Jones has noted, "For all immigrants, immigration was a traumatic experience, resulting in a sense of alienation and isolation. It was nearly always the fate of the first generation immigrant to remain a 'marginal man,' suspended between two cultures but belonging wholly to neither."[16]

Martha remembers her grandmother Katherina Janzen Adrian as "very broad," evidently a driving force, who wore full aprons with cross-stitching a foot wide. In her attic she had a *Kjist* brought from Russia, which had been part of her dowry in addition to "a cow and a couple of horses." This is the same chest which is still in the family of one of Franz and Katharina's descendants.

Martha remembered that this *Kjist* was decorated, that it had "wooden feet" and pegged construction with no nails. "In it Grandma kept handcrafted things, mostly beautiful embroidered head scarves from Russia. In addition there were three *Kjiste* made by Grandpa, to store nightgowns." Martha also remembered that there were "pretty pictures" on the inside of the lids of some of the chests. These chests were plain and simple, "but very pretty and of good wood. He couldn't do the carving [Martha meant inlaid wood]."

The furniture forms built by Franz Adrian reflect one hundred years of past tradition. The pediments and bases of his wardrobes and cabinets still echo Biedermeier style. When compared with the work of other immigrant cabinet-makers, Franz's furniture appears downscaled. His construction method is more simple, but his use of decorative molding and painted graining vies for effect as ambitiously as Heinrich Rempel's furniture painting, even though it is less refined technically. Perhaps the somewhat smaller size of Franz Adrian's wardrobes reflects an adjustment to the modest proportions of his house. With the exception of the pediment and the footed bracket base, his wardrobes are not constructed of component parts which can be disassembled. Instead of dovetailed joints, he made simpler butt joints. Instead of wooden pegs, he used nails. The use of moldings to frame the inset door panels may be a vernacular attempt to create a stylish look. The painted graining imitates contrasting woods, with a preference for strong contrast between dark walnut and "inset" panel effects of light bird's eye maple, outlined in red. The moldings of the cornice and pediment (or gable) details are outlined in solid yellow and black with the occasional use of dark green. A whimsical painted keyhole in the bottom drawer of one wardrobe is not unique to Franz Adrian. It also is found on a wardrobe most likely made by Klaas Hiebert of Mountain Lake, Minnesota.[17] Drawers in the lower case of a wardrobe may reflect an accommodation to wardrobes with bottom drawers available on the contemporary American mass market for furniture in the 1880s.

Franz Adrian's sons Franz and Jacob and grandsons Frank and Bernhard built only occasional pieces of furniture—a utilitarian bench and some footstools. Grandson Frank built a "mission" style stool and side table as part of a high school craft project around 1920. So it is that the vocabulary of the tradition which Franz Adrian brought across the Atlantic was lost.

Heinrich Schroeder, Farmer and Craftsman

Heinrich Schroeder was the oldest of the three craftsmen featured in this chapter. Those pieces of his furniture that survived the past century—all made

Fig.144, Heinrich Schroeder and wife Sarah Schmidt Schroeder (1833-1911), ca. 1880.[4]

for his family's use—constitute the most complete set of the Mennonite canon of furniture by one immigrant craftsman in Kansas.

Schroeder's interpretation of the Mennonite furniture canon is restrained and closely linked to the tradition as it was brought from Prussia to South Russia.

Heinrich Schroeder was born on March 22, 1825 in Alexanderwohl, Russia. He died on May 3, 1908 in his home near Goessel, Kansas. His parents, Johann Schroeder and Sara Tiarth (Tyart, Tiart, Tjart) lived in Podwitz near Kulm in Poland (Map 4) before they migrated to the Molotschna Mennonite Colony in Russia in 1820, to resettle in the village of Kleefeld (Map 6).[18]

On October 21, 1851, at age 26, Heinrich Schroeder married Sara Schmidt (Fig. 144). They immigrated to North America with eight children in 1874,

(above) **Fig.145,** Sarah Schroeder with her daughters Sarah, age 16, and Elizabeth, age 14, for whom their father built furniture, ca. 1886.[5]

(top, right) **Fig.146,** Cradle, 1902, Heinrich Schroeder. Signed and dated on the bottom board. Built for the children of his son Peter at Blumenfeld village, Alexanderwohl, Kansas community. Butted joints, dovetailed joints, pegged pine, red stain, porcelain pulls for blanket fasteners.
H:24" L:37" W:33".
#18.049, Private collection.

(bottom, right) **Fig.147,** Bed headboard and footboard, Heinrich Schroeder. Pine, red stain.
H:37½" W:30½".
#17.020, Private collection.

sailing on the SS *Cambria* and settling in Spring Valley Township in McPherson County, Kansas. They were members of the Alexanderwohl Mennonite Church near Goessel.

In a Schroeder family record Heinrich's occupation is listed as farmer, cabinetmaker and also as casketmaker. The record further identifies him as one who led singing (in church) and who played the accordion well.

His legacy as a cabinetmaker consists of 14 documented pieces, which he built for his family after immigration and which, with the exceptions of a child's folding bed and a table located in the Mennonite Heritage Museum in Goessel, remain in the homes of his descendants.

It is not known what furniture he may have built in Russia, nor is it known whether he built furniture for people other than his large family. Nearly 50 years old when he began a new life in Kansas, he was also farming and his time for furniture building was certainly limited. In addition, his talents as carpenter and cabinetmaker would have been applied to the building and upkeep of houses, barns and fences.

Probably the oldest of the remaining pieces of furniture built by Heinrich Schroeder is a strictly utilitarian child's folding rope bed. The wooden supports are butt-jointed and stained green. According to oral tradition, Heinrich built this bed for his youngest daughter Elisabeth (born January 2, 1872 in Kleefeld, South Russia) to sleep on during the family's voyage in 1874. Perhaps the bed was shared by her sister Sarah, then four years old.[19] Heinrich would build a number of pieces for these two daughters, Sarah and Elisabeth (Fig. 145).

In 1902 he built a cradle for granddaughter Catherine, daughter of his son Peter (Fig. 146). This is known from the writing in pencil on the underside of the cradle: *"Ich Alt Vater Heinrich Schroeder habe diese Wiege...als ich 77 Jahre war...1902...fuer Peter Schroeder Blumenfeld."* He also built a frame and headboard for a single bed (Fig. 147). Of the smaller home furnishings a hat or wall-hung magazine rack has received an honored place in the home of one of his descendants.[20]

A glass cabinet (Fig. 148), in Low-German *Glasschaup* or china cabinet, was made by Heinrich for his daughter Elisabeth Schroeder Enns (Mrs. Jacob J. Enns). The cupboard prominently displays the maker's name and the date 1875—carefully painted in amber-colored fraktur on black background—in a recessed tablet in the center of the cupboard's pediment constructed of five separate component parts (Fig. 149). Elisabeth used it in her "family dining room." After her unmarried daughter Lizzie's death, it was purchased by a member of the family for $50 at the public auction. Heinrich Schroeder's solid cabinetmaking skills are manifest in the dovetailed joints of the two drawers. The dark painted graining may not reflect his original intention, but is believed to have been applied over an original lighter color scheme by Elisabeth's husband Jacob J. Enns, who also was a carpenter and cabinetmaker. There are traces of mustard yellow on parts of the cabinet's five-footed base, as well as on its pediment, and there is evidence of green paint under the top layer of graining.[21]

A single-door wardrobe (Fig. 150), called in Low German *Kjleedaschaup,* literally "clothes cupboard," was made for Heinrich's daughter Sarah (born 1870 in Alexanderwohl, South Russia, died 1938). Her initials S.S. are boldly painted

(right) **Fig.148,** Glass cabinet, 1875, Heinrich Schroeder. Inherited by daughter Elisabeth Schroeder Enns. Pine, painted graining, varnish, traces of mustard yellow visible under dark graining. Separately constructed five-footed bracket base whose component parts are numbered. Pediment constructed of three separate parts—front and two sides. Cabinet refinished with painted graining by Heinrich Schroeder's son-in-law Jacob J. Enns in whose dining room this cabinet was used.

H:96½" W:34" D:Cabinet, 12½", Shelves 7⅝".

#14.005, Private collection.

(above) **Fig.149,** Detail of pediment with Heinrich Schroeder's (maker and owner) name and the date.

#14.005.

Fig.150, *S*ingle-door wardrobe, ca. 1880, Heinrich Schroeder. Built for his daughter Sara Schroeder whose initials "SS" are painted in the center of the pediment. Separately constructed five-footed bracket base with scalloped skirt, separately constructed three-part gable, painted graining, varnish.
H:85½" W:42¼" D:18½".
#11.012, Private collection.

in amber yellow fraktur letters on the black recessed panel in the center of the wardrobe's pediment, which echoes the now familiar neo-Greek pediment form and which was constructed as a separate component. The dark painted graining may have been applied over an original solid color scheme. The inside of the door is stained green. Like Franz Adrian, Schroeder also used nails in his joinery.

The wardrobe stands on a separately constructed base with cabriole legs and a swagged skirt, the type of base typical for most dowry chests and wardrobes made in the Vistula Delta and in South Russia.

Sarah Schroeder married Andreas D. Voth on December 30, 1889, and used this wardrobe in the bedroom of their farm home and later in their home in Goessel where they moved in 1928. A family member purchased the wardrobe at the public auction following Sarah's death in 1938 for $3.25.

(above) **Fig.151,** Resting bench, ca. 1875-1895, Heinrich Schroeder. Pine, painted graining on yellow ground, black paint to accent recessed back panels, black turned armrests, black seat. Note the unusual scrolled feet. A "secret" shelf is mounted under one end of the bench.[6]

H:30" L:80" D:22¾".
#5.006, Private collection.

(right) **Fig.152,** Table, ca. 1880s-1900s, Heinrich Schroeder. Built for his daughter Elisabeth. Pine, painted graining, varnish.[7]

H:29" W:23¼" D:31".
#15.006, Private collection.

Fig.153, Dowry chest, 1891, Heinrich Schroeder. Built for his daughter Elisabeth. Pine, dovetailed joints, key lock, five-footed bracket base with swagged skirt. Crudely executed painted graining may have been done by someone else. Pasted inside the lid are reproductions of engraved portraits of Frederick II of Prussia; Grossfuerst Alexander, heir to the throne of Russia; his wife Alexandrowna; Czar Nicolai of Russia and king of Poland; and his wife Alexandra Feodorowna.

H:23½" L:39½" D:23".
#1.016, Private collection.

A bench or *Ruhbank* built by Heinrich was also purchased by family members at the auction following daughter Sarah's death (Figs. 151). The auction records list an "old bench" and a "bench." It is a fair assumption that this *Ruhbank* was considered old-fashioned and therefore "old" in 1938. This bench has what Heinrich's granddaughter called a "secret" shelf along the underside of the seat in the back. Here, it is said, Sarah kept money (put aside for special things) in a hymn book.

The bench follows the established canon of form and proportion for this furniture type. The amber painted graining contrasts two different grain patterns. The solid black of the seat, the black lathe-turned spindles which form the armrests and the black outlines of the recessed panels in the back and the sides of the bench bind and define the form very effectively. Underneath the present painted finish a dark green color is visible. It is not clear what Heinrich Schroeder's original color concept may have been.

At least five tables built by Heinrich survive. One of these, it is said, was always kept in daughter Sarah's bedroom. It was joined without the use of nails. She kept a lamp on it, turned down very low, to take care of the 12 babies she had. The table had many coats of paint on it. Granddaughter Nada Voth says, "Grandma Sarah believed in paint, according to my father, and, according to him, workmanship was not her strong suit. The table was sold to Pete Reimer for $70 at the sale. Later it was bought back by a descendant, who stripped it and now uses it in her living room."

Heinrich's daughter Elisabeth also reportedly received a table built by her father when she was a young girl in the 1880s (Fig. 152). Along the way, the top was stripped of the original painted graining, which, however, remains on the skirt and the legs.

Each of the daughters also received a dowry chest. Elisabeth's chest, believed to have been made in 1891, is a six-board chest made of pine. The dovetailed joints have wedges, and the chest is finished with painted graining in amber, greys and medium brown (Fig. 153). The painted graining appears rather

Fig.154, Dowry chest, ca. 1890, Heinrich Schroeder. Pine, lid and sides made of one-width boards, four-footed base with slightly draped skirt, no lock, commercial steel handles, screws, nails, few wooden pegs. Painted graining is black on yellow ground.
H:26" W:37" D:20¾".
#1.017, Private collection.

unskilled and may also represent a later attempt at refinishing. It is noteworthy that the chest is smaller than those made in the Vistula Delta and in South Russia. However, it follows the same proportional scheme, includes the conventional till and rests on the separately constructed five-footed bracket base, featuring wooden pegs, not nails. In a departure from the traditional model, it has no handles. The decoration on the inside of the lid is of particular interest with its five portraits of Prussian and Russian royalty, first published in Berlin for the popular market in the 1840s. They are of Frederick II, King of Prussia (Frederick the Great); Prince Alexander, heir to the throne of Russia with his spouse Alexandrowna; and Czar Nicolai I with his spouse Alexandra Feodorowna.

The second Heinrich Schroeder chest (Fig. 154) exemplifies a further departure from the traditional prototype. The joints are no longer dovetailed, but are simple butt joints. The scale is even smaller while the overall proportions depart from the horizontal emphasis of the earlier chests. The measures of depth, height and width do not have a proportionate relationship with each other. The footed bracket base, though still swagged, no longer has a center "leg" and appears more squat. The molding that stabilizes the lid is nailed on; it is no longer pegged. The painted graining gives the illusion of paneled construction with only one large recessed panel on the front of the chest; a complete departure from the traditional scheme of the decorative double frame on the front of the Vistula Delta chest type. The back of the chest shows a forest green stain, and it appears as if the grained painting on yellow ground was applied over an earlier green coat of paint.

On both chests the metal fittings for the hinges, handles and keyplates have ceased to play a decorative role. In fact, this second chest has no lock at all—an eloquent comment on the radically changed social and economic conditions of Mennonite households in late nineteenth century North America. After immigration, the investment of time and resources in a movable dowry of a lifetime supply of goods was transferred to establishing land holdings, for land was abundantly available. Households had few if any servants, and class divisions between hired laborer and master did not exist for Mennonite immigrants in North America.

These two chests by Heinrich Schroeder demonstrate the gradual move toward simplification and coarseness of form, a departure from the original Vistula Delta model and the first stages of "losing" the tradition. The same process is also seen in the dowry chest built by the immigrant Jacob J. Peters of Henderson, Nebraska, for his wife at the beginning of the twentieth century.[22]

The painted finishes of Schroeder's furniture are very inconsistent because all of the pieces appear to have been redone by more or less skilled hands to suit the changing tastes of subsequent owners. It is nearly impossible to know what Heinrich himself would have considered a finished "look" for his furniture.

Heinrich's skills, but not the language of the tradition, survive in the work of his sons and grandsons. Nada Voth, great-granddaughter of Heinrich and Sarah Schroeder reported that Heinrich's son Jacob built the barn that is now relocated to the Mennonite Heritage Museum in Goessel, and that at least three grandsons and a great-grandson became carpenters.[23]

Heinrich Rempel, *Vorwer*, Painter and Cabinetmaker

Heinrich Rempel was the last to immigrate of the three cabinetmakers featured in our study, and he was the youngest at the time. Two wardrobes, one built-in wall cabinet, two china cabinets and one resting bench still testify to his polished skill as a craftsman, and especially as a painter of furniture and woodwork.

Heinrich and his wife Margarethe Neufeld immigrated with their small children Maria and Heinrich to Henderson, Nebraska, in 1884 on the SS *Ems*, departing from Bremen. They arrived in New York on June 14. The ship list gives Heinrich's age in 1884 as 35. There is no document which states from

Fig.155, Heinrich Rempel, age 51, with his wife Margarethe Neufeld Rempel, age 47, and children Maria 20, Cornelius 15, Heinrich 18, Jacob 9, Margarethe 11. Henderson, Nebraska, 1899.[8]

153

(right) **Fig.156,** China cabinet, 1894, Heinrich Rempel. The date is painted in the center gable of the ornate pediment which does not wrap around the sides of the cabinet. Note how two turned finials mark the top corners. As in Rempel's wardrobes, three different kinds of painted graining and three different kinds of wood are imitated. Flower decals applied to the centers of the door panels and to the sides. Black line ornaments are reminiscent of such inlaid or painted patterns on late 18th and early 19th century Vistula Delta wardrobes. The slanted, hinged drop leaf hides compartments perhaps for silverware and food service utensils. A screen is placed in the back of the lower cabinet, possibly to cool or to vent foods stored there.

H:94" W:36" D:20¼".
#14.043, Private collection.

(above) **Fig.157,** Detail of Rempel china cabinet.
#14.043.

which village in South Russia he came. However, other immigrants on the same ship were originally from the village of Lichtfelde, so one may assume that Heinrich also came from this village. Heinrich and Margarethe lost three or four of their firstborn children to black diphtheria while still in Russia. Children born to Heinrich and Margarethe in the United States were Cornelius, Jacob and Margarethe (Fig. 155). Since there is no written family history, very little is known about their life in Henderson. Heinrich reportedly died of a "blood disease."

Fig.158, Wall cabinet front, 1887, Heinrich Rempel. The earliest dated piece of Rempel's work still extant in America, and the most restrained in its decorative scheme. Pine, painted graining of light wood and dark marble, black trim.
H:95½" D:6" W:39".
#14.044, Private collection.

In contrast to Franz Adrian and Heinrich Schroeder, Heinrich Rempel made his living as a full-time cabinetmaker and painter of furniture and woodwork and always lived in town. Rempel did a lot of interior painting and grained painting of woodwork in homes and churches in the Henderson area. He also painted church pews. He grain-painted, for example, the woodwork of the Ebenezer church in Henderson. The Low German term used for grained painting is *oadere*, literally "veining" or the drawing of veins. In addition, he was an excellent cabinetmaker who worked alone behind drawn curtains while painting

(top) **Fig.159,** Resting bench, ca. 1885-95, Heinrich Rempel. Pine, square nails, painted graining imitating light wood and burl graining of dark wood. Flower decals on the two back panels and on the insides of the side panels. Stenciled scroll motif adds further decorative interest to the back rest. Seat stained black, as are the revolving, turned armrests. Geometric black line ornaments on the skirt are also found on his wardrobes and cabinets.

H:34" D:24" L:78¼".

#5.001, Private collection.

(bottom) **Fig.160,** Wardrobe, 1888, Heinrich Rempel. Commissioned by Henry Dueck, great-grandfather of present owner. Initials "HD" (Henry Dueck) and date are painted in the center of the pediment. Wardrobe is constructed of separate elements: five-footed base, lower case with two drawers, two doors, sides, boards for the back, cornice and gable. Gable is assembled from seven separate elements: the front piece, two rounded corner pieces, two side pieces and two end blocks to finish the sides next to the wall.

Very fine painted graining over pine which imitates grain and color of two woods. Inlay and marble, painted decorative lines, oval flower decals applied to the center of the door panels and to the sides, commercial drawer pulls. Columns with black marble effect painted on the sides of the wardrobe. Five-footed base rests on a separate board, decorated with painted graining. Of the four wardrobes Rempel is said to have built in 1888, a second one (#11.030), identical to this one, is recorded.

H:91½" W:51" D:19".

#11.023, Private collection.

156

his pieces "so that no one would steal his secrets."[24] His granddaughter remembers that he was known for doing "very accurate work which others tried to imitate."[25]

This fear of revealing one's technique so that others could take away business was characteristic of other painters at this time. Jacob Harms, an artisan working in the Hillsboro, Kansas, area and the Swiss immigrant painter Emil Kym did not like to be watched as they worked.[26]

In addition to china cabinets (Figs. 156, 157, 158), benches (Fig. 159) and wardrobes (Fig. 160), Heinrich also built little stools which he always dated, cradles which he dated on the bottom and spice cabinets. A child's rocking chair made by Heinrich Rempel is said to still exist in the Henderson community. A great-granddaughter remembers, "My grandmother had a child's rocker that was painted in brightly colored stripes. The stripes went around and were painted free hand. They were ever so even, but my dear grandmother decided she wanted a solid color chair and painted over it."[27] At least two dowry chests documented in the Henderson area may have been repainted by Heinrich Rempel, judging from the style of the painted decoration.[28] A small labor of love still exists in the sewing box Heinrich painted for his daughter Margarethe. It was a commercial box for cotton embroidery floss, recycled for private purposes.[29]

Heinrich Rempel's cabinet work is characterized by refined craftsmanship which presupposes specialized training, and by a Victorian eclecticism which delights in a virtuoso profusion of decorative forms, textures and painted ornaments (Figs. 156, 157, 160). Rempel's range of decorative repertoire embraces variations of Vistula Delta motifs, such as the painted pilasters, the Grecian pediment and the geometricizing linear framing ornaments (compare with the inlaid wardrobe from the Furstenwerder Schulz family farm, Fig. 89). He also employed vegetal corner ornaments, achieved with the aid of copper templates or stencils, and gaily colored flower decals which produced a similar effect to the painted flowers on American Victorian Cottage furniture.

Fig.161, Nettie Vogt with her class, 1911, rural Inman, Kansas.[9]

Fig.162, Teacher's desk, 1910, made by Peter Vogt. Pine, brown paint, commercial drawer pull. The desk has a slanted top with a hinged lid covering a storage box. There is one narrow drawer on the right-hand side. The gallery of this desk has a formal "front" facing the classroom, retaining the tradition's characteristic neo-classical pediment motif as found on wardrobes and cabinets. The basic table shape of the tradition is apparent as well.

H:40" W:36" D:24".
#16.002, KM 88.208.1.

The whole complex scheme seems to have been inspired by a strong need to impress, and, undoubtedly, pleased customers who wished their furniture to express social status. This becomes especially evident when comparing Rempel's ornately painted wardrobe, for example, with Schroeder's severely simple wardrobe.

A unique feature of a Heinrich Rempel wardrobe or glass cabinet is the painted platform on which it stands. The fact that another craftsman from Henderson, Jacob J. Peters, created a miniature dowry chest with its own platform (discussed in chapter seven) suggests that this may have been a more widespread practice than these few remaining examples lead one to believe. Heinrich Schroeder's and Jacob J. Peters' low furniture platforms may indeed constitute the continuation of the same form used for dowry chests in the Vistula Delta and recorded by a German culture historian in the 1920s.[30]

158

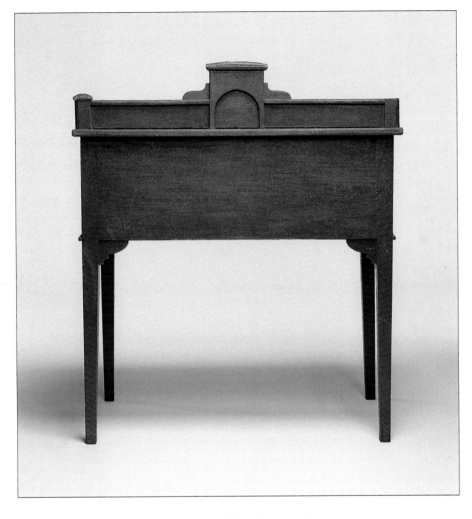

Peter Vogt: A Desk for His Daughter

One of the last pieces built on the central Plains within the formal canon of the Mennonite furniture tradition is the teacher's desk made by Peter Vogt of Inman, Kansas, for his daughter Nettie (Agnes) Vogt Wiens in 1910 (Figs. 161, 162, 163).

Peter Vogt worked at the Inman, Kansas, lumberyard, building houses and barns for his livelihood. For enjoyment he made furniture for his children and grandchildren on his workbench at home. A cradle, designed to ride on a buggy, doll cradles and a downscaled chest are still owned by his descendants.[31]

Some Mennonite emigrants from the Vistula Delta brought commercially produced *secretaires* with them to North America. There is a record of an 1830s Biedermeier *secretaire* in the house of farm number 43 in the Heubuden community.[32] But the type of slant-top desks built by Peter Vogt and by Aron Olfert in the Hillsboro community are the only ones known to have been made by Mennonite craftsmen. A comparable slant-top desk of 1858 made by a German immigrant cabinetmaker exists in Texas.[33]

Peter Vogt's daughter Nettie used her desk to teach four terms in a rural school one mile south and a half mile southwest of Inman and one term of German School in Burrton, Kansas, between 1910-1914. She was 17 when she began teaching, earning $1 a month for each student.[34] After her marriage to Martin Wiens in 1915, she continued to use the desk in her home at Inman.

Painters Who Decorated Homes and Repainted Furniture

Jacob Harms was an 1874 immigrant most commonly remembered as a wall painter in the Moundridge, Goessel and Hillsboro, Kansas, areas. He became a member of the Church of God in Christ Mennonite (Holdeman). An active painter between 1895 and 1922-23, he specialized in marbling, woodgraining and painting borders for plastered interior walls of houses.[35] In his wall paintings he made frequent use of the rose—his specialty and carefully guarded secret—the tulip and grape clusters.[36]

Oral traditions of the Inman, Kansas, area speak of a "painter Harms." Unfortunately, his first name has been lost, and it remains an open question whether this Harms was the Jacob Harms of Hillsboro.

In Inman it is said that P.R. Doerksen learned woodgraining in 1913, when he was eight years old, probably from Harms. Harms also taught several other boys in the Inman community. P.R. Doerksen in turn grained some doors, decorated a sleeping bench and painted some lampshades.[37] About this time woodstains came into common use, and Doerksen finished wood with stains rather than with painted graining.

In addition to Harms and Doerksen, Peter Becker lived near Lehigh, Kansas, and did interior painting and woodgraining professionally between 1898 and 1914. John Wall decorated in the Buhler area.[38] George Bergen, probably also of the Buhler area, did graining of furniture and woodwork from 1890 to 1910. He grained a wardrobe built by Benjamin Boese in the early 1900s. Later Bergen became a mortician.

Conclusion

Most of the Mennonite craftsmen who brought their tradition of furniture making to the Central Plains of North America were from the Molotschna Colony in South Russia; for example, Franz Adrian, Heinrich Schroeder and Heinrich Rempel. A crafts tradition emerged among those who had little or no land, whereas Mennonites who had remained in West Prussia until the 1870s and 1880s continued to be prosperous landowners in North America. Very few cabinetmakers came from West Prussia.

The works of North American immigrant craftsmen and artisans showed little change and innovation within the range of the traditional canon of furniture. Their works simply maintained what was familiar from the West Prussian and South Russian settings and represented first the continuation of the tradition, followed rather quickly by its demise on the Plains.

7

Construction, Decoration and Style

Construction of the Furniture

The methods, tools and materials of constructing a furniture form; the methods, tools and materials of decorating a furniture form; and the form's intended function are the factors which create a furniture style. The style of a piece of furniture is a tangible and a visual language, containing many clues about the cultural and historical origins of the maker and of the user.

The skills required to build the furniture of our study were those of joiners and cabinetmakers trained in the execution of complex joining techniques. The decorative fittings for dowry chests were furnished by smiths and metal working shops, and the more complex, multicolored decorative painted finishes were executed by painters specially trained in the imitation of hardwoods and inlaid motifs.

The dovetailed joints of chests, cradles and case furniture displayed the work of joiners (cabinetmakers) using planes and special saws (Fig. 164), in contrast to carpenters whose primary tool was the axe. Carpenters usually built houses and barns and were seldom involved in furniture making. However, sometimes necessity demanded that the carpenter also build furniture for the family, especially when new homes had to be furnished in North America.

The most commonly used tools of the immigrant cabinetmaker were a rule or yardstick, saw, hammer, mortising chisel, pump drill or drill brace with bits, drawknife, jack plane or different molding planes, mallet, spoke shave, square and scribe or marking gauge. Often the craftsman brought his basic tool set from Europe to North America, and often, as his first task in the new country, he constructed a workbench, a few of which still remain. He purchased all necessary lumber from the lumber yards, supplied by the railroads.

Fig.164, Tools of the cabinetmaker, ca. 1764.[1] Basic tools used in the construction of Mennonite handmade furniture did not change much between the mid-18th and the late 19th century.

1. Double marking gauge
2. Square
3. Trying gauge (template)
4. Cabinetmaker's bench
5. Mallet
6. Hand chisels
7. Veneer saw (ripping)
8. Turning saw
9. Keyhole saw
10. Fret saw
11. Glue clamp
12. Molding plane (hollow)
13. Sash plane
14. Hand chisel (slick)
15. Hollow chisel
16. Mortising chisel
17. Rasp
18. Router
19. Screw clamp
20. Trammel stand
21. Carving knife
22. Jointer plane
23. Trying plane (horned)
24. Hand scraper (rounding)
25. Matching sharpening steel

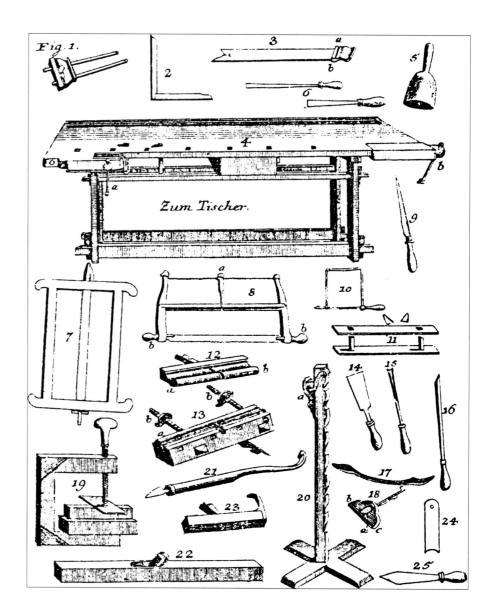

The Chest

Most Mennonite chests from the Vistula Delta and South Russia use the same determinants for their proportions; height, including the base, and depth are equal while the width is twice that measurement. Despite being detachable, the bracket base is included in these proportions. The dimensions of chests brought by Mennonite immigrants are very consistent. Variations of only one or two inches occur. In contrast to framed and paneled chests, Mennonite chests are board chests, with tongue-and-groove or dovetailed joints (Fig. 165), resting on separately constructed footed bracket bases. Many chests employ dovetail joints with very narrow wedges inserted in the dovetail (Fig. 166). The corner joints of the lower cases of wardrobes also feature wedged dovetails, a joining technique that craftsmen continued to use in North America.[1] This technique results in the strongest joint corners possible and is one reason why these chests survived time and major migratory journeys.

The boards which form the lid of the chest are framed on the front and the

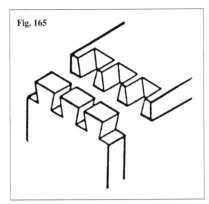

Fig. 165

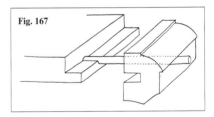

Fig. 167

sides with a molding strip which serves to stabilize the lid, as well as to provide a finger grip that facilitates the opening of the chest (Fig. 167). This molding also functions aesthetically in that it articulates the form of the chest.

The molding strips on the sides are structurally necessary to stabilize the boards of the lid. Held in place by mortise and tenon joints (Fig. 169), they are fastened to the lid with wooden pegs. Molding strips are also fastened in the same manner to the front and sides of the bottom of the chest. On some chests glued joints of boards are strengthened with "butterfly" wedges to deter separation of the boards (Fig. 168).

On the left side inside the chest, there is always a till with a hinged lid, sometimes with several false bottoms serving as secret compartments for valuables. Such tills have been a standard feature of chests since at least the thirteenth century.[2] They are without fail placed on the left side of the chest.

Chests never rest directly on the floor. The construction of chests, as well as wardrobes and other case furniture, always provides a base to raise the bottom of the chest off the floor in order to avoid absorption of moisture and to allow air circulation. If a Vistula Delta or South Russian chest appears without a base, one must assume that the chest is incomplete, that its intended, original base has been lost.

Mennonite chests from the Delta and from South Russia invariably feature five-footed, separately constructed bracket bases (Figs. 170-178). The legs of these bases are either curved in cabriole fashion or they are square, straight and tapered. Both types of legs occur in Biedermeier furniture of about the 1820s to

(top, right) **Fig.165,** Diagram of a dovetail joint.

(middle, right) **Fig.166,** Detail of a wardrobe, 1887. Note the wedge in each dovetail joint.
#11.002.

(bottom, right) **Fig.167,** Diagram of a joint between the lid of the chest and the framing molding.

(top, left) **Fig.168,** Butterfly key joints inside lid of dowry chest.
#1.038

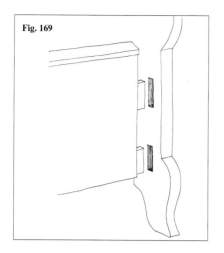

Fig.169, Diagram of a mortise and tenon joint on a Mennonite sleeping bench.

Fig.170, Base of dowry chest. #1.020.

Fig.171, Base of dowry chest. #1.034.

Fig.172, Base of dowry chest. #1.007.

Fig.173, Base of dowry chest . #1.026.

Fig.174, Base of dowry chest . #1.044.

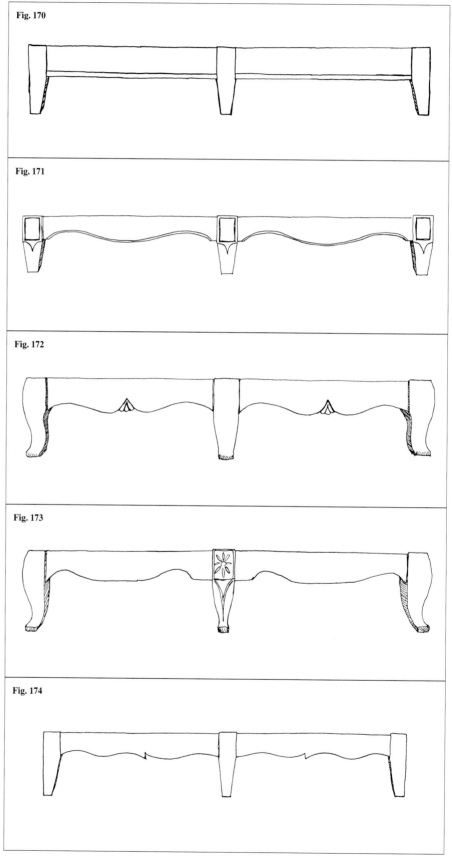

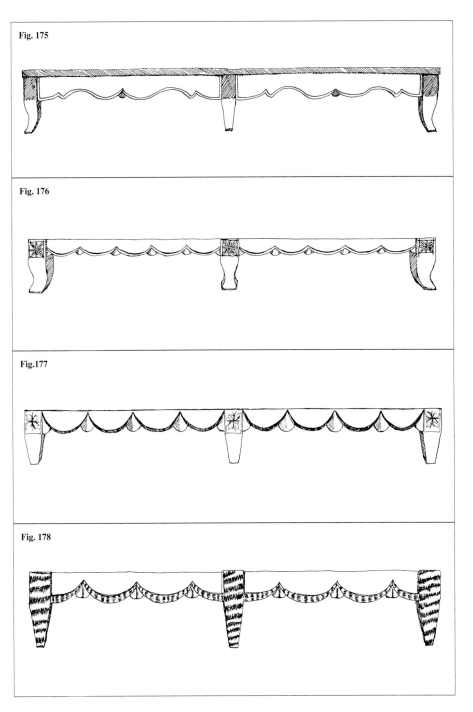

Fig. 175

Fig. 176

Fig.177

Fig. 178

Fig.175, Base of dowry chest . #1.013.

Fig.176, Base of dowry chest . #1.024.

Fig.177, Base of dowry chest . #1.022.

Fig.178, Base of dowry chest . #1.025.

the 1850s. The skirts (also called aprons) of these bases are either straight, or they are variations on a scalloped or swagged motif. They are sometimes given a cut or carved relief profile as well as an accent with contrasting paint for visual emphasis. Wardrobes and chests built in the Vistula Delta in the late eighteenth century and around 1800 often are supported by large, turned ball feet held in place with dowels, a hallmark of baroque furniture design. The only example of this style of support in North America is the wardrobe from Koselitzke, Vistula Delta (Fig. 90).

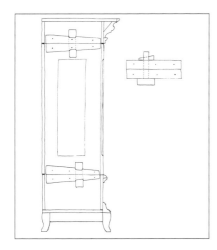

(top) **Fig.179,** Cross section of a Mennonite wardrobe. Note the method of joining bottom and top cases with wooden pins.

(bottom) **Fig.180,** Detail of the interior of a Mennonite wardrobe, with wooden pegs for hanging clothes. #11.002.

(facing page) **Fig.181,** Wardrobe, 1887. The initials "GF" stand for Gerhard Funk, first owner of this wardrobe, of the Bruderthal community, rural Hillsboro, Kansas. Probably made by Gerhard Nickel. Comparing this wardrobe with those drawn in the cross section of the Quiring House in Ladekopp, Vistula Delta (Fig. 73) provides convincing evidence of the style's origin in the Vistula Delta. Pine, painted graining.[2]
 H:90" W:29" D:22".
 #11.002, Private collection.

The relatively few chests built in North America adhere less stringently to this proportional scheme; they tend to be smaller than the Vistula chests. While they retain the separate footed bracket base, the base is often constructed without its front center foot and has only four feet instead of the traditional five. The chests appear more coarse and often look like an abbreviation of the prototype.

The Wardrobe

Characteristic of Mennonite wardrobes is their collapsible construction, which was a general practice for most wardrobes of the early to the late nineteenth century. The two-door wardrobe, which is generally about 90 inches tall or taller, needed to be constructed and assembled of separate components in order to facilitate moving such a large piece of furniture through narrow doors, hallways and sometimes up stairways to its designated place in the home. Such Mennonite-made wardrobes have strongly articulated bases and equally prominent cornices which contribute to rather massive proportions, the whole resting on independent five-footed bracket bases.

This base, the lower case, the upper case, the cornice and the pediment are each constructed as independent elements. The base and cornice, which have dovetail joints just like the chests, are joined to the upright elements of the wardrobe—the doors, the sides and the boards which make up the back—with mortise and tenon joints. Especially important for stability of the assembled wardrobe is the *Keil-Steck-Verbindung,* or "wedged pin connection," found on the lower and upper end of the uprights forming the sides (Fig. 179).

Clothes were not hung on hangers from a horizontal rod, but rather from wooden hooks on a series of short wooden swiveling arms fastened to the back of the wardrobe (Fig. 180), or from metal hooks attached under the shelf board, which ran across the upper section of the wardrobe.

The wardrobe commissioned by Gerhard Funk in 1887 from an unknown cabinetmaker (Fig. 181) is one of the finest examples of a wardrobe made by a Mennonite immigrant craftsman. It is assembled of 16 separate pieces held together with wooden pegs: the five-footed bracket base, the swagged skirt, the bottom box or chest, the two doors, the sides, five boards for the back, the cornice and, finally, the three elements which form the pediment. Joints are wedged dovetails. Clothes are hung from handcarved wooden hooks, doweled into five swiveling "arms."

The surface of the softwood was given a coat of gesso, then a coat of amber paint over which three different shades and two different patterns of brown graining were applied. The dark brown vertical and horizontal lines give the effect of the burl graining of cross-cut wood while the lighter areas suggest the color and grain of ash. The recessed panels on the upper sections of the doors are decorated further, in black and brown, with a formal flower arrangement in a footed vase to imitate inlaid veneer decoration. The two lower recessed panels feature a medallion painted in the same manner. The painter delicately framed the two recessed door panels, tying them into the vertical decorative scheme and rounding the corners of his frame with a scrolled vegetal embellishment.

The corners of the wardrobe are painted with folded pilasters which are related to such motifs on the Vistula Delta chests, except that the pilaster "floats" and allusion to bearing weight is ignored.

(top) **Fig.182,** Pediment and base of the Gerhard Funk wardrobe, 1887. #11.002.

(bottom) **Fig.183,** Pediment and base of a wardrobe by Franz Adrian, ca. 1879. #11.006, KM 6255.1.

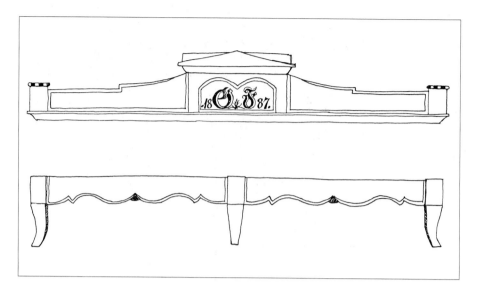

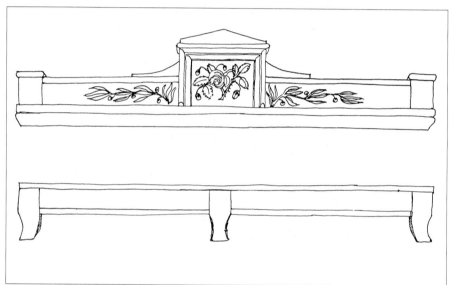

Several other features of this wardrobe are very closely related to the Vistula Delta chest form: the appearance of a chest extended vertically, the five-footed base with a scalloped or swagged skirt, the articulation of the lower "chest" part of the wardrobe into two decorative fields, and the flower motifs which are found on inlaid as well as on painted chests of the Vistula Delta of the late eighteenth century.

The pediment above the cornice evokes architectural pediments adapted by the Biedermeier furniture style of the first third of the nineteenth century. This pediment becomes the "hallmark" or signature of most of the wardrobes and cabinets, including corner cabinets, built by Mennonite immigrant cabinetmakers after the 1870s on the North American Plains (Figs. 182 and 183).

Like the dowry chests, the style of this wardrobe type originates in the Vistula Delta region in the last quarter of the eighteenth century (see chapter three).

Single-door wardrobes seem to have been relatively rare. So far the only known single-door wardrobe is the one made by Heinrich Schroeder for his

Fig.184, *"*Of the heavy burden of children,*"* woodcut by the Petrarca Meister, 1532. Note the cradle and its blanket ties which are held in place by two carved hooks.[3]

daughter Sarah (Fig. 150). Doors of wardrobes are always fitted with a small lock, but these never have the decorative prominence of the locks on the dowry chests. The wardrobe's keyhole blends into the overall painted decorative scheme and does not have the visual emphasis that it receives on the dowry chests.

The lower cases on Mennonite wardrobes have the appearance of dowry chests, especially since the five-footed bracket bases feature the same short cabriole legs and the same swagged skirts or straight skirts as those on the dowry chests. In a fundamental way the wardrobe as case furniture is a vertical extension of the chest.

The Cradle

Characteristic of Mennonite cradles is the simplicity of their construction. The tapered box has dovetail joints and applied bead molding strips which define the horizontal form. Simple identical galleries, also called "pillow boards," at the head and the foot often feature cutout finger holes. Mennonite cradles do not differentiate between a "head" and a "foot" board. Two small handcarved hooks, knobs or ceramic drawer pulls, fastened to each side of the cradle, secure the ties which hold the infant's blanket, as well as the child itself, in place (an age-old practice, as seen in Fig. 184). Slightly scrolled rockers are usually attached to the bottom board with mortise and tenon joints. The slight counter-scroll at the tip of the rockers prevents the cradle from tipping over. Some cradles sit on a platform, probably to prevent the action of the rockers from damaging the floor.[3]

Resting Benches or Sleeping Benches

Characteristic of Mennonite sleeping benches is the continuous upright which is always cyma-shaped—the legs invert the curve of the upright. Typically the arms replicate the curve of the legs and end in a scroll (Fig. 185).

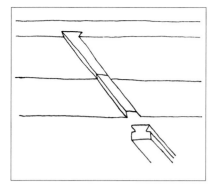

(right) **Fig.185,** Detail of a resting or sleeping bench, by Heinrich Schroeder. #5.006.

(above) **Fig.186,** Diagram of a dovetailed "cleat" under a table top.

Backboards are sometimes shaped with scroll work, sometimes plain and sometimes have a slight rise toward the center. Backs always have two inset panels. Usually, these are plain toward the front and beveled on the back side, a practice also seen in panels of wardrobes and common in furniture construction during this time. Only one bench in the Kauffman Museum survey features beveled inset panels as intentionally visible decoration (see Fig. 6, chapter one).[4]

Skirts of resting or sleeping benches may be scrolled or straight. Some benches have armrests which are integrated with the end panels while others have armrests which are either fancifully turned or are plain. Armrests not integrated with end panels may be stationery or revolve for blanket rolls. The board seats of the sleeping benches can be lifted on a hinge. Sometimes the seats are not hinged but simply lie across the bedbox.

The Tables

Characteristic of the Mennonite table is the dovetailed cleat running across each end of the table top to prevent warping of the boards that form the surface (Fig. 186). Often the table has a single drawer. Legs are square and tapered, often with a curved bracket for additional stability. An applied horizontal bead mold around the straight skirt adds definition.

This form was built in varying sizes, depending on the function of the particular table in each home. Of the larger variant for everyday work and eating,

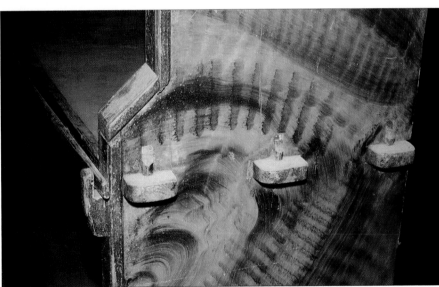

(top, left) **Fig.187,** Table, pinned braces. Wood unknown, recent oil enamel paint finish.

H:31½" W:24½" L:35".

#15.013, Adobe House Museum, Hillsboro, Kansas.

(bottom, left) **Fig.188,** Detail of a pinned shelf in a utility cupboard *(Melkschaup)*.

H:83½" W:47" D of top:12¼" D of base:14¼".

#14.026, Private collection.

only one example has been documented.

The Adobe House Museum in Hillsboro, Kansas, has the only two trestle tables which are documented as having come from Mennonite immigrant homes (Fig. 187). This is an older table form and construction technique, found in the eighteenth and early nineteenth centuries in many of the regions around the Baltic Sea.[5]

Fig.189, Dowry chest hinge. #1.034.

Fig.190, Dowry chest hinge. #1.049.

Fig.191, Dowry chest hinge. #1.007.

Fig.192, Dowry chest hinge. #1.025.

Fig.193, Dowry chest hinge. #1.022.

Fig.194, Dowry chest hinge. #1.010.

Fig.195, Dowry chest hinge. #1.066.

Fig.196, Dowry chest hinge. #1.023.

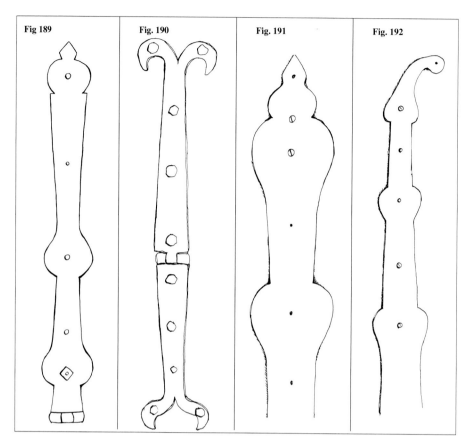

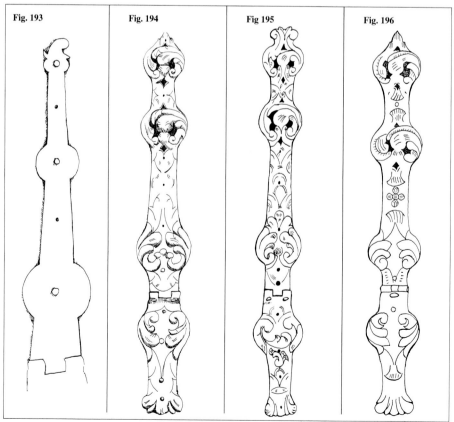

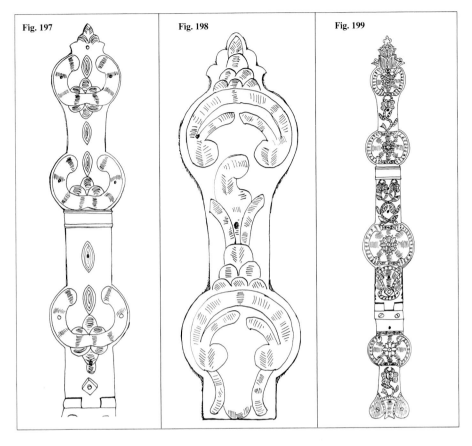

Fig. 197   Fig. 198   Fig. 199

Fig.197, Dowry chest hinge. #1.033.

Fig.198, Dowry chest hinge. #1.013.

Fig.199, Dowry chest hinge. #1.038.

Plain Cupboards or *Schaup*

The characteristic construction feature of the Mennonite cupboard is the pinned shelf. Some of these cupboards alternate a pinned shelf with a shelf fitted into a groove of the upright (Fig. 188).

The Decoration of Furniture

Decorating a form gives it an aura of visual appeal and importance that goes beyond necessity or function, fulfilling the human need for beauty.

The aesthetic appeal of a piece of furniture is determined by the structure of the form—which is part of its function—as it is made up of a series of planes in a three-dimensional space, the proportional relationship of parts to the whole, the individual dimensions in relationship to each other, the decoration of the individual plane or surface and the color of the surfaces.

Mennonite furniture may be finished only in a very simple way—a coat of one color, an application of a simple molding strip, a shaped hinge—or, in contrast, it may receive a very elaborate decoration.

Fittings or Mounts

Keyplates, hinges, lock cases, handles and bosses (to cover screw caps of the lock plates and hinges)add considerable decorative interest to both the interior and exterior appearances of the chests. This hardware often reflects particular historic styles. Hinges on chests vary from simple hand-forged black iron (Figs. 189-193) to those ornately cut, tinned and chased in floral designs (Figs.

Fig.200, Detail of lock case, 1830.
#1.066.

Figs.201 a,b,c, Complete lock system.
#1.019.

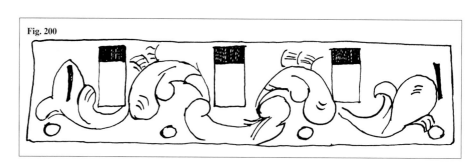

Fig. 200

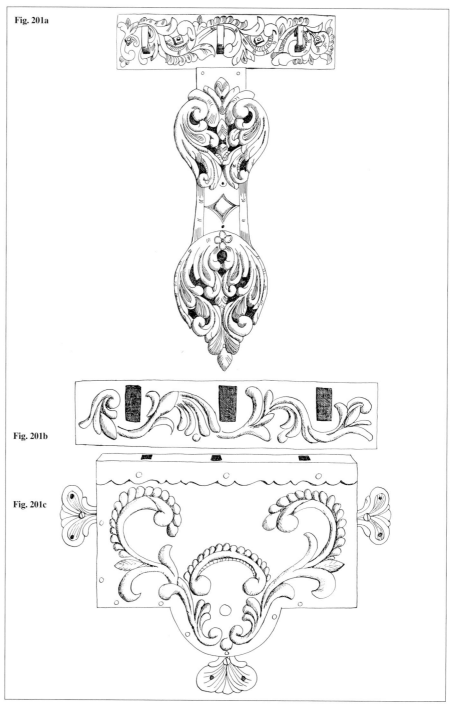

Fig. 201a

Fig. 201b

Fig. 201c

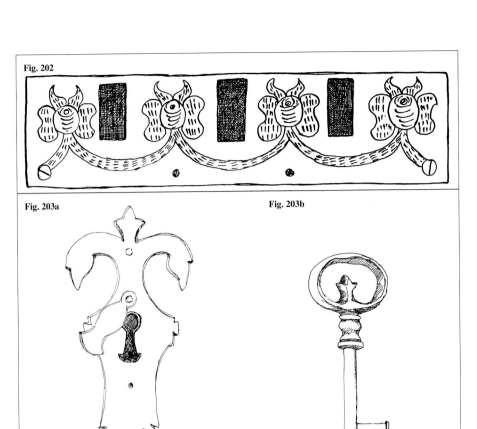

Fig. 202

Fig. 203a

Fig. 203b

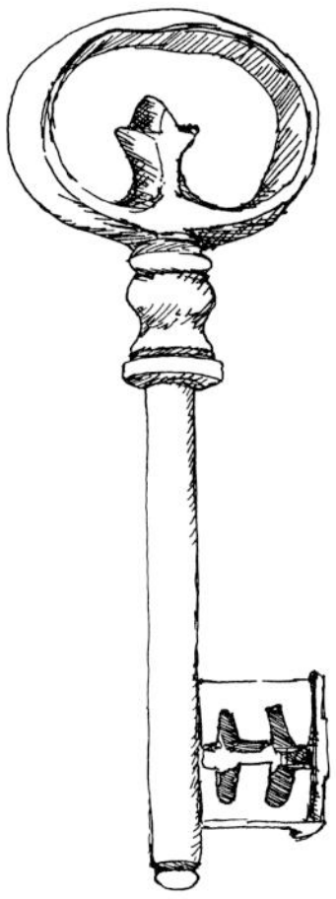

Fig. 204

Fig. 205

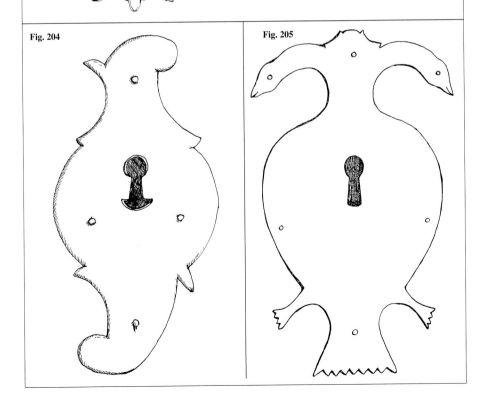

Fig.202, Detail of lock case. #1.038.

Fig.203, Keyhole plate (escutcheon) of cut brass with matching key. #1.013.

Fig.204, Keyhole plate. #1.022.

Fig.205, Keyhole plate. #1.058.

194-199), sometimes accented with narrow horizontal brass bands (Figs. 197-199). Chests featuring elaborately ornamented hinges are generally fitted with lock cases in similar styles (Figs. 200-202). Tinned iron was a favorite material probably because it prevents rust, does not tarnish and lends a jewel-like look to the furniture.

The bolts which hold these hinges to the wood are covered on the exterior of the lid with iron or brass bosses, as are the bolts which fasten the lock to the interior of the lid. Each lock required from two to four bosses. The brass bosses of some inlaid hardwood chests are decorated with engraved ornamental lines.

Central to the decorative effect of the chest is the prominent keyhole plate, also called an escutcheon and usually cut of brass. Matching massive keys are of cast brass or cast iron. The similar shapes of keyhole plates suggests, as does

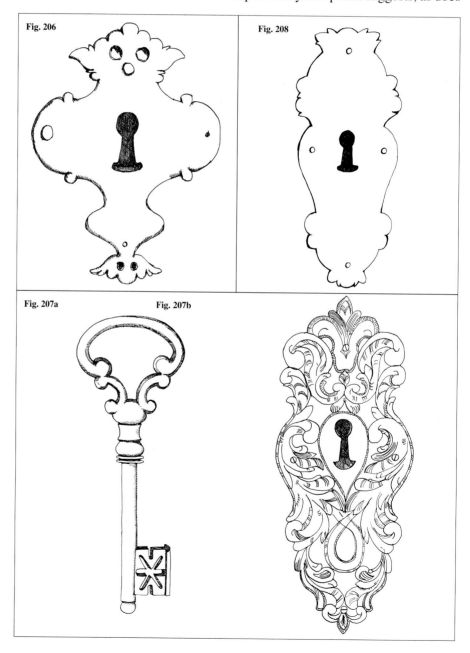

Fig. 206

Fig. 208

Fig. 207a   Fig. 207b

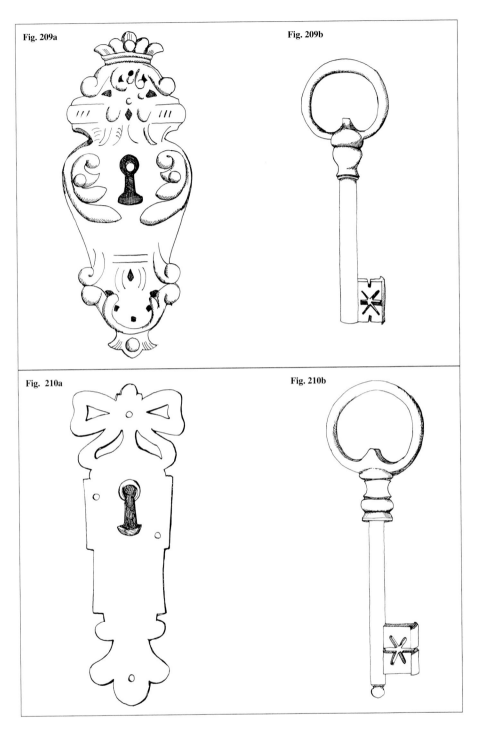

Fig. 209a

Fig. 209b

Fig. 210a

Fig. 210b

Fig.209, Keyhole plate and key.
#1.023.

Fig.210, Keyhole plate and key.
#1.038.

similarity of other style features, that these chests share geographical and
historical points of origin. At least eight distinctly different keyhole plates
(escutcheons) of cut brass and other sheet metal have been documented on
Mennonite dowry chests in this inventory (Figs. 203-210). The few chests made
in North America either do not have locks at all or, if they have locks, the
keyplates are of the mass-produced variety without decorative appeal.

The most common keyplate on Vistula Delta and South Russian chests

Fig.211, Dowry chest handle plate and handle. #1.010.

Fig.212, Handle plate and handle. #1.019.

Fig.213, Handle plate and handle. #1.017.

Fig. 211

Fig. 212

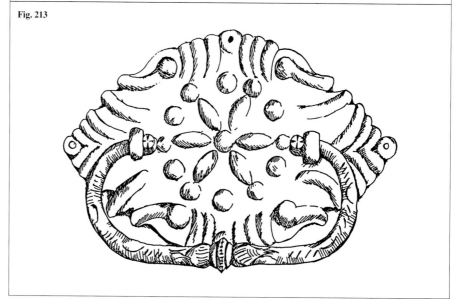
Fig. 213

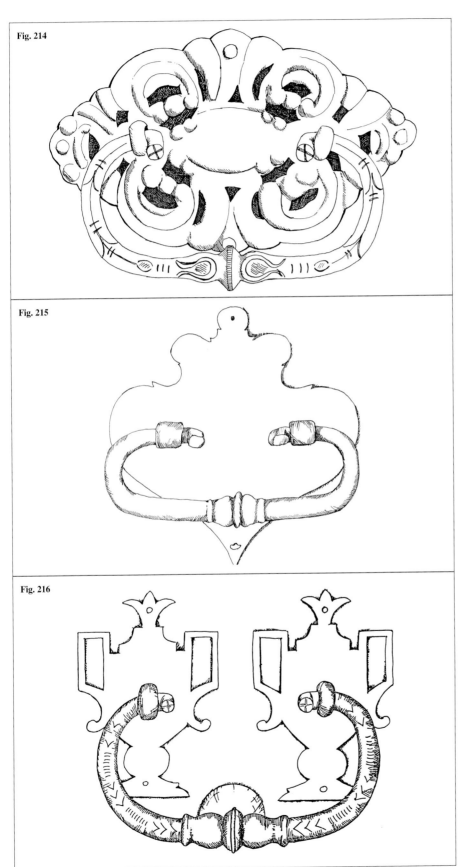

Fig. 214

Fig. 215

Fig. 216

Fig.214, Handle plate and handle. #1.066.

Fig.215, Handle plate and handle. #1.025.

Fig.216, Handle plate and handle. #1.038.

Fig.217, Handle plate and handle. #1.015.

Fig.218, Handle plate and handle . #1.013.

Fig.219, Handle plate and handle. #1.021.

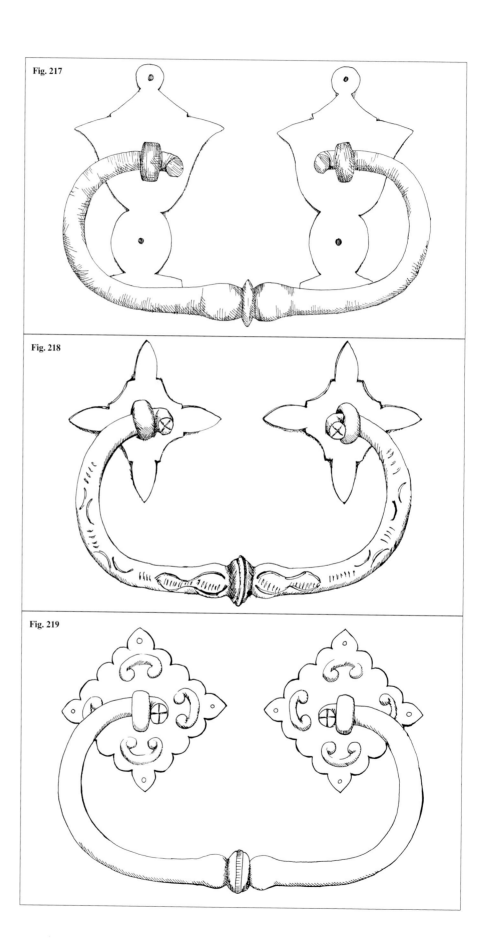

Fig. 217

Fig. 218

Fig. 219

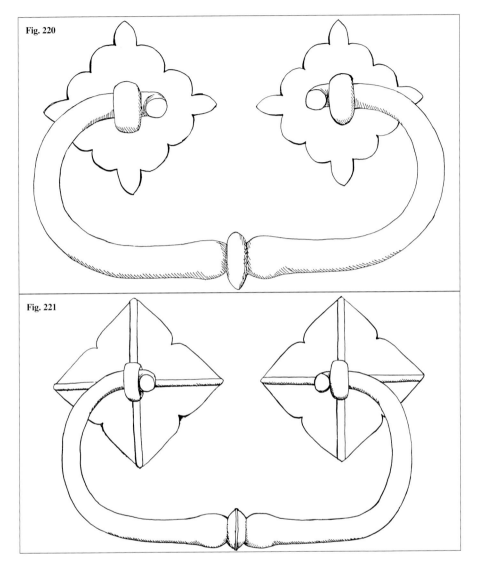

Fig. 220

Fig. 221

Fig.220, Handle plate and handle. #1.059.

Fig.221, Handle plate and handle. #1.014.

suggests an abstract archetypical, stylized plant motif of a trefoil shape (Fig. 203).[6] In its complete state a small bell-shaped plate, fastened above the keyhole, covers the keyhole when the key is removed. A related form, found on three chests from the Molotschna, suggests the stylized double eagle motif on the coat of arms of the royal houses of Poland, Prussia and Russia (Fig. 205). The double eagle also occurs as a decorative motif in Mennonite fraktur paintings. Another common keyplate form found on chests brought from the Molotschna Colony (Fig. 204) reflects the asymmetrical curvilinear form of the late baroque or rococo style. Keyplates on inlaid chests from the Vistula Delta (Figs. 206-209) are especially ornate, evoking late baroque forms.

Handles and handle plates (Figs. 211-221) are of cut or cast brass which are often engraved. They may also be of embossed and cut thin sheet metal, often tinned, with cast-iron handles.

The styles of Vistula Delta-made hardware fittings, especially hinges, handle plates and escutcheons, indicate a style chronology that begins with late baroque (Figs. 211, 212-214) and neo-classical (Fig. 216) forms of the eighteenth century and continues as revival forms throughout the nineteenth century. Chests made in South Russian Mennonite colonies tend to have simpler handle plates and handles than those made in the Vistula Delta (Figs. 215, 217-221).

Shaping the Furniture Form

The simplest, most direct decoration derives from the construction technique itself. For example, framed construction articulates the plane of a wardrobe door or a cabinet door. Pegged or pinned joints of trestle table supports or of the juncture of uprights and shelves on cupboards lend the furniture form three-dimensional visual interest.

Inlaid Decoration

The technique of decorating the surface of a furniture form with designs made of inlaid pieces of contrasting woods or other materials such as shell or animal horn was already practiced in both ancient Egypt and Mesopotamia. This method articulates and enlivens the furniture form by the structure of the grain and the color of the various woods used. The art of inlaid ceilings, wall panels, table tops and chests was introduced to northern Europe by the Italians in the sixteenth century. Inlaid motifs such as pilasters and balusters or frames are tectonic motifs that define the surface structure and style of a furniture form.

One of the best known and best documented regions where inlaid construction was practiced is the lowland area southeast of Hamburg, called *Vierlande* where country cabinetmakers used inlay as ornament on panels, doors and furniture from the seventeenth through the late nineteenth centuries, producing a unique regional style.[7] No comparable documentation exists for the inlaid cabinet work in the Vistula Delta, but the works themselves clearly establish a unique Vistula Delta-style.

Two basic techniques need to be distinguished, namely "core" inlay and marquetry.

In core inlay the contrasting wood or other material is placed directly into the surface of the respective furniture piece, so that a portion of the surface is hollowed out and a thin piece of a different wood is inserted. This is the inlay technique found in all the Mennonite-owned inlaid dowry chests and in the one wardrobe brought from the Vistula Delta to North America. The only known Mennonite immigrant craftsman who was trained in this technique by his father and who continued to practice it in Beatrice, Nebraska, was the cabinetmaker and carver Gerhard Esau (Appendix A).

The other inlay technique, commonly called marquetry, places the inlay pieces into a veneer of the same thickness which is lain over and covers the entire visible surface of the base or core wood.[8] This type of inlaid furniture has not been documented for Mennonite homes, neither in the Vistula Delta nor in North America. Furniture done with marquetry was expensive and was closely associated with the high decorative arts. It would have been found in rich households only. Furthermore, during the Biedermeier era the marquetry technique or veneer inlay fell out of fashion in favor of core inlay decoration. As we will see, inlaid decoration on furniture inspired motifs for painted furniture and was copied by furniture painters.

The walnut veneered wardrobes, cabinets and *secretaires* brought by middle-class Mennonites from the Heubuden community to North America in the 1870s were not handmade pieces. Since they were factory produced, they had become affordable.

Attached Pictures

Furniture builders like Klaas Hiebert of Mountain Lake, Minnesota, and Heinrich Rempel of Henderson, Nebraska, decorated the lower cases, door panels and cornices of wardrobes, as well as the sides and backrests of benches, with commercial, mass-produced flower decals, glued onto the grain-painted surfaces.[9]

Clock faces were often refurbished with new coats of paint, and the addition of such flower decals was a convenient and popular shortcut to achieve the effect of hand-painted floral decoration.

One wardrobe, dated 1878, features decals with narrative scenes, one on each of the four inset panels: a monkey in a zoo reaches through the cage to the warden while a woman acts terrified; a horseman with a rifle rides through the landscape past a woman hanging wash on the line; a boy hunts birds in the forest, in the distance is a church; and people in two rowboats enjoy an outing. These decals may have been added by the owner of the wardrobe. Perhaps it served duty in a room where children slept.[10]

Painted Furniture

All Mennonite immigrant furniture may be considered part of a long and far-reaching tradition of painted furniture. Pharaonic tombs in ancient Egypt contained painted furniture. In Europe painted furniture can be documented in folk and vernacular traditions as well as in upper-class and high-style furniture from Flanders to the Baltic, from the sixteenth century through the nineteenth century. Painted furniture in North America reflected the regional style characteristics of the European homeland of the respective immigrant craftsmen. Painted finishes on furniture were developed partially out of a desire to imitate the grains and color of expensive woods, and to imitate carved or inlaid decorative motifs (Fig. 222).

Mennonite craftsmen brought their painted furniture tradition to North America at a time when mass-manufactured painted furniture already held great popular appeal in Europe, a style which lasted from the mid-nineteenth century to the end of Victoria's reign. But in North America most of this painted furniture, called "cottage furniture," was produced in factories, not by individual craftsmen, for people with modest incomes.[11] For example, in the late nineteenth century "a whole set of cottage bedroom furniture could be had for the price of a single wardrobe of mahogany."[12]

To finish furniture with a painted surface decoration rather than with veneer and carved decoration was for the most part a choice determined by economic factors. Painted furniture was usually made of the less expensive softer woods, such as pine, fir and spruce—woods native to the region where the furniture was made. The painted finish, in addition to being decorative, lent protection to the surface of the wood.

Furniture made by Mennonites in North America, as well as that brought from Europe, embraces three distinctly different modes of painted finishes: (1)

Fig.222, Detail of a painted door panel of Gerhard Funk's wardrobe, 1887 (see Fig. 81). Flowers in a stemmed bowl. The scrolled leaf motif is frequently found as a framing motif in the late 19th century (for example, on printed cardboard frames of photographs).

solid colors, (2) graining in imitation of hardwoods, (3) graining with floral decorations. These techniques for painting furniture can be understood to a large degree as translations or transpositions in paint of other decorative methods which were valued more highly. For example, the painted framing motifs on the lid, sides and front of the Jakob Schmidt chest (see Figs. 114, 115 in chapter five) are derived from raised panels found on late eighteenth century furniture, doors and paneling. But this does not mean that painted furniture was found only in poorer households or only in the country.[13]

Jacob Adrian's list of paints and stains—red, yellow, black, brownish-red, mahogany, scarlet red, green, blue and ebony—given in Appendix C indicates the colors that were probably known to most Mennonite furniture builders and painters in the late eighteenth and early nineteenth century. Little systematic analysis has been made of historical patterns or variations in the use of paint colors in Mennonite furniture. However, according to one connoisseur and collector of Mennonite furniture, the mustard or amber yellow color scheme with black trim is characteristic of furniture made by craftsmen from the Molotschna Mennonite Colony, whereas the red color scheme with black or green trim is characteristic of the Evangelical Mennonite Brethren church people from the Old Colony, that is Chortitza.[14] During an 1889 visit to the immigrant Mennonite setting in Kansas, journalist Noble Prentis recorded the colors in one home he visited. His host:

> took us into a room...which was a perfect copy of a room in Russia, with its sanded floor, its wooden settees painted red and green, its huge carved chest studded with great brass-plated bolts.[15]

The simplest decorative effect was achieved with an application of solid color, notably a burnt-orange, without contrasting trim. The mustard yellow or vermilion with black trim finish has been noted by Bird and Kobayashi as a characteristic of Mennonite furniture in Manitoba and Saskatchewan. Lyndon C. Viel in his collectors' manual also states that these two colors, along with burnt-orange or orange red, are characteristic of Mennonite furniture.[16]

These observations were verified by the Kauffman Museum survey of Mennonite furniture. One of the finest examples of the mustard yellow and black trim finish is the wardrobe made by Dirk Tieszen, now in the collection of Heritage House Museum in Freeman, South Dakota (Fig. 19, chapter one).[17]

Sometimes an original painted finish in a solid color was brought up to the latest fashion standard and grained. Benjamin Boese (1835-1918), of the Alexanderwohl community near Goessel, finished a wardrobe in red with black trim, which was "his way of painting." Around 1900 this same wardrobe was repainted and grained by George Bergen, who later became the first mortician in Goessel.

The parallel occurrence of grain-painting to imitate veneer or hardwood with solidly painted furniture has been observed for much of the furniture produced in many regions of Germany between the 1830s and the 1860s.[18]

In the technique called grain-painting, the craftsperson imitates a specific hardwood such as ash, executing decorative motifs in black or dark brown monochromes and translating via paint the highly prized inlaid hardwood furniture. In grain-painting the base is always a solid ground color. Over this is painted a contrasting glaze color which matches the color of the wood grain to be simulated. Examples include the Sara Schulz dowry chest (Fig. 82, chapter four), the Gerhard and Anna Brandt Dick chest (Fig. 32, chapter one), the Gerhard Funk wardrobe (Fig. 181, chapter seven) and the Heinrich H. Epp bed (Fig. 26, chapter one). Mrs. P.R. Schroeder (1888-1966) remembered that the huge wardrobes with drawers, corner shelves and desks "...were carefully painted to resemble wood grain."[19]

After 1815 the impact of Biedermeier furniture which stresses the innate decorative effect of wood itself, that is the patterns of its natural structure or grain, had significant influence on the development of grain-painting techniques.[20]

The practice of grain-painting wood surfaces was very common in the late nineteenth century and into the first two decades of the twentieth century. Mennonite craftsmen, whether lay or professional, and Mennonite customers followed the general fashion of finishing both furniture and woodwork in homes, public buildings and churches with painted graining.

Painted graining played a major role not only in the finishing and decorating of "movable" furniture, but also in finishing the permanent wood trim of a house—the ceilings, baseboards, wainscoting, window trim, doors and door trim.

One of the most extensive instructions in the techniques of graining and marbling was published in Vienna as a series of leaflets by Ernst Oldenbruch, between 1920 and about 1927. The instructions for painting techniques and recipes included simulations of 15 different woods, including grey maple, five different oaks, German ash, two kinds of mahogany, two kinds of walnut, rosewood and arolla or Swiss pine. Twenty-nine different tools were illustrated for both graining and marbling, indicating the complexity of the process when professional results were to be achieved.[21] In addition to brushes, rollers and combs made of *gutta percha*, cork and steel were used for graining. One English

Fig.223, Ridgley's Graining Tools, an advertisement for painting woodgrain imitations.[4]

185

Fig.224, Pantry door, ca. 1900.
Painted graining, painted floral motifs by
Anna Adrian Buller. From the home of
her brother Franz Adrian II.
H: 71¼ " W: 29".¼".
KM 6255.2.

firm, for example, sold sets of fourteen graining combs.[22]

The art of imitating the grain of hardwoods with paint extended to the similar process of simulating the veins and colors of different kinds of marble. The daughter of Jacob J. Peters, who made several small chests for his daughters in the 1920s, recalls: "He made one chest with a marbled effect on the platform. He did this by painting it white and then streaked smoke with a torch made of newspapers on it before the paint dried." [23]

Both graining and marbling were practiced by trained cabinetmakers as well as by laymen. The slogan of Ridgely's advertisement of one set of five graining tools promised: "Anybody Can Grain!" (Fig. 223).

Many of the grain-painted pieces of furniture originally stood in the "better" homes of Mennonite immigrants, built around the 1890s. In these homes they often matched the grain-painted woodwork of the rooms, including painted doors and wainscoting. The grain-painted pantry door from the home of Franz Adrian's son Franz is an example of this fashion (Fig. 224). Another example features a factory-made walnut dresser, hand grain-painted to "match" the other handmade and hand-grained furniture in the original owner's home in the Buhler, Kansas, area.[24]

Mennonites employed both their own as well as non-Mennonite artisans to decorate their homes, their furniture and their churches. Two examples of such persons are the Swiss immigrant Emil Kym of the Buhler, Kansas community, whose work has been documented by the historian Steve Friesen, and a Mr. Huenergardt, not a Mennonite, who lived near Lehigh and did painting, graining and stenciling for clients in that vicinity. Marie Harms Berg remembered his painting of the woodwork and cabinets in her parents' farm home around 1912 to 1914.[25]

Not all graining stayed close to, nor even aimed at, the imitation of specific woods. Some artisans worked with bold, sweeping, freehand brush strokes, series of powdery, fluffy dabs and swabs or stipples which take on decorative patterns in their own right. One of the most outstanding examples of this type of graining is the work of the unidentified Mr. Harms on the repainting of the Klaas Dick family dowry chest. He also painted a matching wardrobe for Klaas Dick's home (Fig. 225, 226).[26]

These different methods of painting furniture sometimes occur in various combinations on one and the same piece of furniture. The works of Franz Adrian and of Heinrich Rempel exemplify combinations of painted graining, painted floral motifs, stenciled motifs and flower decals.

Comments on Style

We have shown that the sources of the Mennonite material tradition are pluralistic, with elements from Slavic and Germanic traditions, from both the upper class and the common cultures in the southern Baltic region from the sixteenth to the eighteenth centuries. The stylistic characteristics of "Mennonite furniture" reflect a blend of popular or vernacular and mainstream European art historical periods from the seventeenth to the nineteenth centuries.

The styles also reflect the range of the socio-economic standing of Mennonite families. Mennonite furniture of Flemish, Dutch and German derivation cannot be defined as folk art, precisely because of its pluralistic sources and its high

(right) **Fig.225a,** Wardrobe, ca. 1880-1890. From the home of Klaas and Elisabeth Wiebe Dick. Builder unknown. Painted by Mr. Harms to match the dowry chest. Pine, painted graining, black paint, varnish. Grooves above the cornice indicate wardrobe originally had a pediment. Often pediments became separated from wardrobes when they were moved to new houses or into different rooms where ceilings were too low to accommodate the pediment.
H:83" W:57" D:22".
#11.007, KM 89.53.1.

(above) **Fig.225b,** Detail of Wiebe Dick wardrobe.

culture orientation. This becomes very clear the moment one compares a Mennonite dowry chest with a Flemish, Kashubian, Danish, Swedish or Ukrainian painted peasant chest from the same period.

The most dominant stylistic features of Mennonite furniture echo those of the early nineteenth century northern European furniture style called Biedermeier. Georg Himmelheber states that the style was created "by the middle class for the middle class" at the time of the foundation of the German Confederation and the Congress of Vienna around 1815, and it ended with the revolutions of 1848-1849.[27] The term "Biedermeier" refers to a stolid middle class person and was initially coined as a derogatory designation. The "Bieder" man values domestic life above all. Therefore his furniture is scaled to comfort.[28]

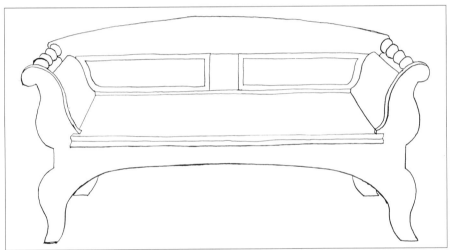

(top, left) **Fig.226,** Dowry chest of Klaas and Elisabeth Wiebe Dick. Brought from South Russia in 1877 on the SS *Vaterland*. Re-painted by Mr. Harms in the Inman area.
H:26½" W:54½" D:28½".
#1.065, Private colletion.

(bottom, left) **Fig.227,** Outline of a resting bench, late 19th century.
H:33½" W:62" D:23".
#5.007, Heritage Hall Museum, Freeman, South Dakota.

Truth to materials and functionalism were key principles followed by the craftsmen who fashioned Biedermeier furniture. They emphasized the inherent beauty of the wood itself, its structure and its grain which emphasized surface flatness, that is the flatness of the plank, and pure geometrical forms.

The applewood veneer with ebonized molding on the wardrobe built by Aaron Claassen of Caldowe near Marienburg in 1869 is a late, yet prime, manifestation of these Biedermeier furniture-style characteristics, albeit with a peculiarly idiosyncratic ornate flare in the unorthodox scalloped crown of the pediment (see Fig. 91, chapter four).

The repertoire of classicism with which furniture makers had been familiar from the time of Louis XVI continued to provide decorative motifs.[29] In Mennonite furniture the classical motifs that filtered through the Biedermeier mode were the Greek urn, the Grecian pediment gables of the wardrobes, the decorative motifs of the column with a simple Doric or with an elaborate acanthus leaf capital, the Greek key framing motif and the stemmed shallow vessel (cantheros) filled with flowers on dowry chests, wardrobes and related furnishings. The spirited cyma-shaped curves of the upright armrest supports and of the legs of Mennonite resting and sleeping benches also took their cues from Biedermeier furniture, particularly the sofas of the Biedermeier era (Fig.

227). Georg Himmelheber has called the sofa "the quintessence of Biedermeier" because it is a "sociable piece of furniture, created for a period in which the middle class gained most enjoyment and intellectual stimulation from social life."[30] In the countryside and especially in the isolated setting of the south Russian colonies, the Mennonite resting and sleeping benches with their characteristic Biedermeier profiles persisted much longer and bypassed several furniture style developments in northern European furniture. The same can be said of the Mennonite *Glasschaup*, which was a vernacular variation of the Biedermeier cabinet, the central showpiece among the furnishings of a Biedermeier living room, which combined a chest of drawers with a glass cabinet.

The Biedermeier preference for warm and light tones of wood and for vivid wood grain was reflected in Mennonite furniture in the preference for the warm blond color of ash. Furniture with painted graining imitated this preferred Biedermeier color. But the rich dark red of mahogany also became fashionable. Since it was expensive to use because it needed to be imported, its colors and grains were copied in stains and paints applied to a range of domestic woods.[31] In the 1830s Jacob Adrian noted two recipes for mahogany stains in his journal (see Appendix C).

Late nineteenth century immigrant Mennonite furniture combined these elements from Biedermeier with the current fashions in furniture which were taking their cues from the eclectic historicism of the Victorian era. The profusion of decorative devices employed by Franz Adrian and Heinrich Rempel in order to give the surfaces of their furniture a "rich" look, for example, contrasts sharply with the spirit of Biedermeier which adheres to classical simplicity if not severity of form. Even so, both cabinetmakers quote the classicizing architectural vocabulary of Biedermeier furniture.

One hundred and fifty years of Mennonite furniture making in the Vistula Delta, in South Russia and in North America mirror the dominant style periods of the late eighteenth to the end of the nineteenth centuries. From late baroque, rococo, neo-classical and Biedermeier periods, along with the revival and layering of historical styles in the Victorian era, Biedermeier forms prevail. When comparing this body of Mennonite immigrant furniture in the Plains states to the handcrafted furniture of Lutheran and Catholic German immigrants in Missouri and in Texas from about 1850-1870, one notes some general similarities in the cyma-curved profiles of the resting and sleeping benches or settees and the shapes of writing tables and pedestal tables. But the construction features, forms and decorations of the Mennonite dowry chest, wardrobe, cradle and sleeping bench remain unique, testifying to their regional and historical derivation in the formative northern European setting of the last decade of the eighteenth century and the first two decades of the nineteenth century.[32]

8

The Waning
of the Tradition

Maunch eena kaun
tjeen Plautdietsch meha
en schaemt sich nich eenmol;
em Jejendeel: he meent sich seha
met siene hoage School,
raed't hoachdietsch, enjlisch, rusch
—so vael,
daut eenem dieslich woat.
Weat es de gaunze Tjlaetamaeh!
nich eene Schintjeschwoat.
Auls etj noch tjleen wea, saut etj oft
bi Mutta op'e Schoot,
en Plautdietsch saed se,—o so oft:
"Mien Jung, etj sie die goot!"
Waut Mutta Plautdietsch to mi saed,
daut klung so woarm en tru,
daut etj daut nimmameha vejaet
bot to de latzte Ruh.[1]

Many a one speaks
no Low German any more
and is not even ashamed.
On the contrary: he thinks himself big
with all his high schooling.
Speaks High German, English, Russian
—so much,
that my head starts to swim.
All put together this gibberish in toto
does not equal in value, the hide of a pig.
When I was small and sat on
my mother's lap,
how often she said, "My son, I love you."
What Mother said in Low German
seems so warm and true,
I will never forget till my final rest.

Not far from Hillsboro, Kansas, H.B. Friesen built a new home for his retirement years near the farm of one of his married daughters. He writes,"In a new house belongs new furniture. So I bought a small cupboard at Julius Gerstenkorn for $3.50, six chairs for $6.00, and some wall paper. We had already bought a wardrobe and a couch before."[2]

The Friesens started building in January, 1908, employing five men for different jobs on the house. In March the house was washed on the inside, the dirt was leveled around it and new furniture was purchased from Mr. Gerstenkorn in Hillsboro. In April they moved in with the help of their many grown children. The total cost was $600, of which $403.50 was spent on lumber, cement, bricks and lime.[3] This new house was not built according to the longhouse tradition in the South Russian Mennonite villages, but followed the prevailing patterns of North American wood frame houses. Behind the choices manifested here, several strong forces are identifiable.

The Advent of Mass Production

The ready availability and purchase of inexpensive factory-produced furniture, instead of commissioning the needed piece from a skilled craftsman in the community, is one of several reasons why the tradition of our study came to an end.

As early as the 1870s in the Vistula Delta and among the well-to-do in South Russia, Mennonites purchased fashionable Victorian-style, factory-manufactured furniture and shipped it to North America when they emigrated. Among these pieces were a *Vertiko* or cabinet with shelves (Figs. 228, 229), wardrobes and linen cabinets, elaborate *secretaires* of walnut or mahogany veneers and a British-manufactured cabinet clock.[4]

Sears & Roebuck mail-order furniture or furniture available at every new town's general store was less expensive than that made by local craftsmen. This meant that the craftsmen who had come to America with the skills for making "Mennonite furniture" did not have enough work to continue making a living from their craft. The incorporation of mass-manufactured furniture into Mennonite homes may be further illustrated in the 1875-1911 Voth/Unruh/Fast family house on the Kauffman Museum grounds. The 1911 addition of a commodious parlor to the house was furnished entirely with factory-produced furnishings which had not been part of the tradition in South Russia. These pieces included an upholstered platform rocking chair and a parlor organ with matching stool. As commercially produced materials became readily available, the investment of personal time and energy in assembling the dowry ceased. In short, the Industrial Revolution, as it affected home furnishings, had a direct impact on Mennonites in Germany (Prussia), Russia and on the Plains of North America.

The Accommodation to Mainstream Taste

American mass market culture was already available to the first generation of Mennonite immigrants. There are numerous cases in which furniture was purchased in St. Louis, Kansas City, Topeka and Omaha on the way to prairie settlements. Those immigrants who came with adequate finances were able to furnish their new homes with purchased pieces. This was not only a matter of convenience, it was also a matter of aesthetic choice, of taste which was often guided by current fashion. There is evidence of individual craftsmen trying to accommodate their work to this mainstream taste.

The work of Hansul Goering of Freeman, South Dakota, seems to have suited the tastes, guided by the advertising catalogues of mail-order firms, of the working middle class. Goering most certainly fashioned his upholstered daybeds (Fig. 230), fainting couches with matching upholstered armchairs, upholstered loveseats and china cabinets after prototypes pictured in the *Sears* catalogue (Fig. 231). Reflected in this preference for upholstered furniture is a changed standard of comfort which mass-manufacturing had made available for "everyman."

(left) **Fig .228,** *Vertiko* (Cabinet), manufactured ca. 1870 in Germany. Purchased in Marienburg, West Prussia, from L. Boettcher's store for furniture, mirrors, upholstered furniture, wood coffins and metal coffins. (The firm's stamp, picturing a coffin and a wardrobe, is on the back of the piece.) Brought to Kansas in 1878. According to family oral history, Anna Claassen received this factory-produced, fashionable piece of furniture for her 16th birthday in West Prussia. Suitable both for storage of linen and for display, it may have taken the place of a dowry chest. In 1878 when she immigrated with her family, the Reverend and Mrs. Peter Claassen, to Newton, Kansas, this piece came along, together with a walnut veneer wardrobe, a spring upholstered sleeping bench and other furniture. Two-door cabinet, fitted with shelves, one drawer above the cabinet. Walnut veneer, varnish, dovetail joints on drawers, mitered joint on front, butt joint on back. The ornately carved top is constructed independently and is fastened with wooden pegs.

H:70½" W:37" D:19¼".
#14.028, Private collection.

(above) **Fig. 229,** Detail of *Vertiko.*

(top) **Fig.230,** Sofabed or daybed, ca. 1910. Made by Johann "Hansul" Goering. Mahogany stain, yellow and gold paint, two round mirrors, blue-green plush upholstery.

H:36½" L:62" D:33".

#10.001, Heritage Hall Museum, Freeman, South Dakota.

(bottom) **Fig.231,** Advertisement for a sofabed in the *Sears & Roebuck Catalogue,* 1902. Illustrates the prototype Hansul Goering tried to copy.

New Tools and New Craft Fashions

Two new saws transformed the techniques of working with wood, leading to new styles of decorative woodworking. With the invention of the bandsaw and the jigsaw, hobby crafts became popular. A flower stand table and bookcase, created by Mennonite craftsmen using these machines, demonstrate that leisure time furniture-making produced objects completely alien to, or divorced from, the tradition (Fig. 232). There is little if any integrity between the form, material and function. The overriding concern in these pieces is effect—to impress with ornament for the sake of ornament—without an understanding of the innate aesthetic possibilities of the material or the beauty of a functional form. To a degree the possibilities inherent in the tool or machine, rather than the craftsman, dictated the design.

Fig.232, Bookcase, 1903. Handmade, wood, varnish, decals, fabric. From Marion, South Dakota.
H:69" W:42" D:12".
#14.038, KM 2203.

Remembering the Tradition in Miniature

The tradition lingered in nostalgic, miniature renderings of the standard pieces of furniture and the architectural forms, such as children's furniture, toys, doll cradles (Fig. 233), doll dowry chests, doll sleeping benches and even a furnished toy model of the Russian Mennonite housebarn. The few known pieces hand built after 1910 (the last dated piece fully in the tradition being Nettie Vogt's teaching desk) merely echo the tradition, reducing and miniaturizing the remembered prototypes.

Fig.233, Doll cradle, ca. 1880-1900. Made by Benjamin Boese. Wood, nails, red stain, black stain trim, dovetail and butt joints.

H:8½" L:14½" W:8".

#18.015, Mennonite Heritage Museum, Goessel, Kansas.

Jacob J. Peters (1863-1942) came to Henderson, Nebraska, when he was 15 years old with his parents, Jacob and Elisabeth Peters from Nikolaithal, South Russia, the second of seven children. After studying in St. Joseph, Missouri, for two years, he taught school in Henderson for seven years. Later, he managed the J.J. Peters General Merchandise in Henderson, which also sold coffins. Jacob Peters did the embalming. He moved to Alta Loma, California, in 1913, where he again was a businessman as well as a rancher. Just before he retired, Jacob made four small chests and footstools for his three daughters and one son, using hammer, saw, coping saw and sandpaper.[5]

One of these small chests bears his initials and the date 1929. It is even decorated with the customary painted rose and tulip bouquet tied with a ribbon (Figs. 234, 235). However, in this piece the bouquet appears on the lid of the till, not on the outside of the chest. According to oral tradition, Jacob Peters also painted a design on the inside of the chest's lid, but it is no longer discernible.

Other hallmarks of the tradition are very distinctly present as well. The little chest sits on a separately constructed, footed base with cabriole legs and a swagged skirt, the molding of the lid and the bottom of the chest approximate the forms of those of the large chests. There is a lock, albeit without decorative keyplate. The colors of the varnished, orange-crate pine and redwood echo the warm amber yellow of ash accented with dark stains. The chest rests on its own separate platform, a feature characteristic of Heinrich Rempel's wardrobes and cabinets, whom J.J. Peters of course would have known.

A toy dowry chest built in 1940 by 71-year-old Jacob J. Enns, complete with till and secret compartment, also still reflects a memory of its full-size prototype.[6]

In 1974 Reverend Abraham W. Friesen (1891-1987) built a doll sleeping bench (Fig. 236) as a commemorative gesture celebrating the centennial of Mennonite immigration to the Plains states of North America. This piece represents a miniaturized evocation of the tradition made at a time of heightened consciousness of roots and heritage.

Abraham W. Friesen was the ninth child of 13. He grew up in a 28'x 30' wood and adobe four-room house with a loft where the children slept. He became involved in carpentry work, and, it is said, after retirement made many toys for his grandchildren as well as cabinets for clocks and wall clocks.[7] The fact that he marked this particular sleeping bench with a stamp bearing his name and the name of his business "Novelties" suggests that he produced these or similar items in quantity for sale.

In a similar evocation of the tradition, B.B. Neumann built a model farmstead (Fig. 237) of his grandfather's place at Altenau, Molotschna, complete with landscaping, a well, livestock and furniture. Neumann built the model in 1946, relying on his memory of the place he and his family left in 1893.[8]

Remembering and Forgetting—Stages of Amnesia about the Tradition

When *Melkschaupe* are thought to have been bookcases; when wall-hung corner cabinets are placed on the floor; when legs of benches are sawn off to approximate the lower height of a sofa and ease the reach toward the coffee table; when dowry chests are painted enamel white over all the metal fittings, stripped to the bare wood, "cleaned up" by removing pictures inside the lids and stored in barns to hold grain or to simply rot; when pediments and bases of wardrobes are taken off because they do not fit in rooms with low ceilings; and when wooden hooks are replaced with rods for clothes hangers; then the

Figs.234, 235, Miniature dowry chest. Made by Jacob J. Peters, signed and dated 1929, Alta Loma, California. Recycled orange-crate wood, lid and platform of redwood, varnish, butt joints. The four-footed base with cabriole legs and swagged skirt is separately constructed. A bouquet of flowers tied with a ribbon bow is painted with watercolor on the lid of the till, with the maker's signature and date. A wreath was painted on the center of the lid, but it is barely discernible anymore. Small lock and key plate, commercial hinges.
H:16½" W:24 ⅝" D:15¼".
#1.055, Private collection.

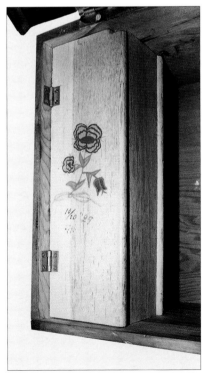

Fig.236, Doll sleeping bench, 1974. Made by Abraham W. Friesen. Stamp on back says, "Abraham Friesen, Novelties, Henderson, Nebraska." The date 1974 is penciled underneath the stamp. The bench pulls out to enlarge its sleeping capacity, just like its full-size prototypes. Plywood, yellow and black oil paint.

H:16½" W:28".

#6.005, Private collection.

tradition has been forgotten.

Just as the crystallization of the domestic furniture tradition was shown to be a reflection of the middle class household among Vistula Delta Mennonites and its manufacture by Mennonite craftsmen in the diaspora a reflection of a continued conscious tradition, so its waning on the Plains can be interpreted in the light of specific socio-economic and cultural determinants, and other less tangible aspects of Mennonite life.

The economic forces of mass culture and accommodation to the prevailing tastes certainly were major factors in the waning of the tradition. However, the differential rate at which elements of immigrant culture were abandoned is tied to the relative lack of importance placed upon them as bearers of core styles, patterns and beliefs in Mennonite identity. The Vistula Delta tradition, so to speak, was the adopted home of these Mennonites who came from elsewhere.

In Low German speaking communities of Kansas, the approximate order in which cultural realms changed to correspond to those of the common American culture were these: 1) agricultural technology and business practices; 2) domestic architecture and furnishings; 3) church architecture and furnishings; 4)language.

Agricultural technology and business practices along with land holding rules changed shortly after arrival. Domestic architecture and furniture continued for a generation, in that most families constructed the characteristic longhouses with their requisite furniture. In the second generation the children of these people (i.e., around 1890 to 1900) built American houses and purchased new mass-produced furniture. At the same time a new group of churches was constructed with the traditional floor pattern to accommodate face-to-face and gender-specific seating, for example, Alexanderwohl in Kansas. These reflected the core of the socio-religious system among Mennonites.

Within this differential rate of change, a nuanced picture of changes in the particular functional types of furniture is apparent. The central hearth and its architecture were undoubtedly discarded because of their impracticality in the quickly-changing Plains climate, and the ready availability of cast-iron wood stoves. The making of dowry chests, although many were brought with the immigrants, virtually ceased, presumably because the chest could be replaced as a piece of furniture by a dresser or cabinet with shelves. Perhaps the dowry chest's demise also had to do with the availability of land and commercially-produced textiles and household items as dowry gifts. Chests lose importance when saving-up is not so necessary because goods are more readily available and hence more expendable. The wardrobes, built-in or free-standing china cabinets, benches and beds could all be purchased in less expensive mass-produced versions. By 1910 many new houses had walk-in closets. Thus the economic and social fabric of household material culture had been altered.

The conclusion one may draw from this analysis of the rise and demise of this particular material cultural tradition—as exemplified specifically in the set of furniture pieces—is that although it had served necessity and expressed a once-contemporary aesthetic, it was no longer at the core of Mennonite identity. Economic and social factors determined its fate. Also, whatever emotional and symbolic load had been projected onto the household furnishings—continuity of family, celebration of rites of passage, thrifty homemade work—was now expressed in the heady new opportunities of the New World, which were

Fig.237, Model of a South Russian Mennonite house and barn. Made by B.B. Neumann, 1946.
KM 90.112.1.

relatively free of constraints. In the prairies of the United States and Canada there was unlimited freedom of religion and education. People were free to propagate their own ideas of the Christian gospel through mission outreach. Identities could be developed around the building and management of hospitals, companies and colleges. There were unlimited opportunities to build one's own home and own one's own land. Many people hoped to turn a profit by working hard. These energies were the new focuses of an emerging Plains Mennonite identity.[9]

The last generation of builders of this furniture struggled with the dilemma of a sharp decline in demand for their work, and the popular attraction to "store-bought" or "catalogue-ordered" replacements. In many cases the hand-made pieces were simply discarded as old-fashioned.[10]

9
Conclusion: Thoughts on Mennonite Aesthetic Identity

At the outset of this work we suggested that furniture making by Mennonite craftsmen became a self-conscious tradition when they began to manufacture the common tradition of the Vistula Delta and took it with them to central Poland, South Russia and, later, the Plains of North America. Did this tradition also constitute an aesthetic tradition, that is "a theory or consistent attitude toward beauty and the beautiful, a standard of value in judging taste?"[1]

Did these Mennonite furniture makers, preceded by the weavers, the lace-makers, the clockmakers and the tile stove makers of earlier centuries, possess a distinctive aesthetic sensibility or judgment about what they made? Is there something in their work that reveals it to have a distinctively Mennonite aesthetic? The Polish historian Kazimierz Mezynski put into words—modesty, honesty, persistence and love of order—the qualities he found in the interiors of Mennonite homes.[2]

According to the anthropologist Edmund Leach, who followed the philosopher Ludwig Wittgenstein, aesthetics and ethics are logically identical.[3] Just as all behaviors have an ethical dimension, so do all dimensions of expressive and material culture possess an aesthetic sense. There are no aesthetically neutral customs. Even those behaviors which are overtly technical, have a dimension of symbolic expressiveness which reveals the ethics as well as the aesthetics of a community.

The inquiry into a Mennonite aesthetic in the domestic setting, examined in this work, may begin with a study of the ways in which furnishings articulate taste, consistent attitudes, rules and conventions about expressiveness and decor. To discern a distinctive Mennonite aesthetic requires especially careful attention, for many of the particular furnishings of Mennonite homes presented in our study are not in their form and style different from the common culture around them, whether that be the vernacular or the finely wrought professional objects emulating the canons of high culture. A Mennonite aesthetic sensibility would be discernible mainly in the way furnishings are presented. Several examples of particular pieces, fortunately well-documented, give us a basis on which to comment.

First, we consider the dowry chest and the way it was used, decorated and perceived. Undoubtedly a central piece of furniture in the household, it was a likely first place to look for the home's aesthetic identity. We have suggested that the floral motifs may be linked to rites of passage, such as adult baptism and marriage, in the life of the young woman for whom the chest was built. All of a family's energies were put into the creation of a vehicle for the launching of the new household. Extra layers of signification were thrust upon the dowry chest and the symbolism of the dowry to give the family persistence, one of the qualities Mezynski mentions. We know of a few instances in which dowry chests were given names that were identical, generation after generation, with the intended inheritor of the chest; thus the "Agatha chest" or the "Anna chest." Often constructed and decorated in a manner to become enduring statements of a particular line, the chests usually followed a matrilineal chain of mothers and daughters or granddaughters through time. Sometimes they were always inherited with a certain house or farm.

And yet, not all chests carried decoration. Along with other furniture pieces, they also reflected the theology of the group in some settings. Scant but suggestive evidence from a number of chests indicates that monochrome mahogany red (see Fig. 113) or black chests (Fig. 108), as well as those of hardwood ash without ornamental inlay (Fig. 238), may have expressed an aesthetic of the plain. Most revealing is the story of the once-plain chest (Figs. 114-116) of Jakob and Elisabeth Schmidt, members of the Old Flemish congregation in Alexanderwohl in South Russia. In their charity to the itinerant painter whom they took in one winter, they let him decorate their chest. For this the elders threatened them with the ban.

How was choice of color and pattern determined by this ethic–aesthetic of the plain? For the Schmidts the ethic of charity outweighed the desirability of

Fig.238, Dowry chest, ca. 1850. Ash, till with two secret compartments, five brass bosses, brass keyplate, ornamental tinned iron handle plates, five-footed separate base. Veneered baluster motif covers dovetailed corner joints.
H:27" W:55" D:29".
#1.007, KM 4318.

adhering to the plain. Or perhaps the ethic of charity toward the beggar justified the decor on the chest.

In these examples we see a certain tension between making the aesthetic moment of founding or commemorating a new household explicit with floral decorations and ornamental lines and of leaving this moment implicit and merely represented in a dowry chest. This tension between the decorative and the plain extended to other aspects of the Mennonite home. There were, of course, additional issues in an aesthetic of the home.

The sitting benches in the canon of Mennonite furniture also reveal an aesthetic and an ethic in the way they were seen and used in the home. More than any other piece of furniture in this Mennonite tradition, suggests George Vollmer, they welcomed the stranger and the visitor, treating him or her as equal to the family. Visiting together expressed a degree of comfort, of welcoming stranger and friend alike at the door. The grace in the form of the sitting bench expressed the physical quality of this welcome, this ethical imperative, to the visitor in the home.

The all-pervasive clock in Mennonite homes in the tradition voiced the widespread cultural value placed on the measurement and stewardship of time, in the era leading to the Industrial Revolution.[4] Certainly, one did not need to keep exact time to be an effective farmer. However, the wall clock in each home in the community created a common punctuality that permitted public meetings such as religious services to be organized more tightly. In the Mennonite setting clocks in every home highlighted the common order and gave to the dimension of time the orderliness of the inwardly-controlled community.

With clocks—although none were completely plain—we also note a progression from the relatively plain, decorated with a few floral sprigs or a date and initials, to those whose faces were highly decorated (see Fig. 34 with flowers, Figs. 92 and 102 with the biblical story of Hezekiah, Fig. 103 with the biblical story of Jephtha, Fig. 109 which is a fraktur drawing of a "spiritual clock" and Fig. 122 with a golden circle and angels). Some of the Mennonite clockmakers in Polish Prussia and South Russia went beyond the mere manufacture of clocks to metaphorize and moralize time through paintings of biblical stories on the clock faces. As we suggested in chapter four, the story of Hezekiah's response to the king of Assyria uniquely commented on the Mennonites' current dilemma with the Prussian government threatening their very way of life and their most cherished scruples about participation in the military. We have few similar Mennonite paintings, but we may infer from the few known painted clocks that visual art was permitted in Mennonite homes of the time if it presented a moralizing understanding of history in which obedience to God was the prime consideration.

A more frequent type of embellishment on Mennonite furniture—one that makes explicit reference to a moralizing order—is the use of scripture text or reference in a prominent location. This aesthetic is exemplified by the 1890s glass cabinet of the Richert family of the Alexanderwohl community in Kansas (Fig. 239). The painting in the center of the cabinet's pediment (Fig. 240) admonishes the viewer to "Search in the Scripture" and take to heart the scripture chapters and verses painted onto the open book. They are: 1) John 5:39, "You study the scriptures diligently, supposing that in having them you have eternal

(right) **Fig.239,** Glass cupboard, ca. 1880-1900. From the Heinrich and Helena Unruh Richert family. Pine, painted graining, gable with carved birds, original glass doors missing. Commercial wainscoting. Note the scripture verses painted into an open book on the gable: John 3:16; Romans 13:13-14; and John 5:39, with the admonitions "Search the Scriptures" and "Take and Read."

H:88" W:38¾" D:16".

#14.024, Private collection.

(above) **Fig.240,** Detail of pediment on Richert cupboard.

life;" 2) John 3:16, "God loved the world so much that he gave his only Son into the world, that through him the world might be saved;" 3) Romans 13:13-14, whose central thought is contained in these solemn admonitions of the Apostle Paul to the Roman Christians: "Let us behave with decency as befits the day: no revelling or drunkenness, no debauchery or vice, no quarrels or jealousies! Let Christ Jesus himself be the armour that you wear; give no more thought to satisfying the bodily appetites." At the center of the pediment the painter wrote these words, "Take and read."[5] Such admonitions to sobriety and salvation on a cabinet for storing and displaying earthly goods remind us of the moralizing tone of much seventeenth and eighteenth century Dutch decorative and academic art in which references to scripture frequently justified the opulence of the Golden Age, as noted by Simon Schama's *Embarrassment of Riches.*[6]

These examples of the plain and the fancy in dowry chests, sitting benches, clock faces and cabinets all demonstrate an aesthetic engaged to articulate an implicit signification concerning: 1) the perpetuation of the family or home; 2) the ethic of openness to hospitality to one's neighbor in the community; 3) the common time frame in the community and the stewardship of personal time; and 4) the moral codes that are to guide thoughts and behaviors in all of life. Perhaps this is too heavy and too consistent an interpretation of the decoration on Mennonite furniture—one in which there is little room for playfulness, the artist's whim or beauty for its own sake, and one in which there is too much moral order. Yet, the burden of signification *is* heavy in a tradition where a cabinet that displays the serving dishes, coffee cups and sugar bowl also warns against giving any thought to satisfying bodily appetites!

With such a strong emphasis on the moral and ethical order, the appearance of the Mennonite sanctuary further revealed a Mennonite aesthetic. The sanctuary is the physical expression of the community of adult believers. During the formative centuries of this tradition in the Vistula Delta, the home was also the place of worship. As we noted in earlier chapters, the transition from worship in the domestic setting (house, shed, barn or even under trees) to worship in prayerhouses occurred only in the eighteenth century, after Mennonites had already been in the area for two centuries.[7] The physical structure created at this moment of transition and the way it was decorated is of special interest to us because it represents an explicit visual statement of the aesthetics of the group.

Ideally we would be able to study this emerging Mennonite architecture and aesthetic in the 1754 Rosenort prayerhouse in the Vistula Delta. It was followed by the construction of four similar buildings in 1768, as we noted in chapter four. However, the late nineteenth century photographs of these buildings (Figs. 60, 61) are only approximations of what they must have been over a century earlier. Nor do we have good visual documentation of the South Russia and American Plains Mennonite prayerhouses which derived directly from the eighteenth century Vistula Delta structures. We know merely that they were plain and the interior seating arrangement was such that the congregants sat in a half circle around the row of preachers and the elder, who sat on a slightly raised platform on the long side of the building.

Through the use of historical comparison and analogy, we may draw insights about Mennonite aesthetics as expressed in their prayerhouses from those constructed in the 1980s in Mennonite settlements in the Soviet Union. In June,

Fig.241, Chancel of the Zhdanovka Mennonite prayerhouse, Orenburg Oblast, USSR. Built and grained by Johann Teichroew, 1982. Glass painting by women of the congregation.[1]

1991 the authors visited many of the prayerhouses in the 22 villages of the Orenburg region in the south Urals. Although the pre-revolutionary Mennonite churches (all of which were closed in the 1920s) were formal brick buildings emulating mainstream European church architecture, the new Mennonite sanctuaries of the 1980s hearken back to the architecture and the interior structure of their Vistula Delta wooden prayerhouse prototypes. The *Kirchliche* prayerhouses of Chortitza or Old Colony origin, as well as those from Molotschna-derived settlements, are from the street nearly indistinguishable from the house-barn-type homes in the settlement. The interior layout of benches again follows the half circle, face-to-face congregational seating, in which everyone can look everyone else in the eye. The preachers and elder sit on chairs in the focal point of this rectangle of congregational members, marked by a screen of painted glass framed in wood (Fig. 241). Each panel is framed with a decorative motif around a brightly colored flower. (The species and sizes varied from prayerhouse to prayerhouse.) The higher central panel behind which the stand for the Bible is placed, features a scripture verse within an ornamental flower frame. Mottos or scripture verses, painted behind glass with brightly colored floral motifs, hang between white lace-curtained windows gleaming with cleanliness. The bright blue benches, the white walls and windows, the lace curtains and the colorful floral verses give the sanctuary the appearance of a *Grosse Stube* polished for Sunday guests.

During Sunday morning worship in June, 1991 the chancel of one such prayerhouse was further embellished with two vases of red peonies, found in nearly every flower garden of every village home. The integrity of the whole configuration—its suitedness to the creative ability, the economic constraints, the ideals of the community and the purpose of the religious service celebrated—constituted the beauty of the place.

If we take the flowers-within-borders motif, seen in the Orenburg prayerhouses, and follow it through a series of settings and functions in this Mennonite tradition, we may distinguish a clear pattern. Whether on dowry chests, clocks, wardrobes, cabinets, wall mottos or in the gardens of flowers between picket fences and houses, we witness a spatial, social and temporal framing of what we may call the sacred centers in the household, family, community and the individual life. These may be moments of transition essential to the long-term life of the social unit (such as the dowry), essential social actions in the community (such as hosting visitors), or auspicious locations in the physical layout of the family, household or congregation (the front yard or the face-to-face encounter).

This "floral framing" tradition may have existed in the early North American Plains Mennonite communities, although there are no records of the visual appearances of the interiors of the first prayerhouses. Wall mottos similar to those we saw in the Orenburg prayerhouses and homes were painted or embroidered and displayed in North American immigrant Mennonite homes. A few that have been preserved carry such verses as these: "*Herr, bleibe bei uns, denn es will Abend werden*" (Lord, abide with us, for it is becoming evening); "*Befiehl dem Herrn deine Wege und hoffe auf Ihn, Er wird's wohl machen*" (Commit your ways to the Lord and trust in Him, He will heal you); and "*Glaube, da Liebe; Wo Liebe, da Friede; Wo Friede, da Segen; Wo Segen, da Gott; Wo Gott, keine Noth*" (Where there is faith, there is love; in love, peace; in peace, blessing; in blessing, God; where God is, there is no want).

These examples help us understand the relationship between form, style and context in the exploration of the nature of a Mennonite aesthetic.

The Mennonite aesthetic is expressed in the interpretive rendering, the choice of emphasis and the use of the object particular to the Mennonite experience. It is not necessarily expressed in the formal style or form, which is usually like that of the common culture surrounding Mennonites.

The concept of order or *Ordnung* in the visual realm represents a pervasive aesthetic concept among Mennonites. When a room, house, barn, workshop, yard, village or field expresses *Ordnung*, it is considered beautiful. When "accurate" is the word used to praise Heinrich Rempel's craftsmanship, it means his work is perceived as beautiful because it is orderly. Descendants of Franz Adrian remembered and praised his orderly workshop. The collective farm worker and Mennonite pastor Penner in Zhdanovka used the word *Ordnung* again and again in our conversations, both in its social sense and in its physical sense. This emphasis on social and physical order was perceived by our Russian travel companion in the Orenburg region Mennonite villages as the single most distinguishing factor between Mennonite villages and Russian villages.

The Polish historian Mezynski conveys his insight into the Mennonite aesthetic, lying not in particular furnishings but rather in the overall presentation of the home, with these words:

> ...as regards house interiors, it was not different from average German houses, but when one looked at them closer, especially among the more orthodox families, one could see the avoidance of very fashionable wallpaper, furniture covering and even pictures in lighter and brighter colours. That, perhaps, gave their interiors a slightly sad look. They did not develop any art—their creed was a little afraid of that. The faces of the inhabitants of those houses reflected something like sadness but at the same time also cheerfulness...the favourable features prevailed: modesty, honesty, persistence and love of order.[8]

For the most part, the particular Mennonite tradition we have presented in this work could be linked to a particular style period—late baroque, rococo, neoclassical, middle class Biedermeier and Victorian. Stylistic forms were adopted from these eras of European art and architecture, carried along and used in a series of migrations and settlements. When the community moved into the North American Plains, the tradition was swept away both by the need to adapt to new political and cultural surroundings *and* by the new phenomenon of cheap mass-produced goods. New expressions of aesthetic sensibility needed to be worked out.

The Mennonite author, storyteller and filmmaker John Ruth, in his book *Mennonite Identity and Literary Art*, stresses the importance of the imagination in Mennonite art and identity.[9] He finds nothing in the theological underpinnings of Anabaptist–Mennonitism to thwart the use of the arts. Rather, he cites excuses and rationalizations for not exercising greater aesthetic imagination. Yet, he notes, Mennonite history is replete with instances of the artistic imagination in the service of distinctive Anabaptist values. Powerful stories have been told with hymns, books, oral traditions and such publishing efforts as the *Martyrs' Mirror*, which also was a massive effort at graphic representation of the Anabaptist–Mennonite story. He maintains that despite the relative control of the sensory in Mennonite and Amish life, especially among the plain groups, there are subtle expressions of beauty in fraktur writing, quilting, clothing and in the order and cleanliness of houses, barns and meetinghouses. There is, in fact, a strong "aesthetic of the plain."

Thus, Mennonite aesthetic identity is not expressed in a particular formal set of styles or objects. Rather, it is found in the use of the vernacular or the academic in ways that speak uniquely to the Mennonite experience and in the underlying tone and control of spatial and societal order, form, color, mood and, wherever possible, an association of sensory expression with a particular piety.

Appendix A

Mennonite Cabinetmakers and Painters

The Kauffman Museum inventory of Mennonite immigrant furniture often reveals the names of the craftsmen, cabinetmakers, carpenters and artists or itinerant painters who created or decorated the pieces. Only two women who painted woodwork and furniture have been discovered. In North America the men usually became farmers. In some cases they had worked exclusively as cabinetmakers in their homelands of Poland, Prussia and South Russia. Because they could no longer support themselves by cabinetmaking alone, they were forced to take up farming after immigration. Following is a list of the Mennonite cabinetmakers and painters known to the Kauffman Museum.

Johann Abrahams, table #15.019.

Anna Adrian Buller (1869-1927), Molotschna, South Russia to Buhler, Kansas. Decorative painting of father Franz Adrian's work. Also painted woodwork and walls in her own farm home. Chimney base cabinet #14.010 (KM 86.375.1), wardrobes #11.006, #11.015.

Bernhard Adrian (1907-1934), Buhler, Kansas. Bench #7.003.

Frank Adrian (1903-1926), Buhler, Kansas. Footstool #8.004, table #15.018.

Franz Adrian I (1836-1910), Molotschna Colony, South Russia to Buhler, Kansas. His grandfather Jacob Adrian (1801-1866) had come from West Prussia to settle in South Russia in 1839. Wardrobes #11.006, #11.015, glass cabinet #14.004 (KM 5894), chimney base cabinet #14.010 (KM 86.375.1), corner cabinet #14.014 (KM 5893).

Franz Adrian (1860-1946), Molotschna, South Russia to Buhler, Kansas. Footstool #8.003.

Jakob Adrian (1862-1958), Molotschna, South Russia to Buhler, Kansas. Footstool #8.002.

Jacob Adrian (1801-1866), son of farmers in Neu Marsau, apprenticed to Heinrich Foth in 1819, immigrated in 1839 to Molotschna Colony, South Russia.

John Albrecht, Volhynia to Turner County, South Dakota. Pull-out bed #17.005, table #15.011.

Peter Balzer, South Russia to Greenfield community, Goessel, Kansas. Doll cradle #18.025.

Franz Banman (1838-1926), South Russia to Goessel, Kansas. Cabinet or bookcase #14.027.

Heinrich Bartel, South Russia to Mountain Lake, Minnesota. Wardrobe #11.016, table #15.017, Heritage House Museum, Mountain Lake, Minnesota.

Abraham Becker, travel trunk #2.005, Adobe House Museum, Hillsboro, Kansas.

Benjamin Boese (1835-1918), South Russia to Goessel, Kansas. Doll cradle #18.015, bench #5.002, wardrobe #11.001, Mennonite Heritage Museum, Goessel, Kansas.

Jacob Buller (1827-1901), cradle #18.009, doll cradle #18.031.

Peter P. Buller, South Russia to Henderson, Nebraska. Bedside table #15.020, child's bed #17.007, cradle #18.030.

Aaron E. Claassen (1850-1929), Caldowe, West Prussia to Beatrice, Nebraska. 1869 wardrobe #11.032, table–bench combination.

Jacob J. Dick (died 1930), Molotschna, South Russia to Mountain Lake, Minnesota. Oval table #15.012.

Jacob J. Enns, Alexanderwohl community, Kansas. Doll or toy dowry chest, #1.053.

Cornelius Epp, Molotschna, South Russia to Henderson, Nebraska. Built-in wall cabinet #14.036.

Gerhard Esau (1876-1951), Samara Colony, Russia to Beatrice, Nebraska. Inlaid tables and carved animals, whereabouts unknown.[1] Carved and painted dogs and blue heron, #153, #154, #155.

Herman J. Fast (1886-1948), Molotschna, South Russia to Mountain Lake, Minnesota. Chest of drawers #12.001.

Rev. Abraham W. Friesen (1891-1987), Beatrice, Nebraska. Miniature sleeping bench #6.005. He also built 40 "grandfather" clocks and at least 10 wall clocks, presumably from kits.[2]

Cornelius Friesen (1771 Prussian census), Tiegenhof, cabinetmaker.

Jacob Friesen (1771 Prussian census), Tiegenhof, cabinetmaker.

Jacob Friesen (1833-1909), Schoenfeld, Molotschna, South Russia to Butterfield, Minnesota. Measurements for an 1866 wardrobe given in diary, table #15.015.

J.J. Friesen, Hillsboro community, Kansas. Commode chair #9.009, Adobe House Museum (60.4.142).

Nicolas Friesen (1771 Prussian census), Einlage, cabinetmaker.

John N. Funk, Bruderthal community, Hillsboro, Kansas. Wardrobe #11.017.

Johann "Hansul" Goering, Volhynia to Freeman, South Dakota. Upholstered armchairs #9.014, #9.015 and upholstered daybed #10.001 in the Heritage Hall Museum, Freeman, South Dakota. Loveseat and chair #9.016 a and b, china cabinet #14.049.

Jacob Harder (1849-1937), Neumuensterberg, West Prussia to Whitewater community, Kansas. Reportedly made beds, wardrobe, table, benches. Whereabouts not known.[3]

Jacob Harms (died ca.1922), South Russia to Gnadenau, Kansas. Two paintings, Adobe House Museum, Hillsboro, Kansas.

Wilhelm Harms (1839-1915), Morgenau, South Russia to Hillsboro, Kansas. Furniture and decorative paintings, whereabouts not known.

"Mr." Harms painted wardrobe #11.007 (KM 89.53.1) and chest #1.065 in the Inman, Kansas area after 1900. A "Mr." Harms also reportedly painted in the Henderson area after 1900. Glass cabinet #14.046. In *The Life and Times of Emil Kym*, Steve Friesen describes an itinerant painter by the name of Harms.

Klaas Hiebert (1834-1920), Lichtfelde, Molotschna, South Russia to Mountain Lake, Minnesota—carpenter, dyer and farmer.

Chair #9.017; wardrobe #11.031 at the Center for Mennonite Brethren Studies, Fresno, California; wardrobe #11.034; probably wardrobes #11.011, #11.025; dresser #12.014; cabinet #14.060; table #15.030; and bed #17.019.

Anton Hoeppner (1771 Prussian census), Alt Schottland, painter.

Isaac Kauenhoven (1771 Prussian census), Koenigsberg, painter.

Jacob Kauffman, Volhynia to Freeman, South Dakota. Cradle #18.003 (KM 2263).

Peter Klaassen, resting bench (*Ruhebank*) #5.004 (KM 1970).

Abraham Kliewer (1771 Prussian census), Tiegenhof, painter.

Emil Kym (1862-1918), Switzerland to Goessel and Buhler, Kansas. Decorative painter who taught Anna Adrian Buller. Probably painted dowry chest #1.013.

Jacob Loewen, cradle #18.010.

Jacob Lohrentz (1851-1919), Elisabethal, Molotschna, South Russia to rural Moundridge, Kansas. Wardrobe #11.010 (KM 89.42.2).

Gerhard Nickel (1855-1935), son of Johann Nickel, Fuerstenau, Molotschna, South Russia to Bruderthal community near Hillsboro, Kansas, cabinetmaker. Wardrobe #11.004, wardrobe #11.021, cupboard #14.006.

Heinrich Nickel, brother of Gerhard Nickel, Molotschna, South Russia to Bruderthal community near Hillsboro, Kansas. Fern stand, hanging shelves #14.015.

Johann Nickel, father of Gerhard and Heinrich, Molotschna, South Russia to Bruderthal–Alexanderwohl, Kansas. Cupboard #14.006.

Aron Olfert (1832-1917), Fuerstenau, Molotschna, South Russia to Bruderthal community near Hillsboro, Kansas. He came to North America with the Nickels and lived with or near the Nickel families from time to time. He was a full-time cabinetmaker and painter, both in South Russia and later in Kansas. His mother was Elizabeth Nickel Olfert. He never married. He was known in the Bruderthal community as "Tischler." His painted graining was fairly crude. Boxes #4.001, #4.002, #4.003, #4.004, #4.005; doll cupboard #14.011, tables #15.001, #15.002, #15.003, #15.004, #15.005, #15.008; desks #16.001, #16.004; and doll cradles #18.014, #18.019.

David Penner, Paulsheim, South Russia to Inman, Kansas. Chair #9.007. He is said to have made more chairs.

Jacob J. Peters, Nikolaithal, Molotschna, South Russia to Henderson, Nebraska to Alta Loma, California. Dowry chest #1.054; small dowry chest #1.055; footstools #8.005, #8.006; and handkerchief box #4.012.

Heinrich Rempel (1849-1902), Lichtfelde, South Russia to Henderson, Nebraska. Wardrobes #11,023, #11.030; china cabinets #14.043, #14.045, built-in wall cabinet #14.044; and painted box #4.011.

Rudolph Riesen (1821-1891), Elbing, West Prussia to Berdjansk, South Russia in 1847 to Marion County, Kansas in 1876. Sleeping bench #6.006 (KM).

Jakob S. Schmidt, cradle #18.008.

David Schroeder, bench #7.002 and bookcase #14.040.

Heinrich Schroeder (1825-1903), Molotschna, South Russia to Goessel, Kansas. Dowry chests #1.016, #1.017; resting bench #5.006; wardrobe #11.012; china cabinet #14.005; tables #15.003, #15.006, #15.016; child's folding bed #17.002; and cradle #18.049.

Henry J. Schroeder, cradle #18.001.

Heinrich Schultz, Volhynia, table #15.007.

Heinrich Sommerfeld (1846-1921), Molotschna, South Russia to Goessel, Kansas. Doll cradle #18.017.

Jacob Thieleman (1771 Prussian census) Schidlitz, painter.

Reverend Dirk Tieszen, South Russia to Freeman, South Dakota. Wardrobe #11.013, Heritage Hall Museum, Freeman, South Dakota.

Peter Unrau (1824-1915), Liebenau, South Russia to Alexanderwohl community, Kansas, minister and cabinetmaker. Table #15.022.

John A. Unruh, cradle #18.007.

Gerhard Rombout Uylenburg (died 1601), royal cabinetmaker to King Sigismund III of Poland. Father of Rombert and Hendrik Uylenburg, both of whom were painters.

Peter Vogt, Molotschna, South Russia to Inman, Kansas. Desk #16.002.

Abraham Walcke (1771 Prussian census), Tiegenhof, painter.

Abraham K. Wall (1860-1932), Molotschna, South Russia to rural Hillsboro, Marion County, Kansas. Doll cradle #18.023, rocking chair with mail order parts from *Sears & Roebuck* #9.003.

Heinrich Warkentin, South Russia to Mountain Lake, Minnesota. Cupboard #14.020.

Jacob B. Warkentin, Molotschna, South Russia to Mountain Lake, Minnesota. Cradle #18.011.

Heinrich H. Wiebe, emigrated through Asia from Prussia to Whitewater, Kansas. Travel chest #2.027.

Jacob Wiebe, West Prussia to rural Whitewater, Kansas. Cabinet #14.017.

"Widow Wiens" (1771 Prussian census), Marienburg, painter.

Appendix B

Kauffman Museum Inventory of Mennonite Immigrant Furniture in Public Collections

The following list represents the inventory which formed the basis of our study. The number behind each category of furniture [for example, dowry chest (1.001-1.072)] indicates the total in the inventory. Thus, 72 dowry chests have been studied. Items housed in public museums are identified by location in the following list. Privately owned items are not listed.

Kauffman Museum, Bethel College, North Newton, Kansas
Mennonite Heritage Museum, Goessel, Kansas
Adobe House Museum, Hillsboro, Kansas
Heritage Hall Museum, Freeman, South Dakota
Heritage House Museum, Mountain Lake, Minnesota
Mennonite Heritage Village, Steinbach, Manitoba
Mennonite Library and Archives, Bethel College
Tabor College Historical Society, Hillsboro, Kansas
Center for Mennonite Brethren Studies, Fresno, California

Chests, Trunks and Boxes

1. Dowry chests (1.001-1.072)
   Kauffman Museum: 007, 025, 026, 031.
   Mennonite Library and Archives: 010.
   Adobe House Museum: 001.
   Mennonite Heritage Museum: 002, 003, 004, 030.
   Heritage Hall Museum: 041.
   Heritage House Museum: 044, 046.
   Mennonite Heritage Village: 047, 048.

2. Travel trunks (2.001-2.048)
   Kauffman Museum: 013, 019, 024, 025, 026.
   Adobe House Museum: 003, 004, 005, 006.
   Tabor College Historical Society: 009, 016.
   Mennonite Heritage Museum: 007, 008, 010, 011, 012.
   Heritage Hall Museum: 034, 036.
   Heritage House Museum: 037, 038.

3. Wicker trunks (3.001-3.009)
   Kauffman Museum: 005, 006.
   Adobe House Museum: 002.

4. Boxes (4.001-4.012)
   Kauffman Museum: 007.

Benches, Stools, Chairs and Sofas

5. Resting benches (5.001-5.013)
   Kauffman Museum: 004, 005.
   Adobe House Museum: 003.
   Mennonite Heritage Museum: 002.
   Heritage Hall Museum: 007.
   Heritage House Museum: 008.
   Mennonite Heritage Village: 011, 012, 013.

6. Sleeping benches (6.001-6.024)
   Kauffman Museum: 006.
   Adobe House Museum: 001, 002.
   Mennonite Heritage Museum: 004.
   Heritage House Museum: 007, 008, 020.
   Mennonite Heritage Village: 021, 022, 023.

7. Benches (7.001-7.007)
   Mennonite Heritage Museum: 001.
   Heritage Hall Museum: 006.
   Heritage House Museum: 007.

8. Stools (8.001-8.006)

9. Chairs (9.001-9.018)
   Kauffman Museum: 001, 002, 003.
   Adobe House Museum: 009.
   Mennonite Heritage Museum: 005.
   Heritage Hall Museum: 011, 012, 013, 014, 015.
   Heritage House Musuem: 008.

10. Couch/sofa/divan (10.001-10.004)
    Heritage Hall Museum: 001, 002, 003.

Cabinets

11. Wardrobes (11.001-11.034)
    Kauffman Museum: 005, 006, 007, 008, 009, 010.
    Adobe House Museum: 003.
    Heritage Hall Museum: 013.
    Heritage House Museum: 016.
    Mennonite Heritage Village: 027, 028, 029.
    Center for Mennonite Brethren Studies: 031.

12. Dressers or chests-of-drawers (12.001-12.014)
    Kauffman Museum: 005.
    Heritage Hall Museum: 007, 008, 009, 010.
    Heritage House Museum: 011.

13. Washstands or dry sinks (13.001-13.004)
    Kauffman Museum: 004.
    Adobe House Museum: 002.
    Heritage Hall Museum: 003.

14. Cupboards, cabinets and shelves (14.001-14.060)
    Kauffman Museum: 004, 009, 010, 014, 029, 038, 039, 040.
    Adobe House Museum: 002, 007, 008, 012, 013.
    Mennonite Heritage Museum: 003.
    Heritage Hall Museum: 030, 031.
    Heritage House Museum: 018, 019, 020.
    Mennonite Heritage Village: 052, 053, 054, 056.

Tables and Desks

15. Tables (15.001-15.031)
    Kauffman Museum: 010, 011.
    Adobe House Museum: 002, 003, 009, 013.
    Heritage House Museum: 017.
    Mennonite Heritage Village: 027.

16. Desks (16.001-16.006)
    Kauffman Museum: 002.

Beds and Cradles

17.Beds (17.001-17.020)
Kauffman Museum: 004, 005, 006.
Adobe House Museum: 003, 012.
Mennonite Heritage Museum: 002.
Heritage Hall Museum: 010.
Mennonite Heritage Village: 015, 016, 017.

18.Cradles (18.001-18.049)
Kauffman Museum: 001, 002, 003, 004, 021, 022, 026, 036.
Adobe House Museum: 005, 010, 018.
Mennonite Heritage Museum: 006, 007, 008, 009, 015, 016, 017.
Heritage Hall Museum: 013, 040.
Heritage House Museum: 027, 028, 038, 039.
Mennonite Heritage Village: 042, 043, 044, 047.

Timekeeping Devices

19.Clocks (19.001-19.031)
Kauffman Museum: 022, 023.
Adobe House Museum: 009, 011.
Mennonite Heritage Museum: 007.

Appendix C

Jacob Adrian's Recipes

Jacob Adrian's recipes for paints, stains and polishes were written consecutively on 15 pages in a notebook which he began in 1819 in West Prussia and which ended with his death in 1866 in South Russia.[1]

Adrian may well have copied his recipes from an eighteenth century printed book. Helmut Ottenjann suggested that there are similarities between Jacob Adrian's recipes and those used by the eighteenth century furniture painter Johann Arndt Mueller (active in the area of Osnabrueck). Mueller's recipes were taken from printed sources.[2] The following pages from Jacob Adrian's diary were transcribed by Helmut Ottenjann and translated by Hilda Voth.

Staining furniture red:

Take ¼ pound *Fernamback* wood shavings, 2 lots [one lot = 10 grams] cream of tartar crystals and 2 lots alum. Soak these three ingredients in good wine vinegar 2 to 3 days. Then cook for half an hour, sieve it through cloth and keep it in a glass. If you add 1 or 2 lots of cochineal [dye from an insect] the color will be intensified and be more durable. With the help of a [sponge?, tool?] apply this stain onto the white, clean wood, for example elm, acorn, birch, and similar woods, polish it later in a way stated following.

On fir wood you should take ½ pound *Fernamback* wood, ¼ pound *Basilicum* shavings [Brazil nut?] and let them cook in wine vinegar for a quarter of an hour. Before applying it you should add 2 lots of alum water. Also you should give the wood a rubbing with alum before brushing on the stain. Put several coats of stain on and polish it after each coat.

To stain furniture yellow:

One takes saffron, mixes it well in a mortar, about 1 *Quentchen* [gram?] to one penny's worth of dye, and then pour strong pure rye whiskey or *spiritus* wine on it and let it evaporate for 12 hours.

This fine yellow extract should be applied several times with a brush depending on how light or how dark a person wants the furniture. When this is lacquered with amber, this stain will last a long, long time [literal translation: "will be of the most beautiful endurance"].

How to stain furniture black:

Mix ½ pound nitric acid with 12 pound well water and stir it once in a while. Divide it into small portions that are convenient to use. During the time this goes on the jar has to be left open because this nitric acid water gets very hot. After it has all dissolved and after it has cooled off, the jar should be sealed with a wax cork. When staining furniture black you have to give it a heavy coat of this first, then let it dry. This way the molten magma has been dissolved. Then before finishing, add 8 lots oak [?] apple juice, add ½ measurement wine, let it cook slowly and then let it get clear. When the above stain is dry, turn the wood and brush it on again on the other side. Keep this up until the furniture is black enough. Then the furniture should be lacquered.

How to paint gun shafts brownish red:

Take seaweed roots, pulverize them and cook a certain portion of them with linseed oil. Rub either old or new shaft with this, but it must be one that has been rubbed clean first.

Advice on polishing furniture:

1. To wax furniture:
Mama usually got her own wax, sometimes with a lot of effort. She took half of a coarse wool cloth and put a glob of wax on it that had been worked to soft stage. Put it on the furniture keeping it all even. For the last part, melt 3 lots of wax in hot water. Then 1 lot *Sal Tartari* and keep stirring until it is right for polishing. This will make it bright and shiny. It will last year after year and it will make the furniture last longer.

2. Furniture with Turpentine Varnish is done in the following way:
Take 8 lots of turpentine oil, keep away from fire because it ignites very easily. but do let it get a bit warm. Put rosin in a glass container until it is completely melted. Add the turpentine and stir hard. This is very effective on soft wood.

How to make a very durable mahogany stain:

Take wood that is to be stained and clean and smooth it with shave-grass and pumice-stone.

Rub it all over with saltpeter and let it dry. Then put 3 lots of thin dragon blood into a half quart of alcohol and a lot of soda salt. Then filter it after it has thoroughly dissolved. Now brush it on the wood with a coarse stiff brush. Then let it get dry enough for all the liquid to soak in, and then let it dry well. Also, melt in a half a quart of alcohol, 3 lots of shellac, and let melt ½ lot of soda salt. Brush this mixture on, like the first time, with the grain of wood. Later when the surface of the wood is dry, polish it with a piece of beechwood which has been allowed to soak in linseed oil. In this way one can give any kind of wood that is used for furniture the color and gloss of mahogany, especially nut and pear trees.

A scarlet red stain:

Pour into a well glazed pot ½ quart of shavings. Scatter in a handful of ground up...lime, stir diligently then pour the clear part that has dissolved over 4 lots of ground up Brazil nut wood. Heat over a low fire until it has cooked down to half. Then it is ready to stain, going over the wood several times, and it should be used while it is still warm and then with ½ lot, dissolved in a little water. *Fernamback* wood should be brushed [with this solution] at most twice, but that has to be done quickly.

How to get a red stain to the wood:

Take one piece [pound?] of yellow wood, one lot dry Orlean [wood] (annatto), 3 lots *Fevarbuk* [Fermebuck, see Kruenitz] 4 lots potash. Put it all together in a well glazed pot. Pour 1½ measurements of water on it and leave it well covered for several days. Then when you want to use it, put the pot on the fire, let the mixture boil for half an hour. Then pour the liquid through a cloth. Brush the wood several times with this. Then pour the liquid through a cloth. Brush the wood several times with this. Then as long as it stays damp go over it with alum-water which has been prepared with 4 lots alum and a quart of water. The wood will turn to a lasting red color from this mixture. Or if you wish to get a light red stain, take 1 piece of Brazil wood and 2 lots clean potash and one measurement of water. Then treat it as it is described above, and finally pour alum water over it.

For staining wood green:

To 9 lots of French *verdigris* [copper acetate] pour $\frac{1}{8}$ quart wine vinegar and 2 spoons urine and let it stand covered for several days until it is clear. Then brush the wood with this. Or you can dissolve distilled *verdigris* in water, or even better, with a grinding stone and pestle which is faster, and brush it on the wood when warm.

A blue stain:

Allow *verdigris* [copper acetate] to dissolve either in water or in wine vinegar. Brush the wood a few times with this, then go over it with a potash solution that is made of 4 lots cleaned potash and $\frac{1}{4}$ quart water. Keep brushing it on until it gets a blue tint.

Making imitation ebony wood with stain:

For this only take hard and smooth woods such as birch and nut tree wood which are especially suitable for this. The stain is made as follows: Take Brazil nut wood shavings, let them cook in hot water until the water is like [?], then throw in a small piece of alum, let it simmer for a few mintues. Apply this warm stain to the wood and brush it on. When after repeated applications of this mixture the stain is sufficiently soaked in take a brush dipped in vinegar and remove the foam.

To make a polish:

Take 3 lots of spar vanish, 2 lots nut oil. Let the spar varnish soften in alcohol, then polish the wood with it.

A furniture polish that can be used on any kind of wood. Take $\frac{3}{4}$ quart *spiritus* wine, 8 lots yellow spar varnish, $\frac{1}{2}$ lot *Gami Elnai,* 1 lot dissolved *capal,* 1 lot turpentine, $\frac{3}{4}$ lot nut oil. Mix these together in a bottle and place it in warm sand or close to a warm stove. Let it stand, stir it often, and wait for it to dissolve. Then pour this clear colored polish into another bottle. The first bottle has to be bound with a rag so it does not get too hot or it will crack.

Notes for Text

Themes in the Interpretation of an Immigrant Tradition

1. Cornelius J. Dyck, ed. *Introduction to Mennonite History* (Scottdale, Pa.: Herald Press, 1967).
2. William R. Estep, *Revolution within the Revolution* (Grand Rapids: Eerdmans, 1990).
3. Jean-Louis Flandrin, *Families in Former Times* (Cambridge: Cambridge University Press, 1979), 92.
4. Edward Shils, *Tradition* (Chicago: University of Chicago Press, 1981) offers a theoretical background for the notion "tradition."

   D. Loewenthal, *The Past Is a Foreign Country* (New York: Cambridge University Press, 1985) has used the concept in charting the historian's task.

   Jan Vansina, *Paths in the Rainforests: Toward a History of Political Tradition in Equatorial Africa* (Madison: University of Wisconsin Press, 1990), 257-60, has applied the notion very imaginatively to language, socio-political, economic and archaeological (material cultural) indices in the western Bantu region of Equatorial Africa.
5. Michael Bird and Terry Kobayashi, *A Splendid Harvest: Germanic Folk and Decorative Arts in Canada* (Toronto: Van Nostrand Reinhold Ltd., 1981).

   Nancy-Lou Patterson, *Swiss-German and Dutch-German Mennonite Traditional Art in the Waterloo Region, Ontario* (Ottawa: National Museum of Man, 1979).

   The Language of Paradise: Folk Art from Mennonite and Other Anabaptist Communities of Ontario (London, Ont.: London Regional Art Gallery, 1985).

Chapter One

1. J.J. Friesen describing his family's first home in Nebraska, from an unpublished manuscript. Printed in *From Holland to Henderson*, Stanley Voth, ed. (Henderson, Neb.: Henderson Centennial Committee, 1975), 42.
2. Charles van Ravensway, *The Arts and Architecture of German Settlements in Missouri* (Columbia and London: University of Missouri Press, 1977).

   Cecilia Steinfeldt and Donald Lewis Stover, *Early Texas Furniture and Decorative Arts* (Trinity University Press, San Antonio Museum Association, 1974).
3. Flandrin, *Families*, 92-111.
4. Some examples of these sources include: a 1748 estate settlement in the Vistula Delta in Horst Penner, *Die ost- und westpreussischen Mennoniten:1526-1772* (Weierhof: Mennonitisches Geschichtes Verein, 1978), 410-12; a 1790 settlement of a modest estate in central Poland of an emigre from the Delta, from archival records identified by Woijech Marchlewski, 1990; an 1855 eye witness account of a well-to-do home in the Ukrainian Mennonite colony of Molotschna in Alexander Petzholdt, *Reise im westlichen und suedlichen europaeischen Russland im Jahre 1855* (Leipzig: Herman Fries, 1864), 151-53; a Canadian Mennonite author's reminiscences of the rooms in the Mennonite house of his early 20th century childhood in Russia in A. Dyck, *Verloren in der Steppe* (Steinbach, Man.: Personal printing, 1944), 5-50; and an account entitled "Furniture" by a well-known Mennonite historian, C. Krahn, *Mennonite Encyclopedia*, II (Scottdale, Pa.: Mennonite Publishing House, 1956), 424-6.
5. J.J. Friesen in *From Holland to Henderson*, 42.
6. H. Worrall, "How the Mennonites Warm Their Houses and Cook with Straw as Fuel," *American Agriculturalist* (1878), 472-3.
7. Personal communication with Dale Schrag and Martha Lepp, July 1991. Kauffman Museum Inventory #9.018.
8. Translated in *Liebe Geschwister II* (1880-1893) by Louis A. Janzen, ed., (Personal printing, 1979), 267.
9. Flandrin, *Families*, 92-102.
10. Flandrin, *Families*, 98-102.
11. *From Holland to Henderson*, 23.
12. Ethel Abrahams interview with Marie Harms Berg, age 88, Parkside Homes, Hillsboro, Kansas, April 18, 1989.
13. N.J. Kroeker, *First Mennonite Villages in Russia, 1789-1943*, 104, Men-

nonite Library and Archives, Bethel College, North Newton, Kan. (hereafter cited as MLA).
14. Peter P. Buller and J.J. Friesen made such chamber pot chairs or stools around 1890, Kauffman Museum inventory #8.001 and #9.009 respectively.
15. Noble L. Prentis, *Kansas Miscellanies* (Topeka, Kan: Topeka Publishing House, 1889), 16.
16. Letter from Helen Mierau Swisher, January 5, 1991.
17. Letter from Jacob E. Friesen, age 84, Hague, Saskatchewan, September 24, 1990.
18. Interview, July 1990.
19. Worrall, "How the Mennonites," 472.
20. The chest was purchased from the family before 1920 by Herman K. Ediger who gave it to the present owner.
21. Personal communication with Agnes Dalke Bryan, June 28, 1990.
22. Letter from Agnes Dalke Bryan, 1990.
23. Ingeborg Weber-Kellerman, *Die Deutsche Familie* (Frankfurt am Main: Suhrkamp, 1974), 197.
24. Doris Janzen Longacre, "A chest, a train, a blizzard and some zwieback," *On the Line* (February 20, 1977).
25. Personal communication with Arthur Kroeger, March, 1991.
26. Interview with Don Huebert, Henderson, Nebraska, July, 1990.
27. In Canada wall-hung pendulum clocks continued to be built by a Mennonite immigrant clockmaker from South Russia.
28. "The Reverend Peter Unrau Genealogy Booklet," unpublished manuscript, 13. Courtesy of Dale Schrag.
29. Letter from Kevin Enns-Rempel, Center for Mennonite Brethren Studies, Fresno, California, October 31, 1990.
30. Marie Voth, "My Great-Grandfather's House," unpublished manuscript, 1959, MLA.

Chapter Two

1. Translation provided by Peter Klassen, Fresno, California, from his research in the Gdansk State Archives, Poland.
2. Arkadiusz Rybak, "Mennonites of the Netherlands in the Vistula Marshland," *Stowrzyszenie Rozwoju Zulaw* (Marshland Development Association Newsletter, Special Edition, July 29, 1987).
3. Cornelius Bergmann,"Das Haus der Urahne," unpublished manuscript, 1907, MLA.
4. Museum exhibits at Gdynia-Oliva, a suburb of Gdansk, and at the Torun Ethnographic Museum show the Kashubian way of life.
5. Rybak, "Mennonites."
6. In conversations with Heinrich Dirks and Jakob Friesen of the settlement of Zhdanovka in the Orenburg Oblast, USSR, in June, 1991, a *Plautdietsch* expression for something that is hastily put together is said to be "Kashubsh." Heard in a colony of Chortitza origin, this would indicate that the expression dates from before 1789, when emigres left the Vistula Delta of North Poland or Prussia. Of more systematic influence upon *Plautdietsch* is the Kashubian phoneme "tj" or "kj" as in *Tjorschemoos*, cherry moos.

   See also Jack Thiessen, "A New Look at an Old Problem: Origins of the Variations in Mennonite *Plautdietsch*," *Mennonite Quarterly Review* (October 1989): 285-296.
7. *Gruenwald in the Memory of the Polish People* (The Gruenwald Social Committee, not dated).
8. Kazimierz Mezynski, *From the History of Mennonites in Poland* (Warszawa: Akademia Rolnicza w Warszawie, 1975), 10-14.
9. See for example Cornelius Neufeldt's drawing of the Marienburg in his arithmetic text, Schoenhorst, West Prussia, 1831-1832, Mennonite Heritage Center, Hillsboro, Kansas. Published in Ethel Abrahams, *Frakturmalen und Schonschreiben*, ill. 91, (1980), 58.
10. Hans Woede, *Alte doerfliche Baukultur in Ostpreussen* (Glueckstadt: Ostpreussisches Landesmuseum, 1980), 12-13.
11. *Die Hanse: Lebenswirklichkeit und Mythos*, Vol. I (Hamburg: Museums fuer Hamburgische Geschichte, 1989), 63-65.

12.Alphonse Verheyden, *Le martyrologie protestant des pays-bas du Sud au XVe siecle* (Bruxelles: Editions de la Librarie des Eclaireurs Unionistes, 1960).

13.*Die Hanse*, Vol. I, 273.

14.Jan Bialostocki, "Die Jagiellonen-Renaissance" and Adam Milobedzki, "Architektur in Polen zur Zeit der Jagiellonen," *Polen im Zeitalter der Jagiellonen 1386-1572* (Schallaburg: Exhibition Catalogue, 1986), 103-111, 112-129.

15.Jan Bialostocki, "Rembrandt's 'Eques Polonus'," *Oud Holland*, LXXXIV (1969), 163-176.

16.*Preussen: Versuch einer Bilanz* (Exhibit catalogue, Berliner Festspiele GMBH, 1981).

17.Ulrich Tolksdorf, "Die Mundarten Danzigs und seines Umlandes," *Danzig in acht Jahrhunderten* (Muenster–Westfalen: Nicolaus Copernicus Verlag, 1985), 313-336.

18.Thiessen, "A New Look," 293.

Cornelius Krahn, "Poland," *Mennonite Encyclopedia* IV (Scottdale, Pa.: Mennonite Publishing House, 1959), 200.

Chapter Three

1. So claims Penner, *Die ost- und west*, 38, 81ff, although Edmund Kizik says there is no verification for this.

2. *Mennonitisches Lexicon* I (Frankfurt am Main: Heinrich Schneider, 1913), 549.

3. Krystyna Mellin, "The cabinetmakers guild in Gdansk in the late middle ages," *Gdanska Studia Muzealne* (Muzeum Narodowe w Gdansku, 1976), 71-84, ill. 267-272.

Krystyna Mellin, "The Gdansk carpenters' and wood-carvers' guild from the middle of the XVIe to the middle of the XVIIe century," *Gdanskie Studia Muzealne* (Muzeum Narodowe w Gdansku, 1978), 49-64, ill. 225-236.

4. See example, "Geschichte u. Landeskunde Ost-Mitteleuropas, No. 3," published in Herbert Wiebe, *Das Siedlungswerk niederlaendischer Mennoniten im Weicheltal zwischen Fordon u. Weissenberg bis zum Ausgang des 18. Jahrhunderts* (Marburg: Wissenschaftliche Beitraege 2, 1952) which is like the example in the Gdansk Art Museum.

5. Nils Claussen, "Der Einfluss hollaendischer Bauweise auf Friedrichstadt," unpublished manuscript (Friedrichstadt Archives, Wissenschaftliche Hausarbeit fuer den ersten Abschnitt des Staatsexamens fuer des Lehramt an Realschulen, 1977).

6. Pictured in Penner, *Die ost- und west*, plate.

7. *Mennonitisches Lexicon* I.

8. Depicted in Wiebe, *Siedlungswerk*.

9. Interviews with historian Edmund Kizik, Gdansk, November 1989.

10.Lecture by Jeremy Bangs at Kauffman Museum, North Newton, Kan., spring 1990.

11.See for example Jerry Dick, *The Russian Mennonite House-Barn of Manitoba: A Study in Cultural Transformations* (Waterloo, Ont.: University of Waterloo, M.A. Thesis, 1984).

Penner, *Die ost- und west*, plate.

12.Woede, *Alte doerfliche Baukultur*, 12-13.

13.Edmund Kizik has defined this so-called "*emphyteutic*" arrangement as a "*gruppenweiser Erbpacht beruhende Siedlungsweise*" (group inheritable rent settlement form) in his article "Die Mennoniten Westpreussens unter Friederich dem Grossen," *Friedericische Miniaturen 1. Forschungen u. Studien zur Friedericizanischen Zeit, Bd. II*, J. Ziechmann, ed. (Bremen, 1988), 24.

14.J. Heise, *Die Bau- und Kunstdenkmaeler der Provinz Westpreussen, Bd. I* (Danzig, 1884-87), 1-4.

Bernhard Schmidt, *Die Bau und Kunstdenkmaler des Kreises Marienburg I: Die Staedte Neuteich und Tiegenhof und die landliche Ortschaften* (Danzig, 1919).

Otto Kloeppel, "Die bauerliche Haus-, Hof- und Siedlungsanlage im Weichsel-Nogat-Delta," *Das Weichsel-Nogat-Delta: Beitraege zur Geschichte seiner landschaftlichen Entwicklung, vorgeschichtlichen, Besiedlung und bauerlichen Haus- und Hofanlage* (Danzig, 1924).

Pauls Kundzins, "Zur Einordnung einiger Bauernhaustypen Westpreussens in die Volksbaukunst der Ostseelaender," *Contributions of Baltic University*, No. 58 (Pinneberg, 1949).

Jerzy Stankiewiez, "Zabytki Budownictwa i Architektury na Zulawach,"

Rocznik Gdanski, xv, xvi (1956-7).

Woede, *Alte doerfliche Baukultur.*

15.Heise, *Bau- und Kunstdenkmaeler* has an interesting floorplan drawing of a T-shaped longhouse of this type built in 1844 by village elder Ediger in Zwanzigerweide, 326, ill. 99.

16.Schmidt's type II (a&b) corresponds to Stankiewicz's I,II,III (after Kloeppel) and is called *typy zulawskich domow podcieniowyeh*. Schmidt recognizes type I by the arcade facing the street and the farm of modest means. Schmidt's IIa and Stankiewicz–Kloeppel type II-III simply add rooms on one or both sides and run the roof perpendicular to the road and back axis.

17.This may be demonstrated by historic houses in the Open Air Museums of Arnhem in The Netherlands and Cloppenburg in North Germany.

18.Penner, *Die ost- und west*, 410-412.

19.Wiebe, *Siedlungswerk*, 13-14.

20.Bergmann, "Das Haus," notes from a 1907 visit to the home his parents had left in the Heubuden community fifty years earlier. Authors' translation.

21.Penner, *Die ost- und west*, 414-68.

22.Petzholdt, *Reise*, 185.

23.Genealogy from Walter Adrian, Prussian census of 1772 as given in Penner, *Die ost- und west*, 417.

24.Jacob Adrian diary, MLA.

25.Reinhild Kauenhoven Janzen, "Sources and Styles of the Material Culture Life of Mennonites in the Vistula Delta," *Mennonite Quarterly Review*, forthcoming.

26.James Urry, *None but Saints: The Transformation of Mennonite Life in Russia 1789-1889* (Winnipeg: Hyperion Press, 1989) details the profound institutional transformation in Mennonite society resulting from these conditions.

Chapter Four

1. Vistula Delta dialect around 1860 by Robert Dorr in Tolksdorf, "Die Mundarten," 333. Translation by Louis A. Janzen.

2. Freiherrn von Reiswitz and Friedrich Wadzeck, *Glaubensbekenntniss der Mennoniten u. Nachricht von ihren Colonien* (Berlin: August Ruecker, 1824), 330.

3. Jack Goody, Joan Thirsk and Eric P. Thompson, eds., *Family and Inheritance* (Cambridge: Cambridge University Press, 1976).

4. The Declaration of Edicts of 30 July 1789 and 12 February 1792 by Friedrich Wilhelm, King of Prussia, spelled out the restrictions on Mennonites who sought to obtain additional land. Any Mennonite who served a term in the military was automatically exempted from these restrictions.

Reiswitz and Wadzeck, *Glaubensbekenntniss*, 208-12.

5. Penner, *Die ost- und west*, 417-467.

6. Reiswitz and Wadzeck, *Glaubensbekenntniss*, 332-3.

7. Curators at Elblag emphasized that the city had a long tradition and wide reputation for its production of inlaid furniture, extending to at least the 17th century when the influence of British inlaid furniture was strong because of trade relations with England. Generally they held that inlaid furniture such as the Vistula Delta chest type dates to the 18th century, whereas the painted variation of the type is more recent. Bun or ball feet were customary for chests in the 18th century, part of "high" or urban tradition, whereas the five-footed pedestals reflect an influence of folk culture and were sometimes a more recent replacement for broken ball feet. The curators said the metal hardware was produced in Elblag. Personal communication with Krystina Laskowska and Maria Kwiatkowska, November 6, 1989.

8. The collections in the National Museum of Gdansk, the museum at Elblag, the furniture collection in the historical museum in the town hall of Torun and the Museum of Kwydzin (Marienwerder) all contain dowry chests of the very same type. Such a chest was also seen in 1989 in the corner of the amber shop at the Malbork (Marienburg) Castle. A chest very similar to the Sara Schulz chest in Kansas was displayed in a corridor of the City Hall of Gdansk.

9. See Mellin,"Cabinetmakers guild," "Gdansk carpenters' and wood-carvers' guild" and her publication "Marquetries from Torun in the collection of the Torun Museum" (Torun: Torun Ethnographic Museum, 1956).

10.Ernest G. Claassen, *Abraham Claassen: Vistula to Plum Grove* (Whitewater: Private printing, 1975) 16-17. There is no proof that this was Sara's chest other than the circumstance that no other person in the extended Abraham Claassen family of the immigrant generation bore the initials SS and the chest was stored in the attic of the Abraham Claassen family home.

11. A chest (inventory #1.047) in the Mennonite Heritage Village in Steinbach has a maker's signature and date on the inside of the lid: "*Anno 1848 Maerz N.24 verfertigt von Jacob Wall N Dorff*" (Made by Jacob Wall in March of the year 1848). "N.24" may indicate the number within a series of chests. "N Dorff" may be the abbreviation for Neuendorf near Gdansk, or Neuendorf in South Russia. Also an inlaid chest in a private collection (inventory #1.038) is marked on the bottom: "*C. Claassen Ww Anno 1819 No.2 Caldowe*" (C. Claassen Widow, the year 1819, number 2, Caldowe).

12. Indeed, we noted at least five painted chests of exactly this type in Polish collections. Painted chests in the "Krebsfelde" style in Polish collections: The Ethnographic Museum at Oliwa–Gdansk, MNG/E/4597 (dated 1879, initials R.S.), MNG/E/1990 and MNG/E/2809 (all have lost their five-footed pedestals); one at the Museum in Elblag, ME/72/MB; and one in the Ethnographic Museum of Torun, #18758 (dated 1879, initialled J.D., on five-footed base).

13. For a thorough study of the Pennsylvania German—Mennonite and Amish—dowry, including numerous inventories, see Jeannette Lasansky, *A Good Start: The Aussteier or Dowry* (Lewisburg, Pa.: University of Pennsylvania Press, Oral Traditions Project, 1990).

14. Claassen, *Vistula to Plum Grove*.

15. Donated by Justina Rempel Epp to the Kauffman Museum, KM 3474.

16. Anna Epp Ens, ed., *The House of Heinrich* (Winnipeg: Epp Book Committee, 1980), 37.

17. Kauffman Museum inventory #9.007, possibly made by David Penner of rural Inman.

18. Kauffman Museum KM 2066 (inventory #11.008), donated by P.M. Penner.

19. Letter from Paul G. Claassen, grandson of the wardrobe's builder Aaron Claassen, April 1990.

20. See Bergmann, "Das Haus," for an account in chapter 3 of his ancestral home at Heubuden #43 which contained a clock from Amsterdam dated 1783. In 1877 Johann Heinrich von Steen brought his London-made, one hundred-year-old cabinet clock from Danzig to Beatrice, Nebraska. A photo of the von Steen clock is filed at MLA.

21. Correspondence with Arthur Kroeger, Winnipeg, Canada, March 1990.

22. Two other round metal pendulum clocks of this style are held in private collections in Kansas and Nebraska (Kauffman Museum inventory #19.012 and #19.026, both with floral decoration). Arthur Kroeger of Winnipeg, collector and restorer of Kroeger clocks and descendant of the clockmaker family, knows of three clocks of this design in Winnipeg alone, as he stated in his letter, September 22, 1990. One of these is in the collection of the Mennonite Heritage Center at Canadian Mennonite Bible College in Winnipeg. All of these clocks, with the exception of the Hezekiah clock, are decorated with flower motifs. However, some of the flower decorations may actually be examples of painting over; thereby, obliterating the original decoration.

23. See Bergmann, "Das Haus," 3, for a description of this bedcovering or *Vorstecksel* displayed in the *Grosse Stube*. This practice is not unique to the Vistula Delta. For example, in Swedish peasant homes the beds in reception rooms were also piled high with bolsters, quilts and pillows to show off the economic status and the textile working skills of the housewife.

24. Kauffman Museum KM 2982, the embroidery spells out "*Glueckliche Reise*" within a bouquet of flowers. It has an interlace frame border of the type painted or inlaid on dowry chests. The pillow was probably made as a good-by present for an emigrant.

25. The curators at Elblag suggested that tulips as well as carnations are typical flower decorations on Vistula Delta inlaid and painted furniture. Ewa Gilewska, curator at the Ethnographic Museum of Oliwa, said 19th century cabinetmaking shops possibly produced two lines of furniture; an expensive one with inlay decoration and a less expensive one of cheaper wood—possibly a soft wood which was then painted to simulate the decorative effect of the classier inlaid chests.

26. See Simon Schama, *The Embarrassment of Riches* (New York: Alfred Knopf, 1987), 351-364 on the "tulip craze" in 17th century Holland.

27. Interview with Tante Anna on the farm worked by her niece Ewa Gabrys, November 6, 1989 near the village Loza near Szropy.

28. Penner, *Die ost- und west*, 256-259; first published in *Mitteilungen Epp-Kauenhoven-Zimmermann* (Limburg an der Lahn: Verlag von C.A. Starke, 1937), 66.

29. There is evidence that originally five turned spindles connected the two back slats. This form is found very frequently in 16th and 17th century paintings and engravings of Flemish and Dutch art. It corresponds exactly to chairs in the Gdansk National Museum, the ethnographic branch of the National Museum in Oliwa, and the Elblag museum which have similar carved motifs, initials and dates.

30. Personal communication with Arthur Kroeger of Winnipeg, January 5, 1991. He suggested that the reds may have been a more recent refurbishing of earlier faded reds.

31. See Kurt Kauenhoven, *Mennonite Life*, October, 1951. The 1933 photograph shows Dutch tiles with religious motifs in the Isaak Schulz farm home built in 1803 in Fuerstenwerder, Vistula Delta.

32. Reprinted in *Der Bote*, July 13, 1938.

33. Kauffman Museum inventory #19.026. The owners had the worn image repainted by a restorer in Kansas City, but they were not aware of the biblical source of the painted story. Their interpretation shared by the restorer was that the figures represented a fairy tale, a "courtly scene" of a knight on a horse, being received by ladies at a castle gate.

34. H.B. Meyer, *Deutsche Volkskunst: Danzig* (Weimar: Verlag Boehlau, not dated), ill. 68.

A fourth clock in this style, but without a pictorial illustration on its face, was seen by the authors in Padolsk museum in Orenburg Oblast, USSR, in 1991. The clock could have come with Mennonite settlers to this region (Neu Samara) directly from the Vistula Delta as early as 1850, or it may have come from South Russia at a later time.

35. Meyer, *Deutsche Volkskunst*, 27.

36. Philippa Lewis and Gillian Darley, *Dictionary of Ornament* (New York: MacMillan, 1986), 219-222.

37. The farmhouse with an arcaded entry is one of two distinct house types found in the Vistula Delta. Kloeppel links this house type to those areas settled by the Teutonic Knights. The question arises whether the arcade or *Vorlauben* house is a vernacular adaptation of the Renaissance arcaded court and the urban arcaded streets—an idea introduced to Poland by Italian architects working for the Polish crown in the 16th century.

Jan Bialostocki, "Manierismus und 'Volkssprache' in der polnischen Kunst," *Stil und Ikonographie* (Dresden: VEB Verlag der Kunst, 1965), 36.

Jan Bialostocki, *The Art of the Renaissance in Eastern Europe: Hungary, Bohemia, Poland* (Ithaca, NY: Cornell University Press, 1976), 88.

38. Schmidt, *Bau und Kunstdenkmaler*, 343, ill. 426. The second house type is the *Langgebaude* or longhouse which combines house and barn under one roof, still found in Flanders and The Netherlands, which was brought to the Vistula Delta by Flemish and Dutch settlers.

39. Schmidt, *Bau und Kunstdenkmaler*, 84. Schmidt states that this practice could have been in place as long as the farms stayed within 4 to 6 *Hufen*.

Personal communication with Arkadiusz Rybak, Stare Pole, and his elderly friend, Tante Anna, November 1989. Each spoke, unsolicited and independent from each other, of the number of supports on the *Vorlaube* being indicators of the number of units of land owned by that farm.

40. Kloeppel, "Siedlungsanlage." 175, ill. 69: *Haus Seedat in Gemlitz*.

41. Sara Voth fraktur, ca. 1840s on the inside of a chest's lid, inventory #1.002 (Mennonite Heritage Museum, Goessel, Kansas).

42. Kauffman Museum inventory #1.016. These lithograph portraits were published by Winckelmann and Sons in Berlin, ca. 1840-46 for the popular market. See Theodor Kohlmann, *Neuruppiner Bilderbogen* (Berlin, 1981), 62.

43. This corner cabinet is now in the permanent collection of the Museum of Man and Nature in Winnipeg.

44. Kauffman Museum inventory #1.059. Pasted inside the lid of the chest are color lithographs published by Gustav Kuehn in Neu Ruppin, ca. 1850. See Theodor Kohlmann, *Bilderbogen*, 14-16.

45. Kauffman Museum inventory #1.028, a chest purchased by an antique dealer in Mexico, resold through the Ottawa auction house in Kansas to an antique store in Newton, Kansas in 1989.

46. Kauffman Museum inventory #1.036.

Chapter Five

1. Wojciech Marchlewski, "Mennonites, Catholics and Evangelicals: Nineteenth Century Interconfessional Relations." Paper presented at the Symposium on Mennonites in Poland and Prussia, Canadian Mennonite Bible College, Winnipeg, July 1990.

2. Comments by Samuel Myovich at the Symposium on Mennonites in Poland and Prussia, Winnipeg, July 1990.

3. Myovich, July 1990.

4. Wojciech Marchlewski provided us with a reading from a microfilm copy of testamentary records in Wymysle from the early 19th century. He is making a longterm study of the Mazovian Hollander settlements.

5. Martin Schrag, "Volhynia," *Mennonite Encyclopedia* IV (Scottdale, Pa.: Mennonite Publishing House, 1959), 844-847.

6. Abe Unruh, *The Helpless Poles* (Montezuma, Kan.: Private printing, 1973), 61, provides a helpful map showing the geographical proximity of the Volhynian Mennonite settlements, all of which lay within a radius of less than a dozen miles.

7. In a foreword to Martin Schrag, *The European History of the Swiss Mennonites from Volhynia* (Newton, Kan.: Swiss Mennonite Cultural and Historical Association, 1974), 10.

8. Schrag, *Volhynia*, 19.

9. Schrag, *Volhynia*, 24.

10. Schrag, *Volhynia*, 32.

11. Schrag, *Volhynia*, 57-77.

12. Schrag, *Volhynia*, 75.

13. Schrag, *Volhynia*, 75.

14. Peter P. Wedel, *Kurze Geschichte der aus Wolhynian, Russland nach Kansas Ausgewanderten Schweizer-Mennoniten* (Moundridge, Kan.: Private printing, 1929).

15. Petzholdt, *Reise*, 185.

16. Jacob Adrian diary. The diary entries have been combined with research to recount a fuller story of the migration overland from the Vistula Delta to Molotschna by Jacob Adrian's great-grandson Walter Adrian, "A Thrilling Story from an Old Diary," *Mennonite Life* (July 1948): 23-44.

17. Jacob Adrian diary.

18. A plain chest in the Kauffman Museum inventory (#1.014), like the one shown here and now in a private collection, has the following pencil inscription on the inside, "Heinrich Schmidt, No. 28, Alexanderwohl, March 31, 1850." It was brought to Henderson by the parents of Peter J. Friesen or by the parents of Peter J.'s wife Eva Abrahams, great-great-grandparents of the present owner. Built of pine, it has a separately constructed bracket base, mahogany red stain, black painted graining, a brass keyplate with movable keyhole cover, a brass key, five brass bosses and handle plates and handles which were more recently bronzed. Pasted inside the lid is a fraktur "New Year's wishes" signed "Catrina Vothin, Alexanderwohl, 1841 and 1842."

19. Simon Schmidt, great-grandson of Jakob and Elisabeth.

20. The Ethnographic Museum at Oliwa–Gdansk has three such chests with nearly identical border field and floral decoration, dated between the first and fourth quarter of the 19th century (MNG/E/4791, MNG/E/2628, MNG/E/2296). One chest of this type bears the painted date 1878 on the front. The Elblag museum's chest of this type is dated 1882 and initialed "MB." Another such chest (undated) is on loan from a private owner near Tiegenhof. The Ethnographic Museum in Torun has one such chest (#29293), accessioned in 1980 from Glina gm. Sadlinki. Polish museums have dated these chests from 1830 to 1880. The similarity between the Jakob and Elisabeth Schmidt chest and the aforementioned chests is likely due to the migration of the crafts tradition with Mennonites to South Russia.

21. Bergmann, "Das Haus."

22. Gerhard Thiessen, *Diary from the Years 1907-1912*, preface by Herman Thiessen, 6, MLA.

23. Gerhard Thiessen, *Diary*, 173.

24. Gerhard Thiessen, *Diary*, 61.

25. Gerhard Thiessen, *Diary*, 33.

26. Gerhard Thiessen, *Diary*, 34.

27. "Memoirs of Peter Jansen," unpublished manuscript, 33, MLA.

28. *The Autobiography of H.B. Friesen*, August Schmidt, trans., 1974, 8, 26, MLA.

29. *Autobiography of H.B. Friesen*, 25.

30. Petzholdt, *Reise*, 153.

31. Peter Epp, *Eine Mutter* (Bluffton: Libertas Verlag, 1932), 79.

32. Epp, *Eine Mutter*, p. 19.

33. Epp, *Eine Mutter*, p. 82-83.

34. Epp, *Eine Mutter*, p. 85.

35. Epp, *Eine Mutter*, 89.

36. Epp, *Eine Mutter*, 227

37. Epp, *Eine Mutter*, 27ff.

38. Epp, *Eine Mutter*, 30-31.

39. Jacob Friesen collection, manuscript 114, MLA. Transcription of the German script by Hilda Voth:

> *Masse zum Kleider Schrank*
> *Breit 4 Schuh 3 Zoll tief 21 Zoll*
> *Unter Kasten hoch 14¼ Zoll ohne Laden*
> *Ober Kasten hoch 8 ½Zoll ohne Deck*
> *Die Thuer hoch 4 Schuh 3 Zoll*
> *Die Thuer Rahmen breit 5 Zoll*
> *Die Bekleid an die thuren 4¼ Zoll breit dick 14 Zoll*
> *Die Unterste Leiste 1⅝ Zoll*
> *Die Andern Leiste breit 1⅛ Zoll dick 1¼ Zoll*
> *Die Oberste Leiste Breit und hoch 2½ Zoll*
> *Das Kapitol auf die Ecken hoch 3 Zoll die mit 6 Zoll*
> *Der Fuss hoch 8½ Zoll dick 2½ Zoll*
> *Jacob Friesen in Schoenfeld, April 2. 1866*

40. *Autobiography of H.B. Friesen*, 28.

41. *Autobiography of H.B. Friesen*, 27.

42. *Autobiography of H.B. Friesen*, 29.

43. *Autobiography of H.B. Friesen*, 29.

44. *Autobiography of H.B. Friesen*, 58.

45. John F. Siemens, "The Johann Siemens Family: Six Generations," unpublished manuscript, 3.

46. *Autobiography of H.B. Friesen*, 41.

47. *Autobiography of H.B. Friesen*, 44.

48. Epp, *Eine Mutter*, 182 ff.

Chapter Six

1. Janzen, *Liebe Geschwister*, 9.

2. Interview Dec. 11, 1989 with Helmut Reimer, Dusseldorf, Germany, son of Gustav E. Reimer of Heubuden, Vistula Delta. The Gustav Reimer family fled the Delta in 1945.

   For an account of apprenticeship and craft practices in the mid-19th century, especially with reference to clock making and cabinetry, see David H. Epp, "Aus der Kindheitsgeschichte der deutschen Industrie in den Kolonie Sudrusslands" reproduced in *Der Bote* (July 13, 1938 through January 18, 1939).

3. *Jacob Claassen Journal 1911*, translated from German by Betty Claassen Miller, (Milo, Iowa: Private printing, 1989) 27. Copy at MLA.

4. Claassen, *Vistula to Plum Grove*, 45.

5. Letter by Anna Janzen, July 7, 1880, in Janzen, *Liebe Geschwister*, 13-18.

6. Abraham Claassen, July 1, 1876, diary entry about debarking the steamer *Rhein* upon arrival in New York harbor in Claassen, *Vistula to Plum Grove*, 24-25.

7. *Memoirs of Peter Jansen*, 33.

8. Interview with Walter Adrian, grandson of Franz Adrian, June 8, 1990.

9. Interview with Terry Klassen, Inman, Kansas. The chest was passed from Franz and Katharine Adrian to their daughter Eva Adrian Klassen (Mrs. Henry Klassen). Her daughter Katharine Klassen (1907) says her grandfather made the chest in Russia, and that dried Zwieback were stored in it on the voyage to North America. Kauffman Museum inventory #1.058. Dimensions: H:24" D:26½" W:51".

10. "The Peter and Marie Kasper Janzen Genealogy," 1974, 78, MLA.

11. Interview with Martha Buller (born January 1, 1898), Newton, Kan., April 10, 1990.

   Steve Friesen does not mention the Buller family as part of the close circle of friends of Emil Kym. That is probably because he interviewed descendants of families whose homes Kym decorated. The Buller home was decorated principally by Anna, and it burned down in 1924.

12. Interview with Walter Adrian, April 3, 1991.

13. Interview with Walter Adrian, June 8, 1990.

14. Interview with Martha Buller, April 10, 1990.

15. Interview with Walter Adrian, April 3, 1991.

16. Maldwyn Allen Jones, *American Immigration* (Chicago: University of Chicago Press, 1960), 127.

17. See Kauffman Museum inventory #11.011.

18. All biographical information on Heinrich Schroeder and his descendants is based on Henry R. Schroeder, *The Heinrich Schroeder Family Record*

(Newton, Kan.: Mennonite Press, 1952) and on personal communication with Nada Voth, great-granddaughter of Heinrich Schroeder.

19.The bed is on loan by Lenora Unruh Johnson, Wichita, Kan. Measurements: H:18" W:32" L:49½".

20.A "hat rack," thought to have been made by Heinrich, is remembered by great-granddaughter Nada as always having been in the entry hall of the farmhouse of her grandmother Sarah. It was a color "we called a Low German name but which would translate loosely to 'repulsive green.' This green was different than the green stain Heinrich used on other pieces." The "hat rack" has been stripped and refinished, placed in an honored position over the piano in the family room in the home of one of Heinrich's descendants. Most likely the intended function of this piece was to hold papers or magazines, or maybe even Heinrich's accordion music. The rack features a scallop or swag–drapery motif commonly found on the bases of dowry chests, cabinets and wardrobes.

21.The separately constructed base with feet is not used for the cupboard since it would make it too tall for the ceiling in the present owner's home.

22.Kauffman Museum inventory #1.054.

23.Personal communication, 1989.

24.Interview with Donald Huebert, Henderson, Neb., July 1990.

25.Interview with Mrs. John R. Doell, granddaughter of Heinrich Rempel, Henderson, Neb., September 1990.

26.Steve Friesen, *The Life and Times of Emil Kym, a Great Plains Folk Artist and the Immigrant Experience* (Cooperstown: Master's Thesis, 1978), 52, MLA.

27.Eloise Cox, letter to Reinhild Janzen, fall 1990.

28.Kauffman Museum inventory dowry chests #1.034 and #1.015.

29.Kauffman Museum inventory #4.011.

30.Meyer, *Danzig*, 20: "*das Empire kennt grosse polierte flache Eschentruhen, mit reichem mehrfarbigen Einlegeornamenten—stehen meist auf flachen, mit schwarz-weissem Schachbrettmuster bemalten Sockeln.*"

31.Personal communication with Anna Grace Flickinger, August 1991.

32.Bergmann, "Das Haus," 2.

33.Steinfeldt and Stover, *Early Texas Furniture*, plates 44 and 44a.

34.Anna Grace Flickinger, unpublished manuscript, 1991.

35.Friesen, *Emil Kym*, 52 ff.

36.Friesen, *Emil Kym*, 30.

37.Friesen, *Emil Kym*, 56.

38.Friesen, *Emil Kym*, 58.

Chapter Seven

1. For examples see the Anna Riesen chest (Fig. 119), the Johann Siemens chest (Fig. 30), the wardrobe from Koselitzke (Fig. 90), the wardrobe by Gerhard Nickel (Fig. 21) and the Gerhard Funk wardrobe (Fig. 181).

2. For example see the 13th century English oak boarded chest in John Gloag, *A Social History of Furniture Design* (New York: Crown Publishers, 1966), 11.

3. For example, Kauffman Museum KM 6258.1&2, and inventory #18.024, private collection.

4. Kauffman Museum inventory #5.004, Fast family bench.

5. This table resembles several found in Polish museum collections: MNG/E/2833 and MNG/E/2834 in the Muzeum Pomorskie in Gdansk-Oliva, both from the Nowy Dwor (Tiegenhof) area of the Vistula Delta.
Illustration 110 MNG in *Dawne Meble Ludowe* of the Torun Museum, Torun, 1976.

6. Suggested by Nancy-Lou Patterson, April 27, 1990.

7. Guenther Heine, *Intarsientischlerei in den Vierlanden* (Berlin, Hamburg: Altonaer Museum in Hamburg: Norddeutsches Landesmuseum; and verein der Freunde des Museums fuer Duetsche Volkskunde, Berlin, 1983).

8. Connoisseurs of inlay techniques differentiate between types of inlay on the basis of the tools used—a knife, an awl, a *Hohleisen* or a fretsaw.
Richard Beittel, ed., "Einlegearbeit," *Woerterbuch der Deutschen Volkskunde* (Stuttgart: Kroener, 1974), 164.

9. Wardrobes #11.023, #11.030; cabinets #14.043, #14.044; bench #5.001 by Heinrich Rempel; wardrobes #11.025, #11.031 by Klaas Hiebert; #11.011, possibly made by Klaas Hiebert; bench #6.003, unknown maker.

10.Kauffman Museum inventory #11.011; an example of application of decals to dowry chests is #1.036, a chest which may have been repainted by Heinrich Rempel, who used decals liberally on his cabinets and wardrobes.

11.Jonathan H. Fairbanks, *American Furniture, 1620 to the Present* (New York: R. Marek, 1981), 408.
Dean A. Fales, Jr., *American Painted Furniture 1660-1880* (New York: E.P. Dutton, 1972), 277-278.

12.Fales, *Painted Furniture*, 278, note 138.

13.*Bemalte Moebel aus Franken*, Exhibition catalogue (Bad Windsheim: Fraenkisches Freilandmuseum, 1980), 40.

14.Interview with Donald Huebert in Henderson, Neb., July 1990.

15.Prentis, *Kansas Miscellanies*, 24.

16.Bird and Kobayashi, *A Splendid Harvest*, 190.
Lyndon Viel, *Antique Ethnic Furniture* (Des Moines, Ia.: Wallace Homestead Publishers, 1983), 149-151.

17.Kauffman Museum inventory #11.013.

18.*Bemalte Moebel aus Franken*, 42.

19.*Mountain Lake 1886-1986* (Mountain Lake, Minn.: The Centennial Committee, 1986), 170.

20.Helmut Ottenjann, *Farbige volkstuemliche Moebel nordwestliches Niedersachsen* (Cloppenburg: Museum Cloppenburg, 1979), 8.

21.Revised reprint with English translation by Barbara Snell of *Die Grosse Wiener Schule* by Ernst Oldenbruch, Vienna, ca. 1925. 1986 Edition "libri rari" Verlag Th. Schaefer, Hannover.

22.Fales, *Painted Furniture*, 198.

23.Martha P. Nielsen, letter of February 6, 1991.

24.Kauffman Museum inventory # 12.002. According to oral tradition this dresser was grain-painted by an itinerant artisan.

25.Ethel Abrahams' interview with Marie Harms Berg, age 88, April 18, 1989. The house decorated by Mr. Huenergardt is located near the corner of Highway 15 and the Menno road, near Hillsboro, Kansas.

26.Kauffman Museum inventory #1.065.

27.Georg Himmelheber, *Biedermeier Furniture* (Winchester, Mass. and London: Faber & Faber, 1973), 33 ff.

28.Today Biedermeier furniture and related decorative arts of the period have seen a revival. Biedermeier furniture is highly prized and also reproduced for the current furniture market, including "Biedermeier lamps." See *Home*, February 1991, 60-61.

29.Himmelheber, *Biedermeier*, 38.

30.Himmelheber, *Biedermeier*, 44.

31.Himmelheber, *Biedermeier*, 39. Favored woods were walnut (never stained) pear and cherry. Jacob Adrian also mentions these woods as suitable for receiving mahogany stain.

32.Steinfeldt and Stover, *Early Texas Furniture*.
van Raavensway, *German Settlements*, chapter 13.

Chapter Eight

1. Tolksdorf, "Mundarten Danzigs," 336. *Mennoniten-Plaut* version written by J.H. Janzen (1878-1950).

2. *Autobiography of H.B. Friesen*, 101-2.

3. *Autobiography of H.B. Friesen*, 103. Friesen gives a detailed list of his expenses for the house including labor costs for five different workers. In addition, his sons helped.

4. See Kauffman Museum inventory wardrobes #11.014, #11.020, #11.024; desks #16.005 (stamped Simonsdorf, which was near Marienburg, on the back side), #16.006; and sleeping bench #6.016. All are from Wiebe, Penner and Claassen families from the Heubuden community near Marienburg (Malbork), Vistula Delta. Also included in this group is a mirror from an Entz family.

5. Personal communication with Martha P. Nielsen, February and March 1991. Mrs. Nielsen suggested that her father may have first learned carpentry skills when growing up on a farm: "Necessity made them quite independent and they needed to know how to do many things." Jacob J. Peters also was a song or choir leader in the church in Henderson. Privately he played the flute and the organ.

6. Kauffman Museum inventory #1.053, private collection.

7. Alan Janzen, "Biography of the Reverend A.W. Friesen," unpublished manuscript, MLA.

8. Kauffman Museum, on exhibit in the Voth/Unruh/Fast house.

9. James C. Juhnke, *Vision, Doctrine, War: Mennonite Identity and Organization in America 1890-1930* (Scottdale, Pa.: Herald Press, 1989).

10.Rachel K. Pannabecker, "Mennonite Parlors and Living Rooms: Objects,

Memories, and Meanings," *Mennonite Life* (June 1989): 13.

Chapter Nine

1. Thomas Munro, "Aesthetics," *Dictionary of Philosophy*, Dagobert D. Runes, ed. (Ames, Iowa: Littlefield, Adams & Co., 1959), 6.
2. Mezynski, *Mennonites in Poland*, 49.
3. Edmund Leach, *Political Systems of Highland Burma* (Boston: Beacon Press, 1954), 12.
4. David S. Landes, *Revolution in Time: Clocks and the Making of the Modern World* (Cambridge, Mass. and London: The Belknap Press of Harvard University Press, 1983).
5. Bible passages are from the New English Bible (Oxford: Oxford University Press, 1970).
6. Schama, *Embarrassment of Riches*.
7. There are several exceptions such as the Danzig churches of the 17th century and the Schoensee prayerhouse near Kulm, which was in fact a plain schoolhouse.
8. Mezynski, *Mennonites in Poland*, 49.
9. John Ruth, *Mennonite Identity and Literary Art* (Scottdale, Pa.: Herald Press, 1978), 46-59.

Appendix A

1. *Mennonite Life* (January, 1949): 12-13.
2. Alan Janzen, *Biography on the Rev. A.W. Friesen*, MLA.
3. Claassen, *Vistula to Plum Grove*, 45.

Appendix C

1. Microfilm, MLA.
2. Personal communication with Helmut Ottenjann, March 12, 1991. Helmut Ottenjann, *Farbige volkstuemlich Moebel,* 16-35.

Notes for Figure Captions

Chapter One

1. H. Worrall, *American Agriculturalist* 472-473.
2. Worrall, 472-473.
3. Worrall, 472-473.
4. Worrall, 472-473.
5. Martha Lepp personal collection.
6. Adobe House Museum Brochure.
7. Photo archive, MLA.
8. Interview with Mrs. Simon Schmidt, June 1990.
9. Photo, private collection.
10. *From Holland to Henderson*, 2nd edition, 1981, 71.
11. The diaries of Johann Siemens and John F. Siemens (Johann's son) are preserved in *The Johann Siemens Family: Six Generations*, 1965, MLA.
12. Marie Voth, "My Great-Grandfather's House."
13. Marie Voth, "My Great-Grandfather's House."
14. Photo by David Kreider, Kauffman Museum photo collection.

Chapter Two

1. Gerhard Nickel, *Rechenbuch*, Montau, West Prussia, 1797, MLA.
2. Similar hinges occur in the Anna Jansen/Helene van Riesen Jansen chest, which would suggest that both chests derive from the same period.

Chapter Three

1. Photo courtesy of Kevin Enns-Rempel.
2. Postcard, Friedrichstadt, Germany, 1991.
3. Nils Claussen, "Der Einfluss," ill. 9.
4. Kloeppel, "Siedlungsanlage," 179, figs. 74 and 75.
5. Kloeppel, "Siedlungsanlage," 123, figs. 11, 12.
6. Photo archive, MLA.
7. Photo archive, MLA.
8. Photo archive, MLA.
9. Kloeppel, "Siedlungsanlage," 168, fig. 62.
10. Manuscript, MLA.
11. Manuscript, MLA.
12. Manuscript, MLA.
13. Manuscript, MLA.
14. Manuscript, MLA.
15. MLA.
16. Courtesy of Duane Schroeder, Summer, 1990.
17. Kloeppel, "Siedlungsanlage," ill. 43.
18. Manuscript SA-II-140, MLA.
19. MLA.
20. Kloeppel, "Siedlungsanlage," 191, fig. 87.

Chapter Four

1. Rudolf Focke, *Chodowiecki et Lichtenberg* (Leipzig, 1901), plate XIII.
2. *Die Holzschnitte des Petrarca Meisters*, (Berlin: Henschel Verlag, 1955), 122.
3. *Jacob Claassen Journal*, 6.
4. Sometimes drawers under the till were hidden by a removable decorative board, as in #1.039.
5. Claassen, *Vistula to Plum Grove*, 16.
6. F.W.H. Hollstein, *Dutch and Flemish Etchings, Engravings and Woodcuts*, Vol. 20, K.G. Boon, ed. (Amsterdam, 1978), 55.
7. Aaron Klassen, *In the Fullness of Time*, 1974, 25, ill. 16.
8. MLA.
9. Kauffman Museum, KM 5657. Several examples of this kind of embroidered insert for a bedcover exist in the Kwydzin (Marienwerder) Museum according to a collection of photographs, folder SA-II-140 (MLA). KM 3132 is an example of painting on paper.
10. Manuscript, MLA.
11. Manuscript, MLA.
12. Schmidt, *Bau und Kunstdenkmaler*, 343.
13. Kloeppel, "Siedlungsanlage," 175, ill. 69.

Chapter Five

1. See Clarence Unruh, "The Benjamin and Catherine A. Siebert Schmidt Family Record," 1980, Manuscript, MLA.
2. Photo courtesy of Ethel Abrahams.
3. Very similar to two travel trunks identified as brought by Andreas Schrag; #2.033, private collection and Heritage Hall Museum #32.036, Freeman, South Dakota. Also similar to the travel trunk #2.026, KM 6308.
4. Jacob Adrian diary, private collection, on microfilm at MLA.
5. This chest is nearly identical in design and painted finish to a dowry chest built by Heinrich Schmidt, Alexanderwohl, South Russia. Written in pencil on the inside of the lid, underneath the middle hinge one reads: "Heinrich Schmidt No.28 Alexanderwohl March 31 1850." The Schmidt chest was brought to Henderson, Nebraska, in 1874 either by the parents of Peter J. Friesen, (who later became first elder of the Bethesda Mennonite congregation) or, more likely, by the parents of Peter J.'s wife Eva Abrahams (great-great-grandparents of the present owner). It has a separately constructed five-footed bracket base. Pine, mahogany red stain, black painted graining, brass keyplate with movable keyhole cover, brass key, five brass bosses, handle plates and handles were bronzed more recently. Fraktur pasted inside the lid are New Year's wishes signed Catarina Voth in Alexanderwohl, dated 1841 and 1842. H:27" W:54½" D:28½". #1.014, Private collection. Published in *Henderson Mennonites*, 1981 and in Ethel Ewert Abrahams, *Frakturmalen und Schonschreiben*, 1980, 116, 117.
6. A chest of the very same style in the Ethnographic Museum in Oliwa–Gdansk is initialled "AK" and dated 1853.
   Dawne Meble Ludowe Polnocnej Polski (Torun: Ethnographic Museum, 1976), ill. 126.
7. Photo of a lost original, MLA.
8. Photo archive, MLA.
9. Gerhard Lohrenz, *Heritage Remembered* (Winnipeg: Canadian Mennonite Bible College, 1977), 65.
10. Klassen, *In the Fullness of Time*, 25, ill. 17.
11. Klassen, *In the Fullness of Time*, 78
12. John Peter Klassen, *Artist as Peacemaker*, (Bluffton, Ohio: Bluffton College, 1989), 8.
13. David C. Wedel, *The Story of Alexanderwohl* (Goessel, Kan.: Alexanderwohl Centennial Committee, 1974).
14. Jacob Friesen collection, MLA.
15. Four other basket cradles brought from South Russia at the time of immigration have been documented in Kansas.

Chapter Six

1. The Kauffman Museum inventory shows travel trunks of this same type from South Russia. They were most likely mass-manufactured in that region.
2. Photo courtesy of Walter Adrian.
3. Photo courtesy of Walter Adrian.
4. Photo courtesy of Adina Meek.
5. Photo courtesy of Joyce Watts.
6. Nada Voth, great-granddaughter of Heinrich Schroeder, correspondence with Reinhild Janzen, January 1989.
7. Two other tables made by Heinrich Schroeder are presently recorded in private collections in Kansas. #15.016 was used by his daughter Sarah in her bedroom, "Sarah kept a lamp turned down very low on it and used the light to take care of the 12 babies she had. The table had many coats of paint on it. Grandma Sarah believed in paint according to my father and according to him, workmanship was not her strong suit." Nada Voth, personal communication, January 1989.
8. Photo courtesy of Donald Huebert.
9. Photo courtesy of Anna Grace Flickinger.

Chapter Seven

1. From Fritz Hellwag, *Die Geschichte des Deutschen Tischlerhandwerkes vom 12. bis zum 20. Jahrhundert*, (Berlin: 1924), 7.
2. In the storage area of the Elblag Museum we photographed the pediment of a wardrobe with these same stylistic features, which further testifies to the presence of this style in the Vistula Delta region in the second half of the 19th century.
3. *Die Holzschnitte des Petrarca Meisters*, 206.
4. From the collection of Bill Hinz.

Chapter Nine

1. Photo by John M. Janzen, authors' collection.

Bibliography

Published and Manuscript Sources

MLA = Mennonite Library and Archives, Bethel College, North Newton, Kansas.

Abrahams, Ethel. *Frakturmalen und Schoenschreiben.* Newton, Kan.: Mennonite Press, 1980.

Adrian, Walter. "A Thrilling Story from an Old Diary." *Mennonite Life* (July, 1948): 23-44.

Autobiography of H.B. Friesen, 1837-1926, The. August Schmidt, trans., 1974, MLA.

Bemalte Moebel aus Franken. Exhibition catalogue. Bad Windsheim: Fraenkisches Freilandmuseum, 1980.

Bergmann, Cornelius. "Das Haus der Urahne." Unpublished manuscript, 1907, MLA.

Beittel, Richard, ed. *Woerterbuch der Deutschen Volkskunde.* Stuttgart: Kroener, 1974.

Bialostocki, Jan. "Die Jagiellonen Renaissance." *Polen im Zeitalter der Jagiellonen* 1386-1572. Exhibition catalogue. Schallaburg, 1986.

_____. "Rembrandt's 'Eques Polonus.'" *Oud Holland,* LXXXIV (1969): 163-176.

_____. "Manierismus und 'Volkssprache' in der polnischen Kunst." *Stil und Ikonographie.* Dresden: VEB Verlag der Kunst, 1965.

_____. *The Art of the Renaissance in Eastern Europe: Hungary, Bohemia, Poland.* Ithaca: Cornell University Press, 1976.

Bird, Michael and Terry Kobayashi. *A Splendid Harvest, Germanic Folk and Decorative Arts in Canada.* Toronto: Van Nostrand, Reinhold, Ltd., 1983.

Bogucka, Maria, *Das alte Danzig.* Muenchen: Verlag C.H.Beck, 1987.

Claassen, Ernest G., ed. *Abraham Claassen: Vistula to Plum Grove,* 1975.

Claussen, Nils. *Der Einfluss hollaendischer Bauweise auf Friedrichstadt.* Manuscript, Friedrichstadt Archives, 1977.

Chodynski, Anton-Romuald. *Malbork.* Warszawa: Wydawnictwo Ardady, 1989.

Dawne Meble Ludowe Polnocnej Polski. Exhibition catalogue. Torun: Torun Ethnographic Museum, 1976.

Dick, Jerry. *The Russian Mennonite House-Barn of Manitoba: A Study in Cultural Transformations.* University of Waterloo:M.A. Thesis, 1984.

Die Hanse: Lebenswirklichkeit und Mythos. 2 Vols. Hamburg: Museum fuer Hamburgische Geschichte, 1989.

Die Holzschnitte des Petrarca Meisters. Berlin: Henschel Verlag, 1955.

Dyck, Arnold. *Verloren in der Steppe.* Steinbach: Personal Printing, 1944.

Dyck, Cornelius J., ed. *Introduction to Mennonite History.* Scottdale, Pa.: Herald Press, 1967.

Epp, David. "Aus der Kindheitsgeschichte der deutschen Industrie in den Kolonie Sudrusslands." *Der Bote* (July 13, 1938 to January 18, 1939).

Epp Ens, Anna, ed. *The House of Heinrich.* Winnipeg: Epp Book Committee, 1980.

Epp, Peter. *Eine Mutter.* Bluffton, Oh.: Libertas Verlag, 1932.

Estep, William R. *Revolution within the Revolution: The First Amendment in Historical Context,* 1612-1789. Grand Rapids: Eerdmans, 1990.

Fairbanks, Jonathan L. and Elizabeth Bates. *American Furniture, 1620 to the Present.* New York: R. Marek, 1981.

Fales, Dean A., Jr. *American Painted Furniture 1660-1880.* New York: E.P. Dutton, 1972.

Flandrin, Jean-Louis, *Families in Former Times.* Cambridge: Cambridge University Press, 1979.

Focke, Rudolf. *Chodowiecki et Lichtenberg.* Leipzig, 1901.

Friesen, John. "Mennonites in Poland: An Expanded Historical View," *Journal of Mennonite Studies,* Vol. 4 (1986): 94-108.

Friesen, Steve. *The Life and Times of Emil Kym, a Great Plains Folk Artist and the Immigrant Experience.* Cooperstown, New York: M.A. Thesis, 1978.

Gloag, John. *A Social History of Furniture Design.* New York: Crown Publishers, 1966.

Goody, Jack, Joan Thirsk and Eric P. Thompson, eds. *Family and Inheritance.* Cambridge: Cambridge University Press, 1976.

Gruenwald in the Memory of the Polish People. The Gruenwald Social Committee, not dated.

Heine, Guenther. *Intarsientischlerei in den Vierlanden.* Berlin: Verein der Freunde des Museums fuer Deutsche Volkskunde; Hamburg: Altonaer Museum, Norddeutsches Landesmuseum, 1983.

Heise, J. *Die Bau- und Kunstdenkmaeler der Provinz Westpreussen, Bd. 1* (H. 1-4). Danzig, 1884-87.

Hellwag, Fritz. *Die Geschichte des Deutschen Tischlerhandwerks vom 12. bis zum 20. Jahrhundert.* Berlin: Verlagsantalt des deutschen Holzarbeiter-Verband, 1924.

Himmelheber, Georg. *Biedermeier Furniture.* Winchester, Mass. and London: Faber and Faber, 1974.

Hollstein, F.W.H. *Dutch and Flemish Etchings, Engravings and Woodcuts,* Vol. 20. K.G. Boon, ed. Amsterdam, 1978.

Home (February 1991).

Iwanoyko, Eugeniusz. *Sala Czerwona.* Wroclaw, Warsaw, Krakow, Gdansk, Lodz: Zaklad Narodowy Imienia Ossdinskich, 1986.

Jacob Adrian Diary, MLA.

Jacob Claassen Journal 1911. Translated from the German by Betty Claassen Miller, Milo, Iowa, May 1, 1989.

Jaehnig, B. and P. Letkemann, eds. *Danzig in acht Jahrhunderten.* Muenster–Westfalen: Nicolaus-Copernicus Verlag, 1985.

Janzen, Alan. *Biography of the Reverend A.W. Friesen.* Manuscript, MLA.

Janzen Genealogy 1789-1944, The Peter and Marie (Kasper). Compiled by Kathryn Klassen, Martha L. Adrian and Walter V. Adrian, 1974, MLA.

Janzen Longacre, Doris. "A chest, a train, a blizzard and some zwieback." *On the Line* (Feb. 20, 1977).

Janzen, Louis. *Liebe Geschwister.* Newton, Kan.: Private Printing, 1979.

Jones, Maldwyn Allen. *American Immigration.* Chicago: University of Chicago Press, 1960.

Juhnke, James C. *Vision, Doctrine, War: Mennonite Identity and Organization in America 1890-1930.* Scottdale, Pa.: Herald Press, 1989.

Kauenhoven Janzen, Reinhild. "Sources and Styles of the Material Culture Life of Mennonites in the Vistula Delta." *Mennonite*

Quarterly Review, forthcoming.

Kauenhoven, Kurt. *Mennonite Life* (October, 1951).

Kizik, Edmund, "Die Mennoniten Westpreussens unter Friederich dem Grossen," *Friedericianische Miniaturen 1. Forschungen u. Studien zur Friedericianischen Zeit, Bd. II,* J. Ziechmann, ed. Bremen, 1988.

Klassen, Aaron. *In the Fullness of Time.* Waterloo, Ont.: Reeve Bean, Ltd., 1974.

Klassen, John Peter. *Artist as Peacemaker.* Bluffton, OH: Bluffton College, 1989.

Kloeppel, Otto. "Die bauerliche Haus-, Hof- und Siedlungsanlage im Weichsel-Nogat-Delta." In H. Bertram, W. La Baume, O. Kloeppel, *Das Weichsel-Nogat-Delta: Beitraege zur Geschichte seiner landschaftlichen Entwicklung,vorgeschichtlichen, Besiedlung und bauerlichen Haus-und Hofanlage.* Danzig, 1924.

Kohlmann, Theodor. *Neuruppiner Bilderbogen.* Berlin: Schriften des Museums fuer Deutsche Volkskunde, Bd. 7, 1981.

Krahn, Cornelius. "Furniture." *Mennonite Encyclopedia,* Vol. II. Scottdale, Pa.: Mennonite Publishing House, 424-6.

Kroeger, Arthur. *Kroeger Clocks.* Winnipeg: Private printing, not dated.

Kroeker, N.J. *First Mennonite Villages in Russia, 1789-1943.* Vancouver: Private printing, 1981.

Kruenitz, Johann Georg. *Oekonomische Encyclopadie, oder Allgemeines system der Statt- Haus- und Landwirtschaft in alphabetischer Ordnung.* Berlin: J. Pauli, 1773-1858 [1782].

Kundzins, Pauls. "Zur Einordnung einiger Bauernhaustypen Westpreussens in die Volksbaukunst der Ostseelaender." *Contributions of Baltic University, No. 58,* Pinneberg, 1949.

Landes, David S. *Revolution in Time: Clocks and the Making of the Modern World.* Cambridge, Mass. and London: The Belknap Press of Harvard University Press, 1983.

Lasansky, Jeannette. *Good Start: The Aussteier or Dowry.* Lewisburg, PA: University of Pennsylvania Press, Oral Traditions Project, 1990.

Leach, Edmund. *Political Systems of Highland Burma.* Boston: Beacon Press, 1954.

Lewis, Philippa and Gillian Darley. *Dictionary of Ornament.* New York and London: MacMillan, 1986.

Loewenthal, D. *The Past is a Foreign Country.* New York: Cambridge University Press, 1985.

Lohrenz, Gerhard. *Heritage Remembered.* Winnipeg: Canadian Mennonite Bible College, 1977.

Marchlewski, Wojciech. "Mennonites, Catholics and Evangelicals: Nineteenth Century Interconfessional Relations." Paper presented at the Symposium on Mennonites in Poland and Prussia. Winnipeg, July 1990.

Mellin, Krystyna. "The cabinetmakers guild in Gdansk in the late middle ages." *Gdanskie Studia Muzealne* (Muzeum Narodowe w Gdansku, 1976): 71-84, ill. 267-272.

_____. "The Gdansk carpenters' and wood-carvers' guild from the middle of the XVIe to the middle of the XVIIe century." *Gdanskie Studia Muzealne* (Muzeum Narodowe w Gdansku, 1978): 49-64, ill.225-236.

_____. "Marquetries from Torun in the Collection of the Torun Museum." Torun: Torun Ethnographic Museum, 1956.

Memoirs of Peter Jansen, MLA.

Meyer, H.B. *Deutsche Volkskunst: Danzig.* Weimar: Verlag Boehlau, Neue Folge, not dated.

Mezynski, Kazimierz. *From the History of Mennonites in Poland.* Warszawa: Akademia Rolnicza w Warszawie, 1975.

Milobedzki, Adam. "Architektur in Polen zur Zeit der Jagiellonen." *Polen im Zeitalter der Jagiellonen 1386-1572.* Exhibition catalogue, Schallaburg, 1986.

Mitteilungen Epp-Kauenhoven-Zimmermann. Limburg an der Lahn: Verlag von C.A. Starke, 1937.

Mountain Lake 1886-1986. Mountain Lake, Minn.: The Centennial Committee, 1986.

Oldenbruch, Ernst. *Die Grosse Wiener Schule.* Vienna, ca. 1925ff. Revised reprint with English translation by Barbara Snell, ed. "libri rari." Hannover: Verlag Th. Schaefer, 1986.

Ottenjann, Helmut. *Farbige volkstuemlich Moebel nordwestliches Niedersachsen.* Cloppenburg: Museumsdorf Cloppenburg, 1979.

Pannabecker, Rachel. "Mennonite Parlors and Living Rooms: Objects, Memories and Meanings." *Mennonite Life* (June 1989).

Patterson, Nancy-Lou. *Swiss-German and Dutch-German Mennonite Traditional Art in the Waterloo Region, Ontario.* Ottawa: National Museum of Man, 1979.

_____. *The Language of Paradise: Folk Art from Mennonite and Other Anabaptist Communities of Ontario.* London, Ont.: London Regional Art Gallery, 1985.

Penner, Horst. *Die ost- und westpreussischen Mennoniten I: 1526-1772.* Weierhof: Mennonitisches Geschichtes Verein, 1978.

_____. *Die ost- und westpreussischen Mennoniten II: 1772 bis zur Gegenwart.* Kirchheimbolanden: Selbstverlag, 1987.

Petzholdt, Alexander. *Reise im westlichen und suedlichen europaeischen Russland im Jahre 1855.* Leipzig: Herman Fries, 1864.

Prentis, Noble, L. *Kansas Miscellanies,* Topeka: Kansas Publishing House, 1889.

Preussen: Versuch einer Bilanz. Exhibit catalogue, Berliner Festspiele GMBH, 1981.

Rempel, Herman. *Kjenn jie noch Plautdietsch? A Mennonite Low German Dictionary.* Winnipeg: Mennonite Literary Society, 1984.

Runes, Dagobert. *Dictionary of Philosophy.* Ames, Iowa: Littlefield, Adams & Co., 1959.

Ruth, John. *Mennonite Identity and Literary Art.* Scottdale, Pa.: Herald Press (Focal Pamphlet 29), 1978.

Schama, Simon. *The Embarrassment of Riches.* New York: Alfred Knopf, 1987.

Schmidt, Bernhard. *Die Bau und Kunstdenkmaler des Kreises Marienburg I. Die Staedte Neuteich und Tiegenhof und die landliche Ortschaften.* Danzig, 1919.

Schrag, Martin. *The European History of the Swiss Mennonites from Volhynia.* Newton, Kan.: Swiss Mennonite Cultural and Historical Association, 1974.

Schroeder, A. *Bemalter Hausrat in Nieder und Ostdeutschland.* Leipzig: Schwarzhaeupter Verlag, 1939.

Schroeder Family Record, The Heinrich, by his grandson Henry R. Schroeder. Mennonite Press, 1952.

Shils, Edward. *Tradition.* Chicago: University of Chicago Press, 1982.

Siemens Family: Six Generations, The Johann. 1965, MLA.

Stankiewiez, Jerzy. "Zabytki Budownictwa i Architektury na Zulawach." *Rocznik Gdanski, xv/svi* (1956-7).

Steensberg, Axel. *Danske Bondemobler.* Kopenhagen: Alfr. G. Hassings Forlag, 1949.

Steinfeldt, Cecilia and Donald Lewis Stover. *Early Texas Furniture and Decorative Arts.* San Antonio Museum Association: Trinity University Press, 1974.

Thiessen, Gerhard. *Diary from the Years 1907-1912.* Preface by Herman Thiessen, MLA.

Thiessen, Jack, "A New Look at an Old Problem: Origins of the Variations in Mennonite Plautdietsch." *Mennonite Quarterly Review* (October 1989): 285-296.

Tolksdorf, Ulrich. "Die Mundarten Danzigs und seines Umlandes." *Danzig in acht Jahrhunderten.* Muenster–Westfalen: Nicolaus-Copernicus Verlag, 1985.

Uebe, F. Rudolf. *Deutsche Bauernmoebel.* Berlin: Richard Carl Schmidt & Co., 1924.

Unruh, Abe. *The Helpless Poles.* Montezuma, Kan.: Private printing, 1973.

Unruh, Clarence, ed. *The Benjamin and Catherine A. Siebert Schmidt Family Record.* Manuscript, 1980, MLA.

Urry, James. *None but Saints: The Transformation of Mennonite Life in Russia 1789-1889.* Winnipeg: Hyperion Press, 1989.

van Raavensway, Charles. *German Settlements in Missouri, a Survey of a Vanishing Culture.* Columbia: University of Missouri Press, 1977.

Vansina, Jan. *Paths in the Rainforests: Toward a History of Political Tradition in Equatorial Africa.* Madison: University of Wisconsin Press, 1990.

Verheyden, Alphonse. *Le martyrologie protestant des pays-bas du Sud au XVe siecle.* Bruxelles: Editions de la Librarie des Eclaireurs Unionistes, 1960.

Viel, Lyndon C. *Antique Ethnic Furniture.* Des Moines, Ia.: Wallace Homestead Publishers, 1983.

von Reiswitz, Freiherrn and Friedrich Wadzeck. *Glaubensbekenntnis der Mennoniten und Nachricht von ihren Colonien.* Berlin: August Ruecker, 1824.

Voth, Marie. "My Grandfather's House." Unpublished manuscript, 1959, MLA.

Voth, Stanley, ed. *From Holland to Henderson,* 2nd edition. Henderson: Henderson Centennial Committee, 1981.

Weber-Kellerman, Ingeborg. *Die Deutsche Familie.* Frankfurt: Suhrkamp, 1974.

Wedel, David C. *The Story of Alexanderwohl.* Goessel, Kan.: Goessel Centennial Committee, 1974.

Wedel, P.P. *Kurze Geschichte der aus Wolhynian, Russland nach Kansas Ausgewanderten Schweizer-Mennoniten.* Moundridge, Kan.: Private printing, 1929.

Wiebe, Herbert. *Das Siedlungswerk niederlaendischer Mennoniten im Weicheltal zwischen Fordon u. Weissenberg bis zum Ausgang des 18. Jahrhunderts.* Marburg: Wissenschaftliche Beitraege 2. Geschichte u. Landeskunde Ost-Mitteleuropas, No. 3, 1952.

Woede, Hans. *Alte doerfliche Baukultur in Ostpreussen.* Glueckstadt: Ostpreussisches Landesmuseum, 1980.

Worrall, H. "How the Mennonites Warm Their Houses and Cook with Straw as Fuel." *American Agriculturalist* (1878): 472-3.

Interviews and Personal Communications

Adrian, Walter. Interview, Wichita, Kan., June 8, 1990; April 3, 1990; June 8, 1990.

Bangs, Jeremy. Lecture, Kauffman Museum, North Newton, Kan., Spring 1990.

Buller, Martha. Interview, Newton, Kan., January 16, 1989.

Cox, Elisabeth. Letter, fall 1990.

Dalke Bryan, Agnes. Letter, June 28, 1990.

Doell, Mrs. John R. Interview, Henderson, Neb., September 1990.

Enns-Rempel, Kevin. Letter, Winnipeg, Man., October 31, 1990.

Friesen, Jacob E. Letter, Hague, Sask., September 24, 1990.

Gabrys, Tanta Anna and Eva Gabrys. Interview, Loza near Szropy, Poland, November 6, 1989.

Gilewska, Ewa. Curator, Ethnographic Museum, Oliwa, Poland.

Harms Berg, Marie. Interview, Parkside Homes, Hillsboro, Kan., April 18, 1989.

Huebert, Don. Interview, Henderson, Neb., July, 1990.

Laenen, Mark. Interview, Bokrijk Openluchtmuseum, Belgium, October 18, 1989.

Kizik, Edmund. Interviews, Gdansk, Poland, November 1989.

Klassen, Terry. Interview, Inman, Kan., 1991.

Klassen, Katharine. Interview, 1991.

Kroeger, Arthur. Letter, Winnipeg, Man., March, 1991.

Marchlewski, Wojciech. Interview on research in Wymysle, Poland, July 1990.

Mierau Swisher, Helen. Letter, Alaska, January 5, 1991.

Myovich, Samuel. Comments to Symposium on Mennonites in Poland and Prussia, Winnipeg, Man., July 1990.

Nielsen, Martha P. Letter, February 6, 1991.

Patterson, Nancy-Lou. Consultant at Kauffman Museum, April 27, 1990.

Reimer, Helmut. Interview, Dusseldorf, Germany, December 11, 1989.

Rybak, Arkadiusz and Zyta Rybak. Interviews, Stare Pole, Poland, November 4-7, 1989.

Voth, Nada. Interview, Walton, Kan., 1990.

Glossary–Index

Adrian, family: in Vistula Delta, and migration to S. Russia, 74; Jacob (1801-1866), cabinetmaker, 74, 116, 117, 137, 184, 190; Jakob (1765-1835), 74; in Molotschna Colony, South Russia, 116-119; migration to America, 137; Anna, painting by, 138, 139, 141-142, 209 (see Adrian, Franz).

Adrian, Franz: 118, 119; portrait with wife Katherine, 135; corner cabinet, 136, 137; cabinetmaker in Kansas, 137-144; chimney base cabinet, 138; wardrobes made, 139; china cabinet, 140; housebarns built by, 141, 142; character of, 143-144, 187, 190, 207.

Aesthetics: sensibilities in furniture, 8; defined, 201; and ethics, 201; of Mennonite home, as described by Mezynski, 201, 207; of the plain, 203; and architecture in prayerhouse, 205.

Akjschaup (see Corner Cabinet).

Akjstow, Eckstube (see Corner Room).

Anabaptism: in Reformation, 7; in first ammendment of U.S. Constitution, 7; and occupations in 16th century Netherlands, 50; beginnings in Vistula Delta, 57; and distinctive church architecture, 64-65; and the arts, 208.

Bad (see Bed, Sleeping bench)

Baroque: style, 59, 61, 208; ball feet of wardrobe, 165.

Becker, Peter: graining painter, 160.

Bed: pullout, 16, 22-24, 31-32, 44; in South Russian context, 129-131; folding rope, for child, 147.

Bedcover: 93-94.

Bench: resting, 16; sleeping, 16, 22, 23; in South Russia, 126; used in *Grosse Stube,* 126; milk, 126, 127, 197; Heinrich Schroeder's, 149, 150, 151; by Heinrich Rempel, 156; construction of, 169-170, 203; Biedermeier, 190; doll sleeping, 197, 198.

Benkj: 16 (see Bench); *Melkbenkj* (milkbench), *Ruhbenkj* (resting bench), *Schlopbenkj* (sleeping bench)

Bergen, George: graining painter and woodworker, 160, 184.

Biedermeier, style: 102; secretary in Vistula Delta, 159; style 188-190, of legs of furniture, 165, 182, 185, 188-190, 208.

Boese, Benjamin: cabinetmaker, 184, 196.

Bookcase: 194, 195.

Cabinet (see Corner, Glass, Wall).

Cabinetmaker (see Craftsman).

Canon: of Vistula Delta derived Mennonite furniture, 11; of Swiss Volhynian, 114.

Central chimney: and hearth in Kansas, 17-20, 18, 21, 40, 41, 61, 141; in Kashubian house, 48; in other Vistula Delta houses, 61, 62, 68-70; in Russia, 125.

Chair: spinning, 7, 16; commode, 30, 87-88; biblical motifs on, 95-98.

Chest, dowry chest: 35-38, 59, 78-83, 104, 110, 112, 118, 119, 112, 134, 151, 152; as moving chest, 3; end of construction on Plains as example of change in tradition, 11-12, 199; in canon of Mennonite furniture, 16; for grain storage, 27; in emigration, 28; dowry, 35-38, 54; by guild cabinetmakers, 52; with flower motifs, 93, 95; pilaster motif, 100, 102; Greek motifs, 102; interior decoration, 103-105; from Karolswalde, 110-112; from South Russia, 118-119; from South Russia, 118-121; from Russia, inlaid, 122-123; construction of, in South Russia, 127; toll taken in transport, 135-137; of Katharine Janzen Adrian, 144; by Heinrich Schroeder, 151, 152, 153; decorated with inlay, 152, 189; painted by Heinrich Rempel, 157; construction of, 162-163; styles of bracket bases, 164-165; fittings and mounts, 172-181; hinges and locks of, 172-182, 189; a decorated with inlay, 182, 189; style not folk art, 188; in miniature, 196-197, 202 (see Dowry).

Church: 3 (see House church, Prayerhouse).

Claassen, Aaron: cabinetmaker, 133.

Class distinctions: rapid exacerbation under Prussian rule, 55; reflected across rural-urban lines in Vistula Delta furnishings and style, 56; and emergence of crafts tradition, 73-74; among Mennonites of South Russia, 116.

Classical orders: 102.

Clock: 16, 30, 35, 37, 38, 39, 203; by Johann Kroeger, in Vistula Delta, 90-93; with biblical motif on face: of story of King Hezekiah, 98-101; of story of Jeptha, 100-101; from South Russia, 125, 183.

Coffins: 39, 127.

About the Authors

Reinhild Kauenhoven Janzen is a native of Goettingen, Germany. She is Curator of Cultural History at Kauffman Museum, Bethel College, North Newton, Kansas, and adjunct professor of art history at Bethel College. Her interests embrace the arts of the northern Renaissance, African art and German art after 1945, as well as the historic antecedents of Mennonite culture of the Plains. Her writings include *Albrecht Altdorfer: Four Centuries of Criticism, For Life's Sake: Arts from Africa* and *The Art of Sharing, the Sharing of Art: Responses to Mennonite Relief in Postwar Germany.*

John M. Janzen is professor of anthropology at the University of Kansas and Director of Kauffman Museum. In addition to his research and writing on Mennonite culture and history, he has conducted field research in central and southern Africa and is the author of the award-winning *Quest for Therapy in Lower Zaire,* as well as *Lemba 1650-1930: A Drum of Affliction in Africa and the New World* and *Ngoma: Discourses of Healing in Central and Southern Africa.* He is co-author and editor of *An Anthology of Kongo Religion.*